MAKING TRACKS

MAKING TRACKS

A Record Producer's
Southern Roots Music Journey

SCOTT BILLINGTON

FOREWORD BY PETER GURALNICK

UNIVERSITY PRESS OF MISSISSIPPI ★ JACKSON

The University Press of Mississippi is the scholarly publishing agency of
the Mississippi Institutions of Higher Learning: Alcorn State University,
Delta State University, Jackson State University, Mississippi State University,
Mississippi University for Women, Mississippi Valley State University,
University of Mississippi, and University of Southern Mississippi.

www.upress.state.ms.us

Designed by Peter D. Halverson

The University Press of Mississippi is a member
of the Association of University Presses.

First printing 2022
∞

Library of Congress Cataloging-in-Publication Data

Names: Billington, Scott, author.
Title: Making tracks : a record producer's southern roots music journey /
Scott Billington ; foreword by Peter Guralnick.
Other titles: American made music series.
Description: Jackson : University Press of Mississippi, 2022. | Series:
American made music series | Includes bibliographical references and index.
Identifiers: LCCN 2021055343 (print) | LCCN 2021055344 (ebook) | ISBN
9781496839152 (hardback) | ISBN 9781496839190 (pdf) | ISBN 9781496839183
(pdf) | ISBN 9781496839176 (epub) | ISBN 9781496839169 (epub)
Subjects: LCSH: Rounder Records (Firm) | Rhythm and blues music—History
and criticism. | Cajun music—History and criticism. | Soul
music—History and criticism. | Blues (Music)—History and criticism. |
Americana (Music)—History and criticism. | Billington, Scott. | Sound
recording executives and producers—United States. | Sound
recordings—Production and direction—History. | Sound recording
industry—United States—History.
Classification: LCC ML3792.R68 B55 2022 (print) | LCC ML3792.R68 (ebook)
| DDC 780.26/6—dc23
LC record available at https://lccn.loc.gov/2021055343
LC ebook record available at https://lccn.loc.gov/2021055344

British Library Cataloging-in-Publication Data available

For Johnette, who brought the music home

CONTENTS

FOREWORD

I THINK THE FIRST THING EVERY READER WILL TAKE AWAY FROM THIS book, apart from its many compelling, sometimes even startling stories and the diversity of its subject matter, is the warmth and compassion of its presentation.

Which is not something to be taken for granted, whether in bitterly divided times like these, or in fact in any age. But it's something that Scott brings to every one of his multifaceted (as producer, writer, designer, and musician) endeavors.

I've known Scott since he was eighteen years old—I was eight years older, and we met, of course, over the blues—and even then he was the same uncommon combination of conscientious application and spirited adventurousness that he remains today. But I'm not sure that he was always this eloquent. (Well, maybe I missed something—certainly he always spoke the unvarnished truth.) Reading this book, though, has been something of a revelation to me, even if I was present for a good deal of it. It's a revelation, in a sense, as much for what it reveals about Scott—about his whole-hearted dedication not just to the music but to self- and social betterment—as it does about the artists he has worked with.

Scott has always been a kind of inspired generalist, with the emphasis on "inspired." If a job needed to be done, if a lesson needed to be learned, Scott was always there to do it, never with anything less than the most intense curiosity and determination to master even its most challenging elements. As the pages of this book make clear, Scott is committed to putting it all out there, to incorporating all of his feeling, all of his knowledge, all of his passion into the music he loves. One of the most interesting things about the book's progress (and it pays to read the chapters in sequence) is how much he learns along the way, as we follow both the arc of Scott's journey and the ever-deepening breadth of his musical knowledge and interests.

Certainly the passion is there from the start, and the focus, too. The intensity of his commitment is evident from the beginning—to the music, to the people that he cares so much about and makes the reader care about, too. But it's not just a single person's journey: he is describing a world that is opening up for him, a world in which, because of all the variables and imponderables, the determinedly idiosyncratic brilliance of so many of the artists he encounters, you have to be constantly on your toes, you have to be constantly committed to "learning and growing" (as the great country singer Dick Curless says)—unless you are willing to settle for a mediocre, or just plain conventional, result. And that is something, it is clear, Scott is never willing to settle for, as much out of his commitment to the artists he is working with as out of any ambition of his own

Humanity, compassion, resourcefulness, creative inspiration, and, perhaps most of all, creative *energy* all enter into it, and they are all evident in the stories and insights he relates, not just about the musicians who are the focal point of each chapter but about their families, too, and about the songwriters and session musicians who contribute so much to the final result. It is in a sense an insider's picture without any of an insider's cynicism. In fact cynicism would be the last word to apply to Scott's approach. Every session is undertaken with the highest of hopes and, whatever the challenges, never abandoned without seeking the highest point of achievement. *Making Tracks* is an unfailingly generous celebration of the creative spirit while never failing to provide a frank account of the challenges, and sometimes even failures (including his own), of a session. Painful personal details are often an inextricable part of the story. But they are always infused with a warmth, an honesty, a tenderness, and the fundamental sense of decency that is the hallmark of this book. And they are always presented with the same scrupulous attention to detail that serves both the artist's and the music's interests.

So many of the stories that Scott tells are both moving and compelling, told with a clarity and focus that never lose sight of their emotional core. These are stories about his *friends*, warmly and affectionately remembered. Some of the profiles that resonate most for me are the story of Beau Jocque, a towering figure in modern zydeco who brought a ferocity of attack never before seen in the music. Then there is Johnny Adams's growing discovery of his own voice not just as the glorious instrument that won him early success but as a means to interpret (particularly through the songs of Percy Mayfield and Doc Pomus) the world around him. The return to prominence of Ruth Brown (Atlantic Records was originally described by its founders as

"The House That Ruth Built" because of her pathbreaking hits) is described in eloquent autumnal colors, as Scott opens with Brown's performance at a casino in Greenville, Mississippi, where, "if her voice was now grainier than on her early hit records, her timing, wit, and charismatic sass left no doubt that she remained a singer and entertainer of undiminished power." "Charismatic sass" just kills me every time.

But Scott does not gloss over difficult times either. There is the tragic and mystifying tale of James Booker. There are the occasional combative moments, none more dramatic than the Solomon Burke session in New Orleans, from which, as Scott writes, both he and Solomon would call me at home each night with their own diametrically opposed version of events. (I've got to admit, much as I loved Solomon—and there was no end to that love—Scott was right.) And then there was the Charlie Rich session, which, for all of Charlie's characteristic misgivings and self-doubt (Charlie wore his nerve endings "on the outside," Sam Phillips observed of one of his favorite artists), somehow magically came together. But I think the portrait that will stay with me longest is the chapter on Boozoo Chavis, probably the artist I knew least before reading Scott's book. Here we get not just an incisive portrait of a zydeco pioneer (his classic "Paper in My Shoe," as Scott describes it, is "one of the most unlikely hit records" of all time, with an indefinable appeal in which only one thing is clear: "that Boozoo and the band are playing in different keys"). Not too many years after that 1954 national hit, Boozoo withdrew from the business of making records, out of the belief that he was not being rewarded sufficiently for his labors, and returned to his mother's racetrack in the Dog Hill area on the outskirts of Lake Charles, Louisiana, where for the next twenty-five years he went back to training racehorses. It's a wonderful story, a wonderful portrait of family and a lost way of life, filled with ribald humor and good cheer—and it brings you around to the music in a way that no sober-sided analysis or recitation ever could.

That for me is the mark of *Making Tracks*, a triumph of empathetic portraiture, in which every one of its subjects is presented with both their humanity and artistry intact. You couldn't ask for a better cast of characters. But perhaps more important, as I think Scott would point out, you couldn't ask for a better group of friends.

PETER GURALNICK

MAKING TRACKS

Chapter 1

HEADING SOUTH

WHEN I WAS SEVENTEEN YEARS OLD, I PAID $200 FOR A RUSTED-OUT 1959 Ford panel truck. The TV-repair company that had abused it for the previous decade deeded me an oil-burning hulk that sagged on one side where a spring had snapped, with a view of the road through the front floorboards. I told my skeptical mother that my objective was restore to it to sufficient roadworthiness to make the drive from Massachusetts to Flagstaff, Arizona, where I had been accepted as a freshman at Northern Arizona University. But my real motive was to head south to hunt for records, and to experience the homeland of the blues music that had come to fill my head.

I bought sheet metal and screws and Sears body filler, patching holes so the wheel wells would no longer shower rainwater into the back of the truck. I paid almost fifty dollars to have a new spring installed at the right rear wheel. After I bolted an aluminum patch onto the floor, I splurged on a new rubber mat at Ellis the Rim Man in Boston. I built a platform of two-by-fours and plywood that would serve as my bed, and my mother made curtains for the back windows. I got a deal on an eight-track tape player at the Automatic Radio factory where I worked as a stock boy. Finally, I painted the interior and bumpers with light gray Rust-Oleum and finished the exterior with two cases of lemon-yellow spray paint. It looked pretty good, and the old tires passed inspection.

In mid-August of 1969, I set out on my journey with a Rand McNally road atlas and all my valued possessions: a Fender Mustang guitar, a Champ amplifier, a Hohner clavinet keyboard, a box of harmonicas, my records, my outdoor gear, and my clothes.

I had come to the blues slowly. I had seen Howlin' Wolf on the television program *Shindig*, with the Rolling Stones sitting at his feet, and was both captivated and puzzled by the immediacy and rawness of his performance, because I had no reference for what I was hearing, other than possibly the Stones themselves. When my mother brought me a copy of the Elmore James record of "Anna Lee" and "Stranger Blues," which she had obtained after waiting in line at a mall, where a local radio station was giving away random 45-rpm singles, I felt the same pull.

My father, Thomas Edward Billington, died at the age of forty in 1966, when I was fourteen years old, after my family had moved to East Brunswick, New Jersey, from Tempe, Arizona, following his promotion by the American Sugar Company to an office job in New York City. I had never experienced an up-close death before, and I could not comprehend that it had happened. I had visited him in the hospital in Philadelphia just the day before he passed away, and he had seemed better. But when I returned home from school the next afternoon, my mother was sitting with the minister from the Congregational church we had attended a few times. I felt scared, embarrassed (because I no longer had a father), and alone. I could not imagine what my mother, Norma (Duncan) Billington was going through. She now a young widow with four children to support. I was the oldest.

In 1967, the "summer of love," my friends and I started making trips into the Village in New York City to hear the Grateful Dead at the Café Au Go Go and the Mothers of Invention at the Garrick Theatre, sometimes telling our parents we were going to a ball game, but it was the Paul Butterfield Blues Band that turned my world around—the musicianship, the groove, and the fluid improvisation.

After my mother moved my sister, my two brothers, and me back to Massachusetts to be near her family, the older brother of a friend lent me the Junior Wells *Hoodoo Man Blues* album. I could not stop playing the record. Junior Wells made playing the harmonica sound as easy as breathing. My mother had given me a harmonica, for which she traded a book of Green Stamps, in my Christmas stocking when I was eleven years old, and I was now determined to learn to play it. I fumbled along as I tried to imitate the sounds of my new heroes.

If my father's death had left me empty and confused, I poured myself into the blues, reading books such as Samuel Charters's *The Country Blues* and subscribing to the British blues magazines *Blues Unlimited* and *Blues World*. I went to hear Muddy Waters, Howlin' Wolf, Buddy Guy, B. B. King,

Rahsaan Roland Kirk, Albert King, and Bobby "Blue" Bland at the Boston Tea Party and the Jazz Workshop in Boston; and at Lennie's on the Pike in suburban Peabody, where owner Lennie Sogoloff roped off a section for his underage customer, and where my mother would drop me off and then pick me up after the end of the first set. While the hippie counterculture was blossoming around me, I found my own alternate world.

Only a week before his death from endocarditis in that Philadelphia hospital, my father had planted an idea in my head. One of my favorite memories from our family's years living in Arizona, where my father had been transferred to help build a beet sugar refinery in the wake of the Cuban nationalization of it sugar plantations, was when my father took me to a fiesta in the Mexican American town of Guadalupe, outside Phoenix. We heard a large mariachi orchestra and ate Mexican food. Now, as he lay dying, he fantasized about the two of us starting a travelogue company that would explore the cultures of the world, bringing back film and recordings and artifacts to present in a lecture format. He was ready to leave behind the corporate world, where he had risen through the ranks from engineer to executive. Our conversations convinced me that it was a working life to which I would never aspire.

If I did not immediately connect my enthusiasm for the blues with my father's idea, I was clearly on a mission. In Massachusetts, after I got off my job each Saturday at noon, I boarded a bus to Harvard Square to buy records. Then, I headed to Skippy White's record shop in Roxbury, Boston's mostly African American neighborhood. Skippy was a goateed hipster who had also been bitten by the blues bug. He had learned the business during his tenure at the nearby (and by then shuttered) College Music, where every touring jazz artist, from Louis Armstrong to Ella Fitzgerald, had left an autographed photo. College Music was owned by "Smilin' Jack" Levenson, who had entered the music business as a sheet music "song plugger" in the days before records, and who was also the first independent distributor of rhythm and blues records in Boston, representing Atlantic, Chess, Specialty, and other labels.

Skippy had his own label—Bluestown—on which he released several singles by a Florida-born Boston bluesman named Guitar Nubbit, and reissues of Otis Rush's Cobra recordings. Skippy befriended me, playing 45-rpm records in which his regular clientele was no longer interested, and turning me on to artists as obscure as Whispering Smith and as important as Percy Mayfield, whose *My Jug and I* album made a crucial impression on me—jazz musicians playing blues and R&B. I came home with orange-labeled Excello singles by Slim Harpo and Lonesome Sundown, and with Clarence "Gatemouth" Brown's "Okie Dokie Stomp," which had a turquoise label embellished with a stylized Peacock. As I played them over and over (much to the annoyance of my younger brother, who was decidedly not a blues fan), I became aware that a door was slowly opening, and that another world was revealing itself.

I began imagining what it would be like to make records, noticing producers such as Samuel Charters, who made the *Chicago: The Blues Today* series for Vanguard; Chris Strachwitz, who owned Arhoolie Records in Berkeley, California; and Bob Koester, the founder of Delmark Records in Chicago. I thought about possible compilations of the 45s I was accumulating.

I was still practicing harmonica every day and was soon brave enough to start my own group, the Picket Fence Blues Band. Our big night was at a battle of the bands in the Boston suburb of Melrose. The three other groups on the bill played Vanilla Fudge and Bee Gees covers, while we opened with Paul Butterfield's "Born in Chicago." I am still not sure what the other kids thought of us, because no one hired us for the dances at which the other bands played, but we came in second.

As I was about to begin my senior year of high school, I answered an ad in the Cambridge folk music newspaper, *The Broadside*. A couple from Austin, Texas, Mike Allen and Lana Pettey, had relocated to Boston to be closer to the heart of the folk music scene, and they were looking for a harmonica player. I sent them a formal resumé and made a little chart telling me which harmonica to use to match the key of the guitar player. I was a sixteen-year-old kid who looked like a fourteen-year-old, but I got the gig.

Mike was (and remains) an accomplished finger-style guitar player with a repertoire learned from reissues of 78-rpm records by musicians like Blind Blake, the Mississippi Sheiks, and Little Hat Jones, and from the songs he heard while growing up in Texas. Lana played acoustic bass. Mike had been an active part of the Austin music scene, playing on some early recordings by Janis Joplin. I had big shoes to fill, because his previous harmonica player had been the wizard-like Powell St. John, who had gone on to become one of the principals in the band Mother Earth. I was initially shy onstage, but I was learning a new side of the blues repertoire from Mike, and my playing quickly got better.

Now, I was performing at Boston's Charles Street folk clubs—the Sword in the Stone and the Turk's Head—and at the Monday night "hoot" at the Catacombs, where musicians such as a young Loudon Wainwright III came to try out new songs. I was hanging out with a group of pot-smoking hippies who were almost a decade older than me. I rallied the courage to sit in with Muddy Waters at a Sunday afternoon jam session at the Jazz Workshop (well, I got to play a few choruses of a slow blues, because there was a line of guitar and harmonica players ahead of me and behind me). It gave me a bragging right, but I had no one to tell except Mike and Lana. My grades went to hell.

That summer, I graduated from high school and went to work full time at my factory job at Automatic Radio, a plant that assembled car radios and auto air conditioners, where I served as one of four stock boys for an ex-army sergeant named Izzy Kyrinski. He allowed us build a sort of clubhouse among the skids of air conditioner coils, but also expected, when he whistled, that we would run as fast as possible to the front of the warehouse and stand at attention, ready for his orders. I also kept up my performance schedule with the trio and continued working on the truck. It would soon be time to leave for college, a mandate from my father that I felt I had to honor. Because I had good memories of our life in Arizona, when my father, my brothers, and I had explored the deserts and mountains together, I enrolled in Northern Arizona University as a forestry major. I was sad to play my last gig with Mike and Lana, a four-day stint at the Yankee Rum Shop in Kennebunkport, Maine.

Now, I was on my way south, with a truck full of my belongings and about $300 cash in my pocket. My mother was understandably worried, so I promised her I would call her every night—two rings on the phone to let her know I was safe and sound, because I did not have the money to pay for actual conversations. Gasoline was under thirty cents a gallon, and I ate food that I bought in supermarkets. I knew I had to economize.

The first leg of the trip was uneventful. On the tape player, Jimmy Reed sang "Going to New York" as I crossed the George Washington Bridge. The truck radio had stopped working long before I took possession, but I had a battery-powered unit that I sometimes propped up on the seat beside me. Junior Walker's "What Does It Take (To Win Your Love)" and Tony Joe White's "Polk Salad Annie" were AM radio hits, and they urged me on. When it got dark, I pulled into a roadside rest area in Pennsylvania, drew the curtains, and went to sleep.

My first musical stop was Nashville. I was not a country music fan, but I knew the importance of the place. Lower Broadway was colorful and seedy, and I enjoyed the Ernest Tubb record shop, where there certainly were treasures to be found that I was too naive to recognize. At dusk, I parked outside the Ryman Auditorium and waited for the radio broadcast of the Grand Ole Opry, because I did not feel I could afford the price of a ticket. When the program ended, I drove out of town and found a rest area, where I parked for the night.

I made it to Memphis early the next morning, where I consulted the Yellow Pages in a phone booth and quickly found the downtown record shop, Poplar Tunes. The salesclerk was mildly helpful and amused as he met my request for blues records by pulling brown-sleeved 45s down from the wall of records behind the counter. He played Lowell Fulson's "Reconsider Baby" on the Kent label, which I bought, but the selection of records did not seem all that different from Skippy's. Then, I got lucky.

An elderly man in a worn suit approached me and said, "If that's the kind of music you're looking for, let me tell you where to go." He scratched out a map on the back on an envelope and sent me to Select-O-Hits, a one-stop distributor that sold records to small retailers. (It is still active in 2021, now as one of the major hip-hop distributors in the South.)

The front room of the warehouse was a clutter of records and cardboard boxes, mostly piled under, on, and around a huge table. The man behind the counter said, "Take your time," and I dived in, while regular customers came in occasionally to pick up their orders. I started seeing the record labels—Duke, Chess, Sun, Savoy, Bullet—and my heart raced. Almost immediately, I found a copy of Buddy Guy's first record, "Sit and Cry (The Blues)" on Artistic Records. There was Elmore James on the Fire label, Slim Harpo on Excello, and dozens of Sun rockabilly records—Jerry Lee Lewis, Billy Lee Riley, and Carl Perkins. Sun 78s were scattered under the table.

As I found what I wanted to buy, I stacked the records neatly at the far end of the counter until I had three substantial piles. I feared that I would not be able to afford them, because Poplar Tunes was still charging ninety-nine cents each for their old 45s. When I was ready, I asked the man how much all of this would cost. He looked me up and down a few times. My hair had remained uncut since high school ended, and it was in need of a good washing. I still looked like I was fourteen years old. Finally, he said, "Aw, give me eight bucks."

Many years later, I realized that I was probably talking with Tom Phillips, the proprietor of Select-O-Hits and the brother of Sun Records founder Sam Phillips, and that the remaining Sun stock was on the shelves in the back, but that never diminished the elation of my eight-dollar score. I also learned that, not many months later, the record collector and Canned Heat lead singer Bob Hite cleaned the place out.

I stepped out of the door and into the Memphis summer with a light heart. If I never found another good record, I reckoned that my trip had been worth it. I stashed the records under my bedframe, worrying about the heat. After a drive up and down the pre-redevelopment Beale Street, which seemed a little too dicey for exploration on foot, I headed south out of Memphis on Highway 61. I planned a route through the Mississippi Delta to New Orleans, keeping my eye out for whatever kind of shop might have old records.

At the time, Highway 61 was a two-lane road. There were no casinos in north Mississippi, and what I mostly saw was cotton. The towns were dusty and quiet. I looked on my map and saw the names of the places where the blues had been conjured—Tutwiler, Itta Bena, and Indianola. At Clarksdale, I veered onto Highway 49, which would take me through Yazoo City to Jackson.

Then, about three miles outside of Greenwood, the motor in my truck abruptly stopped running. I coasted to a halt by the side of the road, where flat cotton fields extended to the horizon on all sides. The temperature must have been close to one hundred degrees. I tried to restart the engine, but it did not make a sound when I turned the key. The metal of the truck's hood was almost too hot to touch.

The reality of my situation began to sink in: OK, here you are, broke down in the middle of rural Mississippi, a long-haired kid in a bright yellow truck from Massachusetts. And now you are going to have to ask for help, if you can get someone to stop. Your records are going to melt.

I locked the truck and stuck out my thumb. To my amazement, the first car that came along stopped—a red convertible occupied by a young couple. I told them my plight. "I know just where to go," said the man who drove the car, because he had a relative who owned a garage in Greenwood. I hopped in the back seat, and they delivered me to a busy gas station and auto repair shop.

The owner had a gentle manner and a deeply creased face. He interrupted one of his mechanics, a young man with a sorghum accent, and asked him to take the Jeep out to see if he could get my truck going. We found it where I had left it, with no police or vandals in sight. The mechanic looked under the hood, into the engine compartment that was almost big enough to step into, but nothing obvious was wrong. We decided to try to jump-start the truck. He aligned the Jeep to give the truck's substantial bumper a push, and once we got rolling I popped the clutch and the motor came to life.

We drove back to the garage, where the combined staff huddled and deduced that the truck would not start or run at high temperature because the starter motor had burned up. "I think I can find you one of those," said the owner. The mechanic again left in the Jeep and came back in about twenty minutes with the part.

It was clear that my vehicle and I were objects of great curiosity. "Look at that," said the owner, with a hint of admiration, "You got you a bed and your records and just about everything you need except maybe a little girl to keep you company." I am sure I blushed.

The truck came down off the lift with the new starter motor installed, and it started right away.

"What do I owe you," I asked.

"Well, I got that part used, so how does twenty-eight bucks sound?" asked the garage owner.

I paid him and shook everyone's hands, astonished both at the price and their kindness. Now, it was an even better day, and I was in love with Mississippi in a way that I never could have predicted. I phoned my mother and let the phone ring twice.

Then, I began thinking about the sorry mechanical state of my truck. It had 130,000 miles on it before the indeterminate time in the past when the odometer cable broke, and I really did have to drive it to Arizona. It was burning a quart of oil with every fill up, despite my regular additions of STP. The motor and transmission appeared to be held together with hardened grease, and there was no telling what might break next.

I made an on-the-spot decision and reluctantly decided to forego the trip to New Orleans. I abruptly headed west across the Mississippi River into Arkansas. The sun had set, so I retreated to the dark recess of a roadside picnic area. After I had turned in for the night, a group of young men pulled in to drink beer and party loudly. They approached my truck, and I became frightened when they commented on my Massachusetts plates, but I kept still until they eventually left.

After that, I did not stop for much of anything except gasoline and the bathroom until I arrived in Flagstaff, once giving myself the luxury of a night in a cheap hotel in Texas, where I showered twice, and stopping to see my cousin Richard in Tucson. The records survived the trip, and the truck kept running for a while longer, at least on cold mornings, until the compression gave out.

Noticing that most of the forestry students at Northern Arizona University were not proponents of the new counterculture, and that there were no women in the program, I spontaneously switched my major to English. My year in college passed quickly, but not without an incident that would hamper the possibility of returning. After reading Carlos Castaneda's *The Teachings of Don Juan*, I decided to experiment with the hallucinogenic cactus called peyote. When I left a dozen peyote "buttons" drying on my dorm room radiator, a fellow student turned me in to campus police. I got busted and was placed on social probation, although I still managed to get into a Ray Charles show when he performed at school. Nonetheless, my formal academic career was over for the time being (years later, I would resume with classes at the Harvard Extension School).

I went back to Massachusetts, where I worked briefly at the E. V. Yeuell nameplate factory (where I became a pretty good spray-painter, and where I met my first wife, Janice Wilson), then got a job at the recently opened New England Music City record store on Boylston Street in Boston. I had gotten to know the store's manager, Ric Aliberte, at another record shop, and he hired me to take care of the blues and folk sections. Within a year, Ric had left to take a promotion job at a record company, and I became the manager. We stocked just about every record in print at the time, and I learned about many less-than-familiar genres of music from fellow employees such as Eric Jackson, who went on to host WGBH's beloved *Eric in the Evening* jazz program. At the same time, I joined Mike Allen in his new band, and I edited a music newspaper called *PopTop*. My daughter Meredith was born when I was twenty-two. I also tried my hand as a freelance writer, placing an article on a railroad excursion trip with *Yankee*, as well as pieces with the *Boston Globe* and the music fanzine *Fusion*. Through the store, I met Bruce Iglauer, the founder of Alligator Records, and Bruce Bromberg, who founded Joliet and Hightone. Both became lifelong friends, and Bruce Bromberg became a true mentor.

I was soon invited to join the Boston Blues Society, a small group that included folklorist Erika Brady, fellow blues enthusiast Steve Frappier, promoter Durg Gessner, writer Peter Guralnick, producer/writer Jack Viertel, and booking agent/manager Dick Waterman. For several years during the early 1970s, we staged concerts by Johnny Shines, Houston Stackhouse, Hacksaw Harney, Joseph Spence, Hound Dog Taylor, Dr. Ross, Roosevelt Sykes, Little Brother Montgomery, and many more. A few of them, such as the Mississippi guitarists Son House and Skip James, had been among the first generation of blues players to record, and I felt lucky to be able to see them. Joseph Spence stayed at my apartment ("Ah, 'tis a punishing place," he commented after seeing snow for the first time), and my car smelled like Roosevelt Sykes's cigars for months after I drove him to his show.

At our Boston Blues Society concerts, I met the three founders of Rounder Records—Ken Irwin, Marian Leighton-Levy and Bill Nowlin—where they had set up a table full of cardboard boxes of records. They were about to release the first Rounder albums and were selling roots music records on various other independent labels to raise funds for their new venture.

At the record store, I started amassing a stock of vintage blues 45s that I scavenged through the network of distributors that supplied the store, and from entrepreneurs such as Chicago's Narvel "Cadillac Baby" Eatmon (Bea and Baby Records), Louisiana's Eddie Shuler (Goldband Records), and a company called Halper's that owned the remaining stock of Cincinnati's King and Federal Records. To sell the records, I asked permission to use the Boston Blues Society's mailing list. I remember when Skippy White's Massachusetts Records Distributors scored one hundred copies of the Otis Rush single "Homework," which had recently been covered by the J. Geils Band. I quickly sold them all, and even reported it to the trade magazines. Yet, as much as I was indulged by my employer, a gentle man named Howie Ring, sales of the 45s eventually waned. Apparently, no one in Boston valued the single of "Hamburger's and Popcorn" [sic] by Boozoo Chavis and his Zodico Accordion as much as I did. When a fire above the store resulted in modest water damage, Howie suggested that I douse the remaining 45s, by the likes of Little Walter, Freddy King, and Jerry McCain, in the sink so the company could collect insurance money for them.

By 1976, I was performing with the swing band Roseland, working three or four nights each week and traveling around New England. As a result, I could no longer hold the record store job. My marriage ended, and I moved in with two of my bandmates. To help make ends meet and to support my daughter, I took a part time job with Rounder Records as a salesperson. It was a natural fit. I loved what Rounder did, as well as the slightly anarchic bent of its roots music mission. Still, it was mostly a practical decision, and certainly not a conscious career move.

As I traveled with the band, I opened Rounder accounts with record stores, head shops, and boutiques, being careful to recommend only what I thought each shop could sell. I stayed in touch with them by phone when I could not be there. Once, when visiting Al Wilson, the buyer for the Strawberries record store chain in Boston, the store owner and label executive Morris Levy (of Roulette Records, among others) saw my selection of new Yazoo Records LP covers. He picked them up and said, in his gravelly New York voice, "You might be in the record hobby, but I'm in the fucking record business," as he tossed them down.

Within two years, I had begun my record production career at Rounder by putting together, with Peter Guralnick, a Johnny Shines album from Boston Blues Society tapes. We edited the songs together at a local studio, where the engineer insisted on fading the applause after each song. I later learned how tape could be edited carefully with a razor blade to make a near-seamless transition. For the package, I designed my first album cover. Overall, the record was a success, garnering good reviews and earning modest royalties for Johnny.

With the informal business culture of Rounder Records, employees were given permission, at least implicitly, to take on just about any task that might help the company. I found that if I tried something and it succeeded, I could keep doing it. That was how I became a graphic designer, when I became intrigued with the album cover "mechanicals" delivered by designer Susan Marsh. I took two graphic design classes at the Art Institute of Boston, and with additional advice from Susan, I learned the basics of the trade. I had been drawing pictures since I was very young, and I loved the design process—working with type and color, and the precision required to prepare the artwork for press.

In 1977, I traveled to the Bahamas with Bill Nowlin and our girlfriends to record the iconoclastic guitarist Joseph Spence on a portable Revox two-track recorder set up in a hotel room. Spence seemed to have invented his complex and syncopated guitar style single-handedly, improvising counter-melodies against darting bass lines while he grunted out the words to pop tunes or hymns. Since his visit to my home for his Boston Blues Society concert, we had kept up a regular correspondence, and he invited us to visit him to record. We walked across Nassau to find his home, Louise Cottage, which he had built by hand for his wife, along with many other houses. She told us that he was "off shoving checkers at Gibbs Corner," where a checkerboard had been set up under the trees behind a small store that sold fresh fruit and live crabs. The session almost did not happen because the Bahamas customs officials were suspicious of the tape machine and demanded that we pay a considerable refundable duty. Thankfully, Bill had brought enough money.

When I proposed to the Rounder owners that Peter and I take an active role in the production of a new album by Robert Jr. Lockwood and Johnny Shines, assuming some responsibility for creative direction, their response was not encouraging. Perhaps they felt that the concept of formal record production that went beyond a purely musician-directed approach was contrary to their mission. I was also a relatively new addition to the staff. But, little by little, I started making inroads.

We went forward with the Robert Jr. Lockwood and Johnny Shines project. Both guitarists had traveled and performed with the pioneering bluesman Robert Johnson in the 1930s, and each had moved forward with creative ideas that made them among the most distinctive players of their generation. Robert's jazzy chord voicings could be heard on the classic Chess label recordings by Sonny Boy Williamson, while Johnny's emotive voice was among the most powerful in Chicago blues. Neither musician had become a blues star, but we realized the responsibility of working with them.

For *Hangin' On*, Robert and Johnny self-produced six band tracks near Robert's home in Cleveland, Ohio, after which the duo traveled to Newton, Massachusetts, to record their acoustic duets at the Mixing Lab, with Peter and me present. We were chagrined when the engineer carelessly erased the second half a brilliant take of a slow blues called "Lonesome Whistle." "Just have them play it again," was his curt retort. But Peter and I knew that something irreplaceable had been lost—that they would not do it that way again—and we were right. Johnny, who knew exactly what had happened, looked at us with amusement and said, "Sure—just play it back for us." They played a new, shorter version, but it did not have the same ethereal, improvised feeling of the first. Nonetheless, the album was a success, and won the W. C. Handy Award for Traditional Blues Album of the Year in 1980.

The following year, we embarked on a follow-up album, but as we were about to begin rehearsals and preproduction at a Cambridge rehearsal facility, Robert dropped an amplifier on his hand and broke a finger. The sessions had to be postponed. Robert and his band drove back to Cleveland, and Johnny to his home in Holt, Alabama, near Tuscaloosa. Then, Johnny had a stroke. He eventually made a medically successful recovery, regaining mobility and speech, but his musical chops were diminished. We reconvened at Dimension Sound in Jamaica Plain, Massachusetts, but the album was, to my ears, a disaster. Johnny's loss of his ability to play the guitar and to control the nuance of his once-powerful voice was heartbreaking. Robert could not be convinced to turn off the phase shifter effect on his guitar, and the recording is poorly focused and mixed. A review of *Mister Blues Is Back to Stay* in the Boston *Phoenix* postulated that Robert and Johnny were bravely confronting their mortality with their new music, while I was thinking I might be confronting the mortality of my incipient career as a record producer.

I recovered with *Electricity*, a record with Arkansas rockabilly Sleepy LaBeef, who was based for several years in the Boston area, after his tour bus caught fire on the Maine Turnpike. I put together an all-star New England band, with brothers Bobby and Russell Keyes on guitar and bass; Harry King, from singer Dick Curless's band, on piano; and Rick Nelson on drums. I had been playing in Sleepy's band on a regular basis, so I planned to add harmonica on a few songs. At Dimension Sound, the chemistry between the band and Sleepy ignited as, on the second day, they laid down an impassioned set of blues, country, rockabilly, and gospel songs. The tracks seemed to fly onto tape in a fervor of synchronous creativity, with Sleepy barely containing his energy while we discussed the arrangement of the next song. Then, at the peak of the session's intensity, the recording console broke down, and we could not continue. When we resumed a few days later at Blue Jay Studio in Carlisle, Massachusetts, the feeling and the spirit were not the same, and we recorded only a few more tunes that were worth releasing. Still, the exhilaration of having captured such a transcendent set in the studio was a kind of rush that I had not experienced before. It was as if nothing had come between the feeling in the music and the recording process, that all artifice and conscious effort had lifted, and that the music simply happened. This feeling was now in my blood as a recording experience—something I might almost describe as an addiction that I would seek to recreate as often as I could.

The Magnetos, a band led by Mike Allen, in the late 1970s. *Left to right:* Bob Anderson (drums), Tim Fiehler (bass), Mike Allen (guitar), Paul Combs (saxophone), Scott Billington (harmonica) (from the collection of Scott Billington).

I was still playing music around New England with a new band, led by Mike Allen, called the Magnetos. We had evolved from a country blues ensemble into a roots rock band, covering songs by Smiley Lewis, Professor Longhair, and Huey Smith and the Clowns, following, perhaps by happenstance, my own developing interests, although the other band members were of like mind when it came to repertoire.

During this time, I completed most of the Berklee School of Music correspondence course, to learn music theory, and I studied ear training with the brilliant jazz pianist and "re-composer" Ran Blake, who taught at the New England Conservatory of Music and who often created exquisite harmonic tension in the standards he deconstructed, opening up new possibilities for an improvising instrumentalist or vocalist. The course with Ran was the most useful I have ever taken, because knowing how to hear may be the most valuable asset a record producer can possess.

In 1977, Rounder released the first of three records by George Thorogood and the Destroyers, and soon the label had a genuine hit on its hands with his version of Bo Diddley's "Who Do You Love?" The follow-up album, *Move It on Over*, was even bigger, as the title track became an FM radio smash. It was not long before many blues-based artists approached Rounder, believing that the company had discovered a magic marketing formula. One of them was the Louisiana/Texas guitarist Clarence "Gatemouth" Brown. Of course, I knew about Brown from the 45s that Skippy White had sold me, and also from his thrilling set at the 1980 New Orleans Jazz and Heritage Festival.

Like so many others, I had begun making a yearly pilgrimage to Jazz Fest, staying with my musician friends Karen Konnerth and Vic Shepherd, who had moved there from New England. I fell in love with the city, where the layers of music and music history were as thick as the humidity. Traditional jazz, rhythm and blues, modern jazz, brass band music, gospel music, Mardi Gras Indians, and a cast of eccentric, one-of-a-kind musicians who seemed at times to cross all genres—Snooks Eaglin, Earl King, James Rivers, the Neville Brothers—all competed for space in my head.

Then, Gatemouth Brown's manager, Jim Bateman, came to Rounder with a proposal and partial funding to make a new record, and I was soon on my way to Bogalusa, Louisiana, to coproduce the album with him. My "record hobby" and my dream of making records was becoming my career, as my father's vision of cultural exploration and documentation morphed into my role as a record producer.

This book is primarily a chronicle of my adventures in that role, in Louisiana and in Memphis (even though I have made records with many talented artists in other parts of the world), and of my relationships with the artists I recorded, both the legends and the upstarts. The chapters are arranged chronologically, based on when I began working with each musician, followed by several wrap-up chapters. Along the way, I offer my perspective on technical elements of the recording craft, as well as the musical and logistical elements that are the foundation of any successful session. However, this book is primarily about a journey that involves the pursuit of something entirely elusive, when the walls of the recording studio become invisible, and when the possibility emerges that we may capture music so filled with immediacy and discovery that the listener will feel the same thing. If we are lucky, we may create something that surprises the musicians themselves, who will break into collective laughter at the end of a take. It is a situation that I have tried to foster in every session, sometimes with success, and occasionally not. Every recording takes its own path, and I hope you enjoy following each one of them with me.

Chapter 2

SLEEPY LABEEF

IT WAS SEVEN O'CLOCK ON A SATURDAY SUMMER MORNING AS I DROVE UP the hill to the property where Sleepy LaBeef had parked his large recreational vehicle, in the circular driveway of the home of his friends Cliff and June Titcomb. We were about to travel from Amesbury, Massachusetts, to a rockabilly festival in Woodstock, New York, where Robert Gordon and Sleepy were the headliners. While the RV was home to Sleepy, his wife Linda, and their two young daughters, he had often driven it to out-of-town gigs.

Today, I found Sleepy across the lawn with a bottle of Formula 409 and a roll of paper towels in his hands, cleaning the musty upholstery of a gold, early-1970s Cadillac. In addition to his stature as one of the last of the original generation of rockabilly singers, Sleepy was an inveterate trader, with a collection of cars, trucks, and other equipment.

"I thought we might take the Cadillac today," he said as he clambered to his feet. I would ride shotgun with Sleepy, while the other band members, bassist Ken Krumbholz and drummer Clete Richards, would drive in the former bread-delivery truck that would carry the equipment.

We pulled out onto Interstate 495 and quickly gained speed, but when Sleepy tapped the brakes, the car shuddered with a harsh metal-on-metal clank.

"Sleepy, that doesn't sound too good. Are you sure the brakes are OK?" I asked. "I'll be happy to drive us in my car, if you want."

"Nah, they're just a little rusty," he replied. "Nothing to worry about at all."

I enjoyed traveling with Sleepy, both for the conversation and for the adventures that were usually in store. His stories about the blues, country, and gospel artists that inspired both of us occupied a great deal of our

Sleepy LaBeef at Blue Jay Studio, Carlisle, Massachusetts (photograph © Scott Billington)

discussion, but he might also talk about his spiritual beliefs. He was a Pentecostal who subscribed to a number of sermons and debates that he listened to on cassette tape. Yet, he retained a reasonably open view of other religions and lifestyles, rendering no judgment when he was greeted by a tattooed and pierced punk rocker, or an inebriated fan at a country bar.

I told him that I was reading Frank Waters's *Book of the Hopi*, in which the author wrote down the stories and beliefs of Hopi elders, including an entry that seemed to mirror the Noah's Ark story—of God giving the world a clean slate. He listened intently.

"How old did you say that book is?" he asked.

"Well, it's not exactly a book, because the stories were passed on from generation to generation, but they could go back thousands of years," I replied.

He turned and said sternly, "Scott, I know of no book that is older than the Bible."

We came to the end of the Massachusetts Turnpike and entered New York. Our exit to the road that would take us down the Hudson Valley to

Woodstock was a long descending ramp. When Sleepy applied the brakes, there was a small popping sound. And then nothing.

"Hold on," he said calmly, in his deepest baritone. We had no brakes other than the parking brake, which did little to slow the heavy car.

As soon as he could, he edged the car onto the grassy shoulder, knocking down a couple of "stop ahead" signs. We came to rest about twenty feet from a busy crossroads, unscathed.

We drove slowly to the service station across the intersection, where the mechanic put the car on a lift and removed the right front wheel, which was wet with brake fluid. The brake disc was so rusty that it had shattered to pieces, sending the piston flying and most of the brake fluid onto the road behind us. It might have been possible to order new parts to repair the brake, but we had a festival to go to. Sleepy's solution was to jam a nail into the brake line and crimp it over with pliers. After refilling the system with fluid and bleeding the air out, we were on our way, now with only one front brake. The road was hilly, especially as we approached Woodstock, and the car pulled violently to the right side every time Sleepy had to stop, but we arrived safely. Sleepy's entrance was grand as he stepped out of the gold Cadillac in his black Western jacket, scarlet shirt, and Stetson hat.

"Hold on" is a good metaphor for what it was like to perform a set with Sleepy. There were a few songs that he played often (Hank Ballard's "Tore Up," Tony Joe White's "Roosevelt and Ira Lee"). But, for the most part, we never knew what was coming next. Every now and then, he would lean over and say, "Get out your harmonica in the key of G," but, usually, everyone had to wing it. Still, there were chord changes to make (or miss, at least the first time through). I think he actually enjoyed a bit of anarchy behind him, and that he was amused by watching his musicians scramble.

One day, after meeting guitarist EJ Ouellette in a local music shop, Sleepy asked if he could make the gig that night at the Fifth Wheel Lounge at Alan's Truck Stop in Amesbury. EJ arrived early and set up his equipment, but when Sleepy took the stage, he directed EJ to an electronic keyboard. EJ fumbled through the night on an instrument he had never played in public, doing his best to keep up. When Sleepy paid him, he commented, "EJ, you're a heck of a keyboard man, but I don't care for your attitude." The negative aspect of the loosely controlled chaos was that the show could come across as amateurish, although as long as Sleepy dashed forward with confidence, I am not sure that many fans noticed.

He did not want us to play anything fancy. He wanted the drummer to play eighth notes on the ride cymbal, the two and four beats on the snare, and the one and three beats on the kick drum. If a drummer dared to play an accent on the hi-hat instead of keeping a steady pulse on the ride cymbal, Sleepy would turn around and give him a scowl. Once, at a gig at Johnny D's in Somerville, Massachusetts, he began playing the Junior Parker (via Elvis Presley) song "Mystery Train," then stopped abruptly and turned to the drummer.

"Now, you might think you're playing 'Mystery Train,' but that ain't it." He then went to the drum kit, sat down, and attacked the groove he was looking for, teaching a lesson the drummer would not forget. Sleepy also played slapped acoustic bass. On any instrument, the sound he made was brash and exciting.

It was precisely Sleepy's unpredictability that made the gig thrilling. We never knew when he would veer into a full set of songs by Ernest Tubb or Jimmy Reed or a country singer—maybe Little Jimmy Dickens—that we had barely heard of. Each set was a stream-of-consciousness ride through a landscape of song that Sleepy may have known better than anyone else in the business. At an outdoor gig in Jackson Square in New Orleans, which was taped for Cox Cable, the skies opened up into a drenching downpour just as we were winding down the set. Sleepy started playing Slim Harpo's "Rainin' in My Heart" as the water ran from the brim of his hat into his guitar. He claimed to know six thousand songs.

But there was another, more transcendent aspect of spontaneity that we all waited for. It did not happen every night, and it could happen on almost any song, but sometimes the music would transport Sleepy to a place beyond the gig, to a realm of pure feeling and energy. His eyes would stare blankly forward, and his jowls would shake. If the song called for it, he might scream, and he would bend chords on his hollow-body Gibson by pulling the whole neck of the guitar back. The intensity of his performance would reach a fervid spirituality that made everyone in the place pay attention, and maybe feel just a little bit lifted. When it was over, he might turn to me or one of the other musicians and say, while catching his breath, "Well, I guess I got a little carried away there."

Born in Smackover, Arkansas, in 1935, Thomas Paulsley LaBeff moved to Houston at age eighteen, where he briefly sang gospel music with his first wife, but when he heard Elvis Presley, he knew he had found his calling.

Peter Guralnick, Scott Billington, and Sleepy LaBeef, ca. 1982 (photograph © Henry Horenstein)

Rockabilly, the hopped-up fusion of country music, blues, and gospel, came naturally to Sleepy, who cited the guitar playing of Sister Rosetta Tharpe as a model for his own. He was an instinctive entertainer who loved his fans, and whose extraordinary memory served not only his repertoire. At a country music bar outside of Bangor, Maine, I watched him greet a fan that he had not seen in years. "Fred, how have you been? And how's Mildred?" He seemed never to forget a face or a name.

When Sleepy signed with Rounder Records in 1979, he had just ended his tenure as the last rockabilly artist signed to the original rockabilly label, Sun Records. After his tour bus caught fire on the Maine Turnpike, he more or less became the house band at Alan's Fifth Wheel Lounge, and a resident of Amesbury. When Steve Morse of the *Boston Globe* discovered him performing there and wrote his first piece about Sleepy, the truck stop gained a new group of regulars, including many area musicians, writer Peter Guralnick, the Rounder Records founders, and me.

Alan's Truck Stop seemed like a place out of another time. Located near the intersection of Routes 95 and 495, near the New Hampshire border, the twenty-four-hour complex included a diner, a sixteen-room motel, a repair garage, a small store, and the nightclub, which featured local and national country artists (we also saw Carl Perkins there). The Fifth Wheel

Lounge felt like it belonged in northern Maine or, perhaps, somewhere in the South a decade or two earlier, where Lefty Frizzell or Hank Williams might be appearing on the next night. It seemed that the truckers might be able to get anything they wanted at Alan's. There were always women at the bar who were available for a conversation or a spin on the spacious dance floor. Sleepy took it all in stride, occasionally calling one of the waitresses or regulars to join him onstage to perform a song.

For Sleepy's first Rounder sessions, label founder Ken Irwin brought him to Nashville and recorded him with an A-list band that included pianist Earl Poole Ball, Elvis Presley drummer D. J. Fontana, and fiddler Buddy Spicher. It is a wonderful record, and a step forward, production-wise, from his recent Sun material, but I felt that it did not capture what Sleepy was truly about. Cliff Parker played most of the guitar solos, as he had on the most recent Sun sessions. Sleepy came across as a pro who was playing it safe.

The first record I produced by Sleepy, *Electricity* (after the gospel song of the same name), got closer to the artist I knew onstage, and if we had not suffered a recording studio breakdown, we might have gotten all the way there. You can hear the fervor in his voice on the title track and on songs such as the Cowboy Copas song "Alabam." His takes on Nancy Sinatra's "These Boots Are Made for Walking" and Clarence "Frogman" Henry's "Ain't Got No Home" demonstrate how the frivolity of rock and roll can be so much fun. And we tried some different production touches, too, such as the harmonized tenor saxes on "Cut It Out" and overdubbed backing vocals by the Questionaries—comprising probably half the Rounder staff—on the Bo Diddley–beat "I'm Through."

On this session, I also saw that for someone who could be so unconstrained, he could be picky about the moral shadings of the lyrics he sang, as when he changed an admiring reference to a dress on a woman from "real tight" to "real right," in Joe Tex's "Cut It Out." Listening to *Electricity* today, the compressed and over-equalized sounds, especially the drums, make the record seem small. I knew even then that we could do better.

I began to think that the only way we were going to get to the heart of Sleepy would be to record him live, and I approached the Rounder Records founders, asking for a modest budget to do so. My friend EJ, the guitar player, had invested in a good eight-track recorder, and we made plans to tape shows at two clubs with Sleepy's hot new rhythm section, drummer

Tommy Lewis and bassist Brent Wilson, who would later be the backbone of the Austin-based band the Wagoneers. Keyboardist Steve Staines would round out the band.

The first night, at the Grog in Newburyport, Massachusetts, did not go well. There was something about the place or the crowd that Sleepy did not like, and nothing was going to change his attitude. Perhaps he had his mind set on the next venue, Harper's Ferry in Allston, Massachusetts, because there he played one of the best shows I had ever heard him deliver. I joined him occasionally on harmonica, while running back and forth to the modest studio space that EJ had set up above and behind the stage. The club was packed, and midway through the evening, Boston mayor Raymond Flynn and his entourage arrived with great fanfare, as the mayor took the stage to sing "Elvira" with Sleepy. Sleepy reached one of his deepest states of transcendence on his wild version of "Let's Talk About Us," while the autobiographical "Boogie at the Wayside Lounge" channeled John Lee Hooker. I was elated that we finally had captured on tape what I most appreciated about Sleepy.

However, when we listened back to the tapes the next day, the improvised nature of the set became apparent. While Tommy never missed a beat, keeping up with every one of Sleepy's twists and turns, no one else had. The beginnings and endings of songs were often a mess, and some of the chord changes were not right. We also discovered a buzzing noise on the bass track that had not been audible in the "control room" at the club, with the din of the live show around us.

As I thought about the situation, I realized that if this had happened in a recording studio, we would simply fix everything. The only difference was that we were not likely to have gotten this kind of performance from Sleepy in the studio. So, at the expense of presenting an unvarnished live concert, and in service of a better listening experience for Sleepy's fans, I asked EJ and Steve to recut almost all the bass and keyboard parts. We also added EJ's rhythm guitar to many of the songs, and I recut several of my harmonica tracks with a more defined sound. When we were done, we took the tapes to engineer Gragg Lunsford at Blue Jay Studio, where he created an ambient environment for the final mix that was as exciting as Sleepy's performance.

I've carried this philosophy forward over the years. A recording is not a live performance, but it often is the illusion of one. Recording is its own

Scott Billington and Sleepy LaBeef at Tipitina's, ca. 1983 (photograph © Rick Olivier)

medium, and if a technological trick will enhance the listening experience, I'm usually all for it. There is absolutely no substitute for a genuine and emotive performance or vocal, which is impossible to fake. The craft of record production is to use the studio in a way that is invisible, so nothing distracts from the feeling and the art.

Sleepy went on to record several more albums for Rounder, and I think the two he made with Jake and Peter Guralnick as producers are the best of his studio work, with wonderful song choices and musicians. Those sessions made me think about all the little and often intangible things that can get in the way of an artist giving his or her best in the artificial environment of the studio. During a session for *Strange Things Happening*, on which I played harmonica, Jake was working on Sleepy's headphone mix, which was very loud, but still not to his taste.

"Jake, I think you'd better send out for another can of reverb," Sleepy joked.

And with just the right amount of echo added—actually, a whole lot—the session was off and rolling. The headphone mix is critical to what musicians will play, and how they will communicate with one another—probably the most important basic step of recording to get right.

Holding court in his motor home with a cup of black coffee in his hand (he brewed a commercial-sized urn every day), Sleepy sometimes seemed bemused by the visits of the fans, journalists, and musicians who sought him out, although he was appreciative of every one of them. He kept rocking until his death in 2019 at the age of eighty-four, playing songs that meant something to him, and if he never had a major hit record, the integrity of his presentation was timeless. He loved his family, and he was adored around the world, bringing honest and soulful American roots music to people who were undoubtedly moved and possibly changed by it.

And about that gold Cadillac. A few months after our trip to Woodstock, Sleepy drove it down to Harper's Ferry for a gig.

"Man, I'm glad you got those brakes fixed," I said.

"Fixed?" he replied. "Nah, if it ain't broke, don't fix it."

RECOMMENDED LISTENING:

"Let's Talk About Us" from *Nothin' But the Truth*
(*Electricity* has not yet been released digitally.)

Chapter 3

CLARENCE "GATEMOUTH" BROWN

WHEN I ARRIVED IN BOGALUSA, LOUISIANA, FOR THE FIRST TIME IN JUNE 1981, I had become happily acclimated to the cultural hodgepodge and decaying elegance of New Orleans. But Bogalusa was different, and it was unsettling. Jim Bateman, the manager of guitarist Clarence "Gatemouth" Brown, had picked me up at the New Orleans airport, and we drove north on the 26-mile-long causeway across Lake Pontchartrain before joining Route 21, which eventually became a two-lane road that passed small, ramshackle farms and the occasional new ranch-style brick home, shaded by tall longleaf pine trees. As we reached the outskirts of the small city, the air became heavy with the sour stench of the Crown Zellerbach paper mill. Then, one of the first buildings I saw was the local KKK headquarters. Between the smell of the Armor All in Jim's vintage Mercedes and the inescapable odor of the mill, I felt that I might not be able to breathe. That night, at a local restaurant, I noticed an Italian "Wop Salad" on the menu. What kind of place was this?

I had come to Bogalusa to coproduce an album, with Jim, by the guitarist and singer Clarence "Gatemouth" Brown at Studio in the Country, where Stevie Wonder, the Neville Brothers, Kansas, and Professor Longhair, among many others, had made wonderful-sounding records. It was a destination studio, and a world-class facility. It had been founded by Bogalusa native Bill Evans, with acoustic design by Los Angeles heavyweights Tom Hidley and George Augspurger, including a separate building constructed as a live reverb chamber. Jim, also a Bogalusa native, and new studio owner Gene Foster gave me a tour of the studio and its grounds, where the trees

Clarence "Gatemouth" Brown at Studio in the Country, Bogalusa, Louisiana, 1981 (photograph © Scott Billington)

and the carpet of pine needles made the smell of the paper mill less objectionable, or maybe I was already getting used to it.

I had previously met Gate, as everyone quickly learned to call him, only briefly, backstage at the New Orleans Jazz and Heritage Festival, and at a club in Cambridge, Massachusetts, so I knew him primarily through his recordings. Born in Vinton, Louisiana, in 1924, he made a series of blazing and highly influential blues records for Houston's Peacock label from the late 1940s through the 1950s, with his overdriven guitar often sparring with a tightly arranged horn section. When he moved to Nashville in the 1960s, he became the musical director of the television show *The !!!! Beat*, emceed by the pioneering R&B disc jockey Bill "Hoss" Allen, where he backed artists such as Otis Redding and Freddy King.

After a challenging and fallow period when he lived in New Mexico, he began to travel overseas, recording several very good albums in Europe. Back in the States, he became friends with the virtuoso guitarist and country entertainer Roy Clark, leading him to an association with the Tulsa-based booking agent Jim Halsey. He made a series of appearances with

Sticker from the 1979 USSR tour (courtesy of Joe Sunseri)

Clark on the television show *Hee Haw*, on which he played violin as well as guitar, and the duo made an excellent album together in Nashville, *Makin' Music*. During this time, Gate and his band, Gate's Express, embarked on a forty-five-day tour of the Soviet Union booked by Halsey through the Soviet agency Gosconcert, whose talent buyers had seen him at a Halsey showcase in Tulsa. It was the first tour of an American artist in the USSR that had not been booked by the State Department. Gate's most recent recording, *Blackjack*, was a set of jazz, blues, and country tunes that showcased his multi-instrumental prowess, produced by Jim Bateman, on which he was backed by the band Louisiana's LeRoux, who would soon have a hit with "Louisiana Ladies." It was a good fit. He continued to tour extensively with his own hot young band, whose members would be the core musicians on our new project.

I do not know what expectations I had in getting to know Gate, except that the mythological name on the turquoise-labeled Peacock record I had bought as a teenager was about to materialize as a real, living person. He drove up to the studio in the Grey Ghost, his touring van, which was decorated with bull horns mounted above the windshield. As Gate's baritone saxophonist Joe Sunseri recalls:

Somewhere in the Midwest, we stopped for lunch in the downtown of a small town. Gate came out with these self-sticking metal rectangles that had the letters of the alphabet on them. He proceeded to put on the side of the van—not too straight: "Clarence Gatemouth Brown . . . Kicking Ass and Taking Names." He got that saying from David Hickey, who was booking us [having superseded Halsey]. Within twenty-four hours the band was adjusting the signs to say "Ate Out Own" and whatever else we knew how to spell. The signs were on both sides of the van.

Gate's lean figure emerged from the van, dressed in black Western clothes, boots, and a cowboy hat. He was not a large man, but he walked with a swagger, like someone who knew how good he was, and who expected to be acknowledged. He was confident, but, as I would learn, he also carried a chip on his shoulder, and could be downright cantankerous.

Jim and I had done a fair amount of preparation for our sessions. With Gate, we had conceptualized the record as an extension of the big-band blues sound he had developed at Peacock Records, which itself was an extension of the horn-driven Texas blues style popularized by T-Bone Walker. This idea appealed to Gate, who liked nothing better than a big horn section riffing behind his explosive, staccato guitar runs.

Yet, I quickly realized that it was not a good idea to mention the word *blues* around Gate. He had grown up in the midst of one of the most musically rich environments in America, where, on any weekend night, Western swing, Cajun, pre-zydeco Creole, big-band jazz, country, and blues musicians might all be performing within a fifty-mile radius. As Gate recollected, his father was a professional string band musician who played mandolin, banjo, and fiddle, in a style that may have been akin to old-time country music. Gate idolized the big-band jazz of Duke Ellington and Count Basie, as well as the early R&B of Louis Jordan. T-Bone's music was blues, but it had a swinging and urbane sophistication about it. Young Clarence learned a little bit of all of it, becoming especially adept on fiddle, and developing an eccentric, highly recognizable guitar technique that used open tunings to allow for rolling, rapid-fire arpeggios, played with his fingers almost fully extended. Yet . . .

"Blues is the sound of ignorance," he told me. "You listen to somebody singing about misery and alcoholism and all that low-down moaning shit, it'll make you want to kill yourself. Music should be uplifting." I once heard him mimic the pronunciation of European audience members who would shout out for him to play "the bleeuuues," which he interpreted as a diminution of his music, and which might provoke him to play a fiddle tune instead (he had one called "Six Levels Below Plant Life," which seemed tailor-made for those occasions). I do not believe that Gate actually hated the blues, because he had such a deep understanding and feeling for the style, but he resented that he was constantly stereotyped and pigeonholed that way, especially when the music he grew up with had been so wide-open. He felt it was disrespectful that his music was perceived as raw and intuitive when, in fact, it reflected professionalism, practice, and a serious work ethic. And now, we were about to make a blues record.

Gate and his band had been performing many of the songs we would record on the road, including his own new songs "Sometimes I Slip" and "Dollar Got the Blues" and a few of his older numbers, newly arranged. I had brought along a few new/old songs from the Texas blues songbook, such as T-Bone Walker's "Strollin' with Bones" and Junior Parker's "I Feel Alright Again." We augmented the road band with trumpet player Stanton Davis Jr., who had played with Gate in Europe, and tenor saxophonist Alvin "Red" Tyler, a veteran of hundreds of New Orleans sessions.

However, I had made a major miscalculation, because the only horn charts the band members had written were for the songs they already knew, and then for only three horns. When I realized this, we quickly got to work. We divided up the songs between saxophonists Bill Samuel and Joe Sunseri, and trombonist Jim McMillen. Joe had played in the highly regarded Three o'Clock Lab Band at North Texas State University, from which Gate had recruited several band members (including bass player James Singleton, who would become my first-call bassist in New Orleans, but who by now had left the band). After running through arranging ideas with Gate, because many of the horn parts would be based on his guitar lines, our arrangers went off to separate rooms, scribbling away until each chart was done. In the meantime, we worked on refining rhythm section arrangements, and going over lyrics with Gate. When a horn chart was ready, all the musicians would convene in the main studio, where, for the most part, we cut everything live, with Gate sitting in the center of the room and conducting with his guitar neck as he played.

The music was spectacular, as Gate reveled in the big sound behind him. He had taught the rhythm section of drummer Lloyd Herman, bassist

Myron Dove, and pianist David Fender to swing like mad, and we worked on the horns until they did the same. In many ways, I was reminded of Percy Mayfield's recordings with the Ray Charles band, and we even cut one of Percy's songs.

I learned not to push Gate too hard if he was initially unreceptive to an idea, waiting until he voiced his own version of what I was suggesting. He had a strong ego, the positive side of which was that he was going to rise to this occasion and show the world what he was made of. With its return to swinging, big-band blues, this would be the rebirth of Gate's music, in his favorite musical setting.

On the slow blues "Sometimes I Slip," Gate played his trademark "shock wave," a full chord played with a thirty-second-note trill that builds in intensity over the first four measures of the solo, before dropping to near silence on the chord change. It's a cathartic effect. Red added a sweet and lyrical solo based on the old folk blues tune "Black Gal." It is a masterful performance by all that stands with the best of Gate's blues recordings.

Spirits kept getting higher. Actually, we all kept getting higher as Gate brought out his special blend. I usually have no tolerance for drugs in recording sessions, but in this environment, a hit of marijuana every now and then seemed right. Gate was magnanimous as he imagined building a ranch where we all could live, with a recording studio where we could record whenever we wanted. A family environment had coalesced, and we enjoyed immensely our dinner breaks, with a soul food buffet prepared and catered by Mrs. Green Andrews. Maybe Bogalusa was the place to be, after all. I realized how intimate and familial a recording session could become, except it was not really like a family, because all of us would go our separate ways in just a few days.

At Studio in the Country, I met engineer David Farrell for the first time, beginning a relationship that endures to this day. In addition to his acute ears and audio engineering skills, he is one of the most patient and calming people I have known. His contributions to our sessions over the years have been as much about his positive vibe as his creativity in crafting sonic landscapes.

After Gate and the musicians had gone, David, Jim, and I spent four days mixing the record. No matter how much I might enjoy the camaraderie of a successful session, I usually breathe a sigh of relief when the musicians and artist leave, because the concentration required to maintain awareness of all the musical nuances, personal needs, and shifting moods can be exhausting. I am not by nature an outgoing or gregarious person, so assuming the role of a leader who is responsible for making final decisions and, hopefully, for sustaining an inspiring and positive atmosphere, requires a certain amount of internal gearing up each time, even after four decades in the producer's chair.

The day we finished, there was a reunion at Tipitina's in New Orleans, where the full studio band played the repertoire from the album. They were on fire, so much so that I almost wished we could go back and record the songs again, as if the recording session had been a rehearsal for the real world.

Alright Again! was released that fall. The album may have surprised some critics and blues fans who were accustomed to a more down-home blues sound from Rounder Records. To our amazement, it was nominated for a Grammy award (although I remember one of the musicians commenting, with pot-induced enthusiasm, "Damn. This is good enough to win a Grammy.").

On Grammy night, I was performing with Sleepy LaBeef at the Grog in Newburyport, Massachusetts. I had never considered that our album might actually win, and, anyway, I did not own a television. Between sets, an acquaintance approached me and said, "Man, I think your album just won a Grammy." And it had—the first Grammy win for Gate, for Rounder Records, and for me. When I went to the offices the next day, I was regaled as a hero, with my foot now firmly in the door as a producer. Talk about a lucky break.

With all the excitement surrounding *Alright Again!*, we decided that we should waste no time in planning a follow-up album. To have time to work on song ideas with Gate, I decided to meet the band at their gig at Fitzgerald's in Berwyn, Illinois, outside Chicago, then to travel back to New Orleans with them. Gate was now touring in a large motor home that pulled an equipment trailer, and I would ride with him.

The Fitzgerald's gig was the last show in a long run, and everyone was ready to go home. Since the last album, Gate had acquired the talented young rhythm section of bass player Miles Kevin Wright and drummer Robert Shipley, in addition to veteran sax player and composer Homer

Brown. His old road manager, soundman and driver, Jim Glasscock, was also back in the fold.

The day of the gig, I was hanging out at their motel with Miles, Jim, and Robert. Miles had written a tune that the band had been using as a set opener during the tour. Jim recorded almost every show on a cassette deck connected to the output of the sound console, so Gate could listen as they drove to the next show, but he had yet to record Miles's new song, putting the deck into record only after Gate had come to the stage.

"Jim," asked Miles, "Do you think you could record my song tonight? Here, I bought a cassette tape that you can use."

"I'll record what I damn well choose to record," he drawled in response.

"C'mon, man. What's your problem?" asked Miles. "I just want to hear what it sounds like."

Just as their voices began to escalate in volume, Gate walked into the room.

"What's going on here?" he asked.

"You stay out of this, boy," was Jim's reply.

Gate exploded. "You called me 'boy'? Jim Glasscock, you'd better run, because I'm gonna get my gun and blow your motherfucking head off," he said as he ran out the door and down the balcony.

"Oh shit," muttered Jim. Once Gate was out of sight, he left the room.

Sure enough, Gate returned with a pistol, and then spied Jim in the parking lot below. Before long, Gate was chasing Jim around the parked cars, holding his gun by the barrel like a dirty sock, and raining expletives on Jim, who ducked from car to car. It was an employer-employee relationship I could not understand, and it was painful to observe. Yet, by showtime that night, things seemed to be back to business as normal. Jim recorded the song.

The ride to New Orleans in the comfortable motor home was productive. Gate had hired a photographer to join the tour, to make prints of live photos for Gate to sell at the merchandise table, and the bathroom had been used a mobile darkroom, so black-and-white prints were hanging from clotheslines strung through the cabin. We were able to listen to demos of many of the songs we were considering for the album, and to talk about direction, which would be broader than *Alright Again!* Both Gate and Homer Brown had new songs ready to go, while Jim Bateman brought Hoyt Garrick's "Sunrise Cajun Style." I proposed Roy Milton's "Information Blues" and Junior Parker's "Stranded." I was still using my record collection as a song library, and I found some good material, but I also realized that it would be better if I were finding new songs.

We pulled up next to the side entrance of Gate's home on Grand Route St. John in New Orleans, where we were greeted by his wife, the pianist Yvonne Ramsey Brown, and their young daughter Renée. They had created a welcoming space, with a grand piano and a fireplace in the living room, in one of the most beautiful neighborhoods in the city. I would be staying with them for a couple of days, sleeping in the motor home.

When Gate and a couple of the band members began to unload the equipment from the trailer, it became apparent that something extra had been stored there. Along the way, Gate had purchased a substantial lot of African wooden sculptures, and Yvonne was aghast as more and more of it was removed. She deemed it junk, and when she found out how much her husband had paid for it, she became angry. As the disagreement escalated, a raucous fight ensued. Yvonne called the police, who hauled Gate off to jail on a domestic disturbance charge.

Now, that was quite a homecoming, I thought to myself.

Jim Bateman arrived and was able to get Gate out of jail relatively quickly, but Yvonne had decamped with Renée to her family home in Baton Rouge. I stayed on with Gate. While he certainly had lost his temper, he maintained that he had not physically harmed Yvonne, but it had not been a pretty argument. On good days, which had been frequent, Yvonne played onstage with Gate, and she was a talented photographer who was a cheerful presence at our sessions. I could not understand exactly what had happened, except that Gate's art purchase probably came at the expense of supporting his family, and that his marriage may have been an unfortunate outlet for his simmering frustration with the world at large.

We got on with the production of the record, *One More Mile*, this time augmenting the live band with pedal steel player/guitarist Tommy Moran, in addition to expanding the horn section. Homer Brown and Bill Samuel had written most of the horn charts before we arrived in Bogalusa, which allowed us to spend more time on capturing the best performances instead of working on arrangements. Gate would play more fiddle this time, on "Sunrise Cajun Style," and on his own songs "Song for Renée" and "Near Baku" (written during his tour of the Soviet Union, during which Gate told us he had found a field of potent Russian marijuana growing by the side of the road). This album, I thought, would come closer to reflecting Gate's

David Farrell, Clarence "Gatemouth" Brown, and Scott Billington at Studio in the Country, 1983 (photograph © Rick Olivier)

description of his synthesis of genres as "world music, Texas-style"—a wholly original vision that embraced all his influences.

Homer Brown was a key part of the record—a contemporary of Gate's who added a second voice of experience and who commanded the respect of the younger musicians. This was one of the best bands that Gate would ever front, with the talented New Orleans pianist Craig Wroten rounding out the rhythm section. Gate was relaxed enough to wear a polo shirt and Birkenstocks to the studio, and Yvonne took photographs.

The recording sessions were everything that a good session should be, with everyone united in the objective of supporting Gate, so when the music coalesced, he was inspired to give his best. *One More Mile* won a second Grammy nomination, solidifying a musical direction that would prevail for the remainder of Gate's career, which included a big-band record arranged and conducted by Wardell Quezergue, on Verve Records.

Rounder Records released one more record with Gate, recorded live at the Caravan of Dreams club in Fort Worth, and then my professional relationship with him was over. My great regret, in retrospect, is that I did not follow through with the idea to record him in an acoustic setting with bluegrass musicians in Nashville, but I lacked the connections (although I could have made them through Rounder's Ken Irwin) and possibly the confidence to make such a bold move. Once, when paying Gate a social visit, I brought him a stack of LPs of old-time fiddle music from the Rounder Records catalog, and his face lit up when he listened, especially to the Kentucky fiddler Ed Haley. It brought him back to his father's music. Making such a record would have helped break him out of the box in which he felt entrapped, and it probably would have been a lot of fun, too.

I continued to see him perform whenever I could and was always floored by his musicianship and his ability as an entertainer. He was magnificent as he directed the band, firing off impossible guitar licks against the horns, or getting everyone in the audience on their feet with a fiddle tune. He inhabited the stage like he owned it, and he did.

Yet, he could be melancholy and bitter offstage, whether disparaging drunken nightclub audiences or the "negative" music of blues musicians. He was angered by the one-dimensional caricature of a bluesman that he felt was so often forced upon him, no matter how accomplished he was at this aspect of his music. Sometimes he brought his attitude into his show. I once watched him taunt an intoxicated college-aged audience member, telling him, "OK, now I want you to really go ape. I want you to bang your head against that post." The kid complied. As I think it is for many great performing artists, life was never as perfect for Gate offstage as it was onstage, where he was in control.

In his later years, I visited him in the small house where he lived alone, along on the edge of the marsh surrounding Lake Pontchartrain, in Slidell. By the early 2000s, his marriage had ended, but he still was touring constantly, and this home was his refuge, where his numerous awards occupied the shelves. He would often drive his Cadillac twenty miles west to New Orleans, where he parked in the no-parking zone in front of the House of Blues (and where he was never ticketed). The club had constructed a restaurant booth to honor him, to which he had loaned a painting of himself as the Drifter (after one of his songs), in full Western regalia, riding a rearing black stallion as he confronts the Devil at the brink of hell. He could sit at the booth and entertain guests, and order anything on the menu, gratis. I once joined him there for lunch. He got his due from the House of Blues, at least for a while.

In 2019, House of Blues undertook a renovation of its restaurant, when the booth was donated to Habitat for Humanity. Renée Brown made the discovery that the booth was gone at a Yelp event when the restaurant's new menu was revealed. She was eventually able to acquire the booth. The Drifter is also in her possession.

In his later years, Gate was clearly lonely, and he was not taking care of himself. After years of avoiding the dentist, he lost his teeth, and he was now smoking during all waking hours. He was still as proud and as grouchy as ever, but he was frail. In 2005, Hurricane Katrina destroyed his home completely, and he died a couple of weeks later in Orange, Texas, at the age of eighty-one.

I learned so much from working with Gate, both about the responsibility of supporting an iconic artist who had already built a legacy, and about organizing a session to get the most out of the time we would spend in the studio. The musicians I met and the relationships I formed at these sessions were the foundation of my work in Louisiana. And what a pleasure it was to work in such a first-class studio. I even warmed up to Bogalusa.

RECOMMENDED LISTENING:

"Frosty" from *Alright Again!*
"Ain't That Dandy" from *One More Mile*

Chapter 4

JAMES BOOKER

THE PIANO POPE. THE BAYOU MAHARAJAH. GONZO. THE IVORY EMPEROR.
Little Booker. The Piano Prince. The Bronze Liberace. Music Magnifico.

James Carroll Booker III was one of the most flamboyant and idiosyncratic characters in the colorful pantheon of New Orleans musicians, and
one of the preeminent pianists of the twentieth century. He was a prodigy
who first recorded at the age of twelve, who could play many Chopin
pieces by memory, and who sometimes made the claim that he was the
reincarnation of Jelly Roll Morton. He often performed in extravagant wigs
and capes, along with an eye patch decorated with a star. Fellow musician
Earl King claimed that Booker could play a song backwards. His technical
ability as a pianist left most musicians scratching their heads. He was the
Vincent van Gogh of New Orleans—a brilliant and troubled artist who was
only fully appreciated years after his death—and the only person I have
met who might have been what we call a genius.

Booker (as everyone called him, although I usually addressed him as
James) was a small man with a scrawny frame who seemed older than
forty-two, probably the result of his long history of substance abuse. In
the 1970s, he was arrested on a drug charge and sent for a short time
to Louisiana's notoriously brutal Angola Prison, where he ran a music
program for inmates, and where he told me he acquired the nickname
"Madame X" (after the 1966 Lana Turner character and film). Many of
his acquaintances believe he suffered from undiagnosed psychological
problems. There are many conflicting stories about how he lost his left eye,
which filmmaker Lily Keber documents in her extraordinary film *Bayou
Maharajah: The Tragic Genius of James Booker*.

Scott Billington and James Booker, Ultrasonic Studio, New Orleans, 1982
(photograph © Scott Billington)

When I set out for New Orleans to make a record with him, in October
1982, I had little idea of what I was getting myself into, for I understood
neither the challenge of working with a musician with so many foibles and
shifting demons, nor the full scope of his talent.

In fact, I was feeling a bit cocky, especially following the Grammy
award with "Gatemouth" Brown. Yet, as much as I trusted my ears and my
instincts, I remained a novice in the art and craft of music production. My
experience at this point had been with musicians with healthy egos who
operated with a certain level of steadiness. I would listen to their ideas
about what they hoped to achieve as we embarked on our collaboration,
and they would consider my thoughts as well. We would work together as
we planned our strategy to get there. Even if the magic of a perfect, inspired
take was unpredictable, we tried to optimize our chances.

At my instigation, Rounder Records had licensed James Booker's *New
Orleans Piano Wizard: Live!* from the Swiss Gold Records label in 1981.
Just one year earlier, I had heard Booker in performance for the first time
at the Maple Leaf Bar in New Orleans, after my friend Tom Smith told
me, "You have to hear this piano player, James Booker, who is playing in

the window of this laundromat" (the Maple Leaf had an array of washing machines and dryers in the back at the time).

I caught his performance on a good night, because it was a dizzying experience. Just like on the Swiss record, Booker swept through blues, pop, classical, and classic New Orleans R&B songs, with his left hand covering ground that would have occupied both hands of any other pianist, while his right hand soared into precisely slurred arpeggios and syncopations. His singing was soulful and direct—not a great voice, in the sense of a person who had been born with a remarkable physical instrument, but one that could acutely evoke the pain and the joy he found in the songs he played.

It was easy enough to approach him to ask if he would like to make a record. His manager was John Parsons, who also managed the Maple Leaf Bar, and both were enthusiastic. At the New Orleans Jazz and Heritage Festival in May 1982, Booker appeared with one his students, the young Harry Connick Jr., sitting next to him on the piano bench. When I told him afterward that I had never heard anyone play the piano quite like he did, he smiled at me, with a glint in the corner of his good eye, and said, "Well, I know I can play the pee-AN-ah."

A formal recording agreement was quickly drafted and signed, overseen by Booker's New Orleans attorney Gene Fulghum. Over the next few months, Booker planned to work on material he wanted to record, and to "rehearse" each Wednesday night at his Maple Leaf gig with the band that would accompany him in the studio.

Saxophonist Alvin "Red" Tyler, whom I had met at my Gatemouth Brown sessions, would be his instrumental foil. Red was a legendary presence in New Orleans music who had supported Little Richard on his hits in the fifties. The horn parts he played, often in tandem with fellow sax player Lee Allen, were a propulsive chug that contributed to the exciting second wave of New Orleans R&B in the early sixties, on hits such as Shirley and Lee's "Let the Good Times Roll" and Huey "Piano" Smith and His Clowns' "Sea Cruise." He also recorded his own instrumentals, such as "Snake Eyes," and was a brilliant modern jazz musician and composer who played gigs around town with the hippest musicians in the city. Yet he was never a full-time musician, choosing instead to keep a job as a liquor salesman to support his family, opting for steady income over the constant hustle for gigs. A couple of years later, I would produce two albums of his own modern jazz compositions.

Bassist James Singleton and drummer Johnny Vidacovich together remain one of the most sought-after rhythm sections in New Orleans, known for their work with the preeminent New Orleans improvised-music ensemble, Astral Project. Both had performed with Booker before our sessions, and he was enthusiastic about playing with them again.

James Singleton is a whirr of motion when he plays, throwing his full being into the music and always making a gorgeous, fat sound. "We played daily duos at the Toulouse Street Theatre annex," he recounted about his experience with Booker: "He would play the first set without alcohol (to prove he could do it?), hands shaking like a leaf but still sounding flawless. At the first break he would have a *water* glass of brown liquor followed immediately by a glass of water. His face would be covered in sweat, but his hands were rock steady."

Johnny V has the New Orleans street beat in his blood, raised to a nuanced level that reminds me of an impressionist painter. I've watched him play the drum shells, the hardware, and even the walls of a recording studio booth. James and Johnny were just right for Booker's freewheeling rhythmic and melodic shifts. I came to love working with Johnny and James, and we would collaborate on many future projects.

The gigs went well, with the band hitting a stride on many nights that added supple and fluid support to Booker's sound. I began to think the recording would be easy.

At the time, Booker seemed to be making a great effort to move forward with his life in a positive way. He put away his more colorful clothing in favor of a suit and tie, and his eye patch in favor of dark glasses. He had overcome his addiction to heroin and was faithfully taking the drug Antabuse to help him stop drinking. Yet he was still prone to erratic behavior, such as taking a twenty-dollar cab ride to the Maple Leaf to borrow twenty dollars from John. And the Antabuse did not stop his drinking. He might drink a full tumbler of gin while sitting at the piano at the Maple Leaf, continuing to play brilliantly until he became intensely sick. He developed peptic ulcers.

He kept an apartment in the French Quarter, on Decatur Street, a short walk from the Toulouse Street Theatre, where, in addition to his gigs with James, he had played in the lobby before each performance of the Vernel Bagneris musical *One Mo' Time*. He had traveled widely in the 1970s, playing on recording sessions in New York and Los Angeles, with artists as diverse as Ringo Starr, the Doobie Brothers, T-Bone Walker, and Aretha Franklin, who recorded his composition "So Swell When You're Well." He played many of the piano parts on Fats Domino's *Fats is Back* album, working with producer Richard Perry. He had also toured Europe as a solo artist, where he recorded several live albums (in addition to the Swiss disc). Yet, by the time of our recording, his health was generally not good. His traveling days were over, and he seldom left Orleans Parish, supporting himself with gigs at clubs such as Tipitina's, Rosy's, and the Maple Leaf Bar.

A month before our scheduled sessions, I was in Bogalusa, Louisiana, recording my second album with Clarence "Gatemouth" Brown. John Parsons called to tell me that Booker had suffered some sort of breakdown and that he was now confined to a bed at Baptist Hospital in New Orleans. When I called Booker on the phone, he seemed only marginally coherent.

"Do ya know what I really want?" he asked me.

"What, James?"

"A lukewarm bath."

A few days later, when I visited Booker in his hospital room, he was in a frail and fragile state. Yet he wanted to go forward with the sessions. Upon his discharge, only a day before our studio date, a problem emerged. The hospital had lost his upper dental plate, without which he could not sing well. John came to the rescue, remembering that when Booker's dentist had first made the plate, he had placed the requested gold star on the wrong front tooth. John found the extra plate, which had not been properly fitted, in Booker's sock drawer.

Booker, John, the musicians, engineer Jay Gallagher, and I gathered at Ultrasonic Studio in New Orleans on October 18, 1982. After an hour or so of microphone checks and sound level adjustments, we were ready to go. One of the songs Booker had chosen to record was by Paul Gayten and Annie Laurie, "If You're Lonely," and that was how we started. Because he needed a lyric sheet, he wrote most of the words in my notebook, in his elegant penmanship. We never got all the way through a fully realized arrangement, with all the verses intact, but we finally got an acceptable take. It took a long time, but Booker seemed satisfied with it.

I was trying to conduct the session in an easygoing and methodical way, as I had Gatemouth's—to have the musicians talk through or run through an arrangement, then hopefully to capture the final performance in a couple of takes, before it became overworked and wrung out of feeling.

James Booker's elegant handwriting and Scott Billington's scribble (courtesy of Scott Billington)

Even though Booker had participated in numerous sessions that ran that way, this approach clearly was not in the cards for him on that day. As the session progressed, he became distracted and would not play any of the songs we had planned. He began engaging in a cat-and-mouse game with the musicians, randomly starting songs until they caught on, only to switch abruptly to something else. Then, he stopped communicating entirely.

The next day was not any better. Booker decided that he was lacking songs, and requested that his musician and songwriter acquaintances Cyril Neville, Earl King, and Allen Toussaint show up at the studio with material for him. Remarkably, Cyril and Earl, both of whom were friends who had great respect for his talent, came over right away, and the secretary from

Allen's office dictated the lyrics to the song "Viva la Money" to me over the phone, which I wrote in my notebook. Cyril wrote out the words to his song "Such Is Life," giving half the credit to Booker. Earl sat at the piano and made a couple of on-the-spot demos. Yet Booker ultimately ignored them, too, and then he stopped talking to everyone.

Booker went to the piano and we did our best to record everything he and the band played. Somewhere in the midst of his verbal silence and the confusion over what he would play next, he launched into his remarkable version of "Angel Eyes," a dark and virtuosic reading of the standard, but the session was out of control. During regular pauses, Johnny was doing headstands while James and Red waited patiently. At one point, after Booker left the piano and crouched in a corner, Red and I walked over and picked him up. I said, "Look, you're either going to play the piano, or I'm going to cancel the session and you're not going to get paid." He looked at me sheepishly and returned to the piano bench. His ill-fitting dental bridge was not helping and was making him uncomfortable. At one point, in the middle of a take, it fell out and landed on the keyboard. He picked it up with his mouth, without missing a beat.

Perhaps he was perversely enjoying all the fuss that was being made about him, and my coddling approach to coaching him was not the best tactic. I kept trying to guide him back to songs he had rehearsed and, in the process, may have failed to appreciate some of the tangents he was taking. I still wonder what would have happened if I had said, "OK, that's a piece of Les McCann's 'Swiss Movement.' Let's start that again and get a clean beginning. Go for it, Booker." Probably not. Whenever I did ask him what he wanted to do next, or suggested a song, he would simply start playing.

I was struck with panic at the thought that our final day of recording might not be any better, while trying to imagine that it could be. I asked Jay if we could start early the next day, so I could listen to everything we had recorded to determine if there was anything beyond "If You're Lonely" and "Angel Eyes" that was worth releasing. I was afraid I was going to spend thousands of dollars of the record company's money and come back with nothing.

I did not sleep much that night, as the chaos of the previous two days kept playing in my head, and I was bleary eyed when I showed up at the studio at ten the next morning. Jay had not yet arrived, but, to my astonishment, a smiling James Carroll Booker III was waiting by the door.

"Scott, is it OK if I play now?" he asked.

"Sure, James. I mean, that's great!" I replied.

Jay arrived a few minutes later. Booker asked if I would sit by him in the studio, instead of in the control room, so I brought a chair over by the piano. And then he started to play. Over the next two hours, he performed all the solo piano material on the record. John Parsons arrived at about eleven. The night before, he had taken Booker out for a meal of boiled crabs, and Booker had slept well. He occasionally stumbled over a piano passage that he would have nailed at midnight on a gig, but we were capturing take after take of very good James Booker.

In the early afternoon, the other musicians arrived. They were surprised to see me grinning. We cut several tightly focused band arrangements, including the remarkable slow-burn version of "Lawdy Miss Clawdy" that is a highlight of the session, but then Booker's focus began to drift. He asked me if I would pay him. Knowing that we had a record, I agreed, and gave him his check for $3,000. He returned to the piano bench for a few more songs, but then abruptly stopped playing, resting his forearms on the keys. He asked, "What time does the bank close?"

"About three o'clock, Booker" said Red.

Without saying a word, he got up and quickly left the studio, and that was the last anyone saw of him for several weeks. One story told was that he bought a car, wrecked it immediately (he did not have a driver's license, nor did he know how to drive), and was subsequently arrested. He stayed in jail at New Orleans Central Lockup, under an assumed name, until John finally found him and got him out.

After the sessions, he began calling me on the phone, usually in the middle of the night, collect. He told me a story about being on the road with Fats Domino, when he became stranded in Las Vegas. He decided that his best way home would be to get arrested and subsequently deported, so he knocked over a mailbox in front of a police officer while he pleaded his case. It did not work. In another conversation, he asked me if I would like to go sailing with him on Lake Pontchartrain the next time I was in New Orleans. Later, I found out that his friend Thorny Penfield had indeed taken him sailing, and that he loved it. Thorny said that Booker sat in the prow with his nose to the wind, like a grinning figurehead.

Once, as I was heading back to bed after an hour-long talk, the phone rang again. It was another collect call from James Booker.

"Scott, I had something really important to tell you," he said.

"Sure, James. What was it?"

"I can't remember," he replied, and hung up.

It was then that I began to appreciate how lonely Booker was, and how he struggled to maintain any semblance of a balanced life and connection with other people. Without knowing him, any listener can hear the soulfulness and pain in a vocal performance such as "If You're Lonely." He once told John Parsons, "I'm a lonely motherfucker."

The album, *Classified*, was released in May 1983. We celebrated with a party at the Maple Leaf, during the New Orleans Jazz and Heritage Festival. Booker seemed genuinely proud. He gave a good performance that night, with Red Tyler, Johnny Vidacovich, and George French substituting for James Singleton on bass. The album attracted a fair amount of international attention after it was licensed for release in the UK and Europe by Demon Records.

Classified is by no means James Booker's best album. In fact, that mythical recording is still out there, on the tapes that fans around the world have recorded to cassette or burned to CD and traded for the past thirty-five years. My favorite is a live set recorded at Rosy's in New Orleans, before an audience that could not have numbered more than a dozen. For me, it is akin to listening to, say, Vladimir Horowitz or Glenn Gould in a perfect concert setting. I believe that Booker was their equal.

Yet *Classified* offers material and perhaps an attitude that can be heard nowhere else in Booker's discography. "Angel Eyes" may be the biggest surprise. With his command of harmony, Booker could have held his own in any modern jazz combo. There are also the light classical pieces. Booker sometimes referred to himself "the Bronze Liberace," and these performances show that this was no mere boast. He plays "Warsaw Concerto" as written, complete with the dissonant note after the opening flourish. "Madame X" (mistakenly titled "Swedish Rhapsody" on the first edition of the record) is the theme from the 1966 Lana Turner film.

There are also the quirky pieces that show the scope of his repertoire and his sense of humor: "King of the Road," "Hound Dog," and "Theme from The Godfather" (which was released on a 2013 expanded edition of the album). "Yes Sir, That's My Baby," also released in 2013, is the only song we recorded with Booker playing the Hammond B3 organ. If it begins with a circus-like tone, it soon settles into a groove that would have any New Orleans native

James Booker, with George French on bass, at his album release party at the Maple Leaf Bar, May 1983 (photograph © Scott Billington)

second-lining down the street. Booker never recorded extensively on organ, although his 1965 hit on Houston's Peacock Records, "Gonzo" (a reference to a drug dealer in the film *The Pusher*) was an organ instrumental.

The title track, which Dr. John also recorded as "Qualified," with different words (the sequence of authorship is unclear), offers a look into Booker's view of himself as a "classified" person that others would seek to put in a box or categorize. He sings, "I know it's real, what my mind keeps telling me. I know it's real, what this one light lets me see." He sometimes expressed paranoia about being watched by the CIA and the FBI. Once, when John Parsons booked him to open a show for Marcia Ball, Booker asked, "Is that Marsha with an "S-H-A?" When John replied, "No Booker, it's with a C-I-A," Booker got up and left.

Not long after the album's release, Booker surprised everyone by taking a job at the Office of Economic Analysis at New Orleans City Hall. As Earl King told me, Booker had a "photo mind," and was very good with numbers. Booker had several high-placed friends in New Orleans who recognized his genius and who looked out for him, including the district attorney, Harry Connick Sr., and his new supervisor, Lee Madère, who found him "a hell of a typist."

It was a big enough local story to catch the attention of David Leser of the *Times-Picayune*, who wrote, "If James Booker hadn't actually discarded his satin capes for a three-piece suit and tie, and taken up employment at City Hall five days a week, three to four hours a day, the very thought of it would almost defy comprehension."

Madère, who was also a fan, told Leser, "If I give him an assignment I know he will do it. What more can I ask of an employee? People come up to me and say they have never seen him in better shape—that some change has come over him. City government can take some credit for helping James put his life in order."

Said Booker, "This job is a big help. You don't want to stay at the piano all the time. Too much piano ain't good for you. Too much water ain't good for you, either, it makes you drown."

Yet he was not well. His performances at the Maple Leaf became increasingly erratic. In perhaps one show out of half a dozen, he could still play the most inspiring and moving music that anyone could hope to hear. But on other nights, he would barely play, walking around the almost empty club with his hands thrust down, staring up at the tobacco-stained tin ceiling. Or he would sit at the piano and ramble on in his Béla Lugosi voice, or speak fractured Spanish. He would follow his pattern of taking Antabuse, drinking, and getting sick. During the photo session for *Classified*, he had been stricken with a seizure. Because of his shaky health, he declined an offer to travel to Chicago to play on PBS's *Soundstage* with his friend Dr. John (with whom he had once shared a Hammond organ gig on Bourbon Street, and with whom he went on the road in the early 1970s).

On November 8, 1983, Booker died of renal failure at Charity Hospital in New Orleans, at the age of forty-three. He was found dead in a wheelchair in the emergency room, waiting to be seen, without his eye patch or glasses. It is likely that a combination of freebased cocaine and alcohol killed him. The person who brought him to the hospital and left him there has never been identified.

I was not able to attend the funeral, but friends such as Red Tyler and Jeff Hannusch reported that it was a desultory affair, with few people in attendance. Instead of his reaching-to-the-heavens piano, the funeral home played their standard piped-in hymns. He was interred in a crypt at the Providence Memorial Park and Mausoleum in Metairie, Louisiana, the same resting place as Johnny Adams, Fats Domino, and Mahalia Jackson.

Unlike other New Orleans legends such as Professor Longhair and Dr. John, Booker received no second-line parade, and no tribute set at Jazz Fest, at least not until many years later. In his day, he was not a beloved figure except among the small group of sympathetic artists and steadfast followers who recognized the brilliant musician in their midst. Yet, his status and mythology have grown each year, and now his unmistakable, eye-patched visage can be found on murals, in galleries, and on T-shirts. He has metamorphosed into a true New Orleans icon.

For the first few years after his death, Booker's estate was represented, in a manner, by Joe Jones, the singer whose hit "You Talk Too Much" made the national charts in 1960, after Booker's three heirs signed a document authorizing him to do so. Jones had founded a company called Theatrical Management Consultant, which sought to recover unpaid royalties, occasionally with success, for rhythm and blues artists. He began by going after John Parsons, seeking to prohibit John from selling James Booker posters or albums at the Maple Leaf, and to forfeit any memorabilia he might have. In his opening letter to John, he wrote, "Like James Booker is deceased, the Maple Leaf Bar and John Parson [sic] has also deceased concerning James Booker."

John's attorney responded with a letter asking that, until Jones had received proper judicial sanction, he stop harassing John.

Joe Jones countered with a letter complaining about John's attorney, which he sent to the Louisiana Bar Association, copying the US Drug Enforcement Administration, the Louisiana State Police, District Attorney Harry Connick Sr., Rounder Records, and several newspapers. He began by outlining his case, citing the authorization he had received from Booker's heirs, and making several claims that John had abused Booker and supplied him with narcotics. By the third page, he was relating a story of an encounter he claimed to have had with John while Booker was alive.

"I told John Parson and I quote, that if he ever put his hands on James Booker, I would personally put a whipping on his ass, a whipping he would never forget," he wrote. "I requested him in front of James Booker to dare hit James Booker in my presence in order for me to give him a whipping that he will always remember." He also made claims of racial discrimination, but no legal complaint or other legal document was ever filed. It was a further inglorious marker of the end of James Booker's life, for, in every instance that I observed, John had been a good and gentle friend to Booker, and an honest manager. Later, the assets of the James Booker estate and his song catalog were acquired by music publisher Don Williams, who continues today to represent Booker's heirs.

While insiders traded live Booker cassettes and CDs, many of the people who owned tapes of his live recordings were covetous of their holdings, and no new material was released for several years. In 1993, John Parsons and I culled two albums of live material from over sixty hours of cassette tape recordings that John made at the Maple Leaf Bar. The upright piano and the noisy recording quality are not enough to get in the way of the remarkable performances (and the many nonremarkable performances that we chose not to include) that John preserved. I brought transfers of the cassettes to engineer Joe Gastwirt at Oceanview Digital Recording in Los Angeles, where he used the Sonic Solutions NoNoise system to bring out as much of the music as possible. While this software was soon superseded by better noise-reduction technologies, I was glad this tool existed at the time.

Don Williams has since overseen the release of a number of excellent James Booker recordings. The pianist George Winston, who is a great fan of Booker's music, purchased a collection of live recordings made at the Toulouse Street Theatre. And someday, perhaps those Rosy's tapes will surface.

In 2013, the filmmaker Lily Keber premiered her documentary *Bayou Maharajah: The Tragic Genius of James Booker* at the South by Southwest film festival in Austin, overcoming years of frustrating legal issues. She interviewed many of the key people in Booker's life, including Harry Connick Jr., Cyril Neville, James Singleton, John Parsons, and me. It is a remarkable achievement that most of Booker's acquaintances would say gets it right, because his importance as an artist is never overshadowed by his troubles as a person. In the process of making the film, she kept asking me if she could hear the entire *Classified* sessions, which I had avoided revisiting for over twenty-five years. Finally, my wife, Johnette Downing, brokered a deal, and I made copies of my original reference cassettes. Rather than finding that they elicited difficult memories, I actually enjoyed listening to them, and there were definitely some previously unheard moments that were worth sharing. Thus, a two-album set drawn from the sessions—an expanded version of *Classified*—was released on LP and compact disc, just in time for the New Orleans premiere of the film at the New Orleans Film Festival.

Among the hundreds of recording sessions I have conducted over the years, none have continued to haunt me as this one has. There was no second chance to record Booker, and no opportunity to refine what might have been needed to get it right. One can imagine so many "if only . . ." moments that might have led James Booker down a different path, but perhaps the life he lived was the only one possible for him, and perhaps his recklessness was the counterbalance to the musical heights he could so often achieve. As Red Tyler said to me after Booker left the studio, "It's like trying to capture the wind."

RECOMMENDED LISTENING:

"Classified" and "King of the Road" from *Classified*

Chapter 5

BUCKWHEAT ZYDECO

DRIVING WEST FROM NEW ORLEANS ON INTERSTATE 10, PAST THE SPRAWL of Baton Rouge and the heavy industry that dominates the horizon as you cross the Mississippi River bridge, there is a perceptible change as you enter the Atchafalaya Basin. The causeway through the dense swamp lasts for miles until it bisects Lake Bigeaux, with its open waters and cypress trees. When the road finally meets dry land, you have entered an area that is culturally distinctive from the rest of the state, and a world apart from the generic Southern ethos of Baton Rouge.

Southwest Louisiana was one of the more isolated parts of America until the 1960s, when the interstate was built. The people who settled there over the years—including Cajuns (Acadians) who were forcibly expelled from Canada by the British in the 1755; Creoles who escaped political turmoil in Haiti in the 1800s; and an assortment of Germans (in Roberts Cove), Spaniards (in New Iberia), and French, may have colonized the region for exactly that reason. Native Americans such as the Coushatta had fled to the area to escape encroachment on what had been their territory in the east. French is still spoken in Southwest Louisiana, where students in many communities are given the option of enrolling in modern French immersion programs. The French identity of southwest Louisiana is persistent. I was once surprised when I heard zydeco accordion player Nathan Williams conversing in Creole (or Kreyòl) with a drummer from Haiti, who had stayed on after Lafayette's Festival International. It was then that I realized that this distinct but related language is also part of the area's heritage.

Outside the cities of Lafayette and Lake Charles, southwest Louisiana still has a rural ambience, where many people raise, grow, trap, or catch at least part of their food supply, the legacy of a subsistence culture that

Stanley "Buckwheat" Dural (photograph © Rick Olivier)

has not entirely disappeared. In the flat "Cajun Prairie" around Eunice (so-called for the endangered tall grasses that once covered the area), rice fields are flooded and transformed into crawfish ponds in the winter, while cattle graze in wide-open fields. In parishes to the south, sugarcane and oil dominate, with the industries of oil rig construction and shipbuilding concentrated along US Route 90 between Lafayette and Morgan City. In the Atchafalaya Basin, trappers and fishermen wend their way through the maze of waterways. People in the region work hard and are not afraid to get their hands dirty. And, until recently, no matter how you earned your living, Saturday night was spent in a dance hall. The area is rich with some of the most idiosyncratic music in America.

In 1982, I made my first trip to south Louisiana to meet Stanley Dural Jr., the upstart musician who called himself Buckwheat Zydeco, for his childhood resemblance to the *Little Rascals* film character. The sun went down as I sat in the lobby of the Day's Inn in Lafayette, Louisiana, waiting for his manager, Peggy Below, to pick me up to take me to his Saturday night show at Richard's Club in Lawtell, about thirty miles away. This would be my first visit to a zydeco club, and I was excited. A new blue Cadillac driven by Peggy's father pulled up, and I sat in the back seat with her, while her parents sat in front. There was not much to see in the darkness along the way, because the fast food restaurants that now light the road from Lafayette to Opelousas were just beginning to pop up at the exits along Interstate 49.

The post–World War II music style called zydeco is the fusion of traditional French Creole music with rhythm and blues. In southwest Louisiana, the people who describe themselves as Creoles are the descendants of French- or Creole-speaking people of color (as opposed New Orleans Creoles, who may cite French and Spanish ancestry), and zydeco is one of their primary cultural rallying points. The accordion is always present, as is the rubboard or *frottoir*, a variation of the laundry-room washboard, which is used as a percussion instrument. It was invented by zydeco pioneer Clifton Chenier, who sketched his idea in the dirt for Port Arthur metalworker Willie Landry. The now ubiquitous corrugated–sheet metal instrument that he fabricated hangs on the player's shoulders and is usually played with bottle openers.

I had seen Buckwheat's performance at the 1981 New Orleans Jazz and Heritage Festival, and I was floored. At the time, zydeco bands were traveling to New Orleans at least a few times a month, so I had seen Rockin' Dopsie at the Maple Leaf Bar, as well as both well-known and obscure musicians, from Clifton Chenier and His Red-Hot Louisiana Band to Marcel Dugas and the Entertainers, at Tipitina's. But Buckwheat was different. He played the large piano accordion, like Clifton, but delivered his music with the flair of a rhythm and blues star like Joe Tex, and with the precision of James Brown. He performed Creole dance music, but it was also Southern soul music and Louisiana funk, with a Caribbean edge, all in one package. It was the distillation of folk tradition into something that I knew was bound to reach a larger audience.

We pulled up to Richard's, a long, low-slung wooden building with an unpaved parking lot that was already filled with shiny pickup trucks, with the overflow deflected to the shoulder of US 190. The club had been built in 1947 by the father of current owner Kermon Richard. In the 1950s, it became a regular stop on the Chitlin' Circuit, where artists such as B. B. King, Muddy Waters, Big Mama Thornton, and Jimmy Reed performed. Kermon had seen the potential in zydeco and began booking artists such as John Delafose and the Eunice Playboys on Friday and Saturday nights. I would visit Richard's many times over the years, and I would become good friends with Kermon and his wife, Ann, but I can recall few musical experiences to match the exhilaration of that first night.

It was a modest place. The bar was at the front, near the door, and the stage was at the opposite end. The large dance floor was abutted by railings that set off small tables and chairs along the sides of the building. The wooden ceiling was so low that I could reach up and touch it. There was no air conditioning except for a few struggling window units. Restrooms were in the back, behind the stage, and were surely in violation of one building code or another.

Yet there was something about the building and the acoustics that made a zydeco band sound better there than almost anywhere else, with a big, pulsating low end that never overwhelmed the detail of the vocals and the accordion. As we entered and made our way through the crowd that huddled around the bar, I could see that the dance floor was packed with Creole couples of all ages, some dressed in matching Western outfits with pressed jeans. The athleticism of many of the younger dancers reminded me of the best salsa and swing dancing I had seen, but it was more intense. The floor moved up and down, so much so that the building seemed in danger of shaking loose from its foundations. It was a festive place, dimly illuminated by Christmas lights and bare light bulbs, and many of the women had brought food—fried chicken, turkey necks, and sandwiches. It seemed that the ritual of the Saturday dance was not only an entertaining way to spend a weekend night, but an affirmation of life and identity in this very specific corner of the world.

Buckwheat played old-time two-steps, albeit faster than any traditional band would have dared, interspersed with Southern soul hits by Z. Z. Hill and Tyrone Davis, along with an occasional waltz (which the audience demanded). His popularity with local dancers would eventually wane as the sound of the small diatonic accordion came to dominate the scene, but that night he ruled Richard's.

When I met him after the show, there was no sign that he was tired, and he was eager to talk about a relationship with Rounder Records and what that might mean for him. He had released a few records locally, on the Crowley-based Blues Unlimited label, but he felt he was now ready to make a move to a national label and national stages. He might have been the most focused and driven musician I have ever met, with a solid business sense, a never-say-no work ethic, and a high level of musical creativity—qualities that seldom reside in the same person. He sometimes spoke with a stutter, but never when he was singing (he eventually became stutter free).

Buckwheat was born to a farming family in Lafayette in 1947. When he was in his teens and early twenties, he played piano and organ in the Lafayette bands Sammy and the Untouchables, and Lil' Buck and the Top Cats, led by his friend and, in later years, oft-time guitarist Paul "Lil' Buck" Sinegal. At times, they provided backing for touring artists such as Barbara Lynn, Clarence "Gatemouth" Brown, and Solomon Burke. He next did a stint with the swamp pop/R&B band Lil' Bob and the Lollipops, known for their 1965 hit, "I Got Loaded," which was later covered by Los Lobos. (I saw the singing drummer Camille Bob—Lil' Bob—in 1983, at a bar improbably located near a back entrance of a now abandoned mall along the Evangeline Throughway in Lafayette.)

In fact, Lafayette has remained a stubborn outpost of Southern soul music and traditional rhythm and blues. You can hear it in two albums that I was fortunate to make in the 1990s with the Lafayette singer Dalton Reed, who, to my ears, ranks with the best of the classic soul singers. You can hear it in 2020 in the songs of many of the zydeco piano accordion players, such as Nathan Williams Sr. and Clifton's son C. J. Chenier, as well as in the music of southwest Louisiana artists Tucka ("The King of Swing"), Marc Broussard, and Roddie Romero. Even the swamp pop sound, which blossomed in the masterful songwriting of Bobby "Charles" Guidry, is derived from Fats Domino–style New Orleans rhythm and blues. Buckwheat's father was an accordion player, so Buckwheat was aware of the Creole music around him, but his music was also shaped by the sounds of the day, and by the rhythm and blues side of Lafayette music.

In the early 1970s, he founded a fifteen-piece show band that he called Buckwheat and the Hitchhikers, covering songs by groups such as the Ohio Players and Parliament-Funkadelic, and backing touring artists such as Betty Wright. During this time, he discovered and hired the then-thirteen-year-old bass player Lee Allen Zeno, finding a musical partner who would become one of his greatest assets. Yet the logistics of keeping such a large ensemble together were formidable, and the Hitchhikers disbanded after five years. Lee Allen joined the R&B band Sky, and Buckwheat surprised everyone by following Lil' Buck Sinegal to join Clifton Chenier's band, playing Hammond B-3 organ with the zydeco master.

It was a revelatory experience. During his time on the road with Chenier, he watched doors open and barriers fall away as he performed the kind of "old fashioned" music that he had heard his father play, and that he associated with his father's generation. He began formulating his vision for zydeco as something bigger. After woodshedding material and practicing accordion for many months, he put together Buckwheat Zydeco and the Ils Sont Partis Band (from the announcer's "they're off" at the Evangeline Downs racetrack).

Concurrent with signing him to Rounder, I introduced him to the Massachusetts-based booking agent Paul Kahn, whose Concerted Efforts company would book Buckwheat for the remainder of his career. Paul wanted to bring the band to the Northeast, so we made a plan to record at Blue Jay Studio in Carlisle, Massachusetts, during the tour.

Blue Jay is a secluded studio that was built underground by Bob and Janet Lawson in 1979. Chief engineer Glenn Berger had been the legendary producer Phil Ramone's engineer in New York. After he joined the Blue Jay staff, the studio quickly gained a reputation as one of the best in New England. It became a destination, much like Studio in the Country in Bogalusa. With its Sony MCI console and well-tuned acoustic space, it was the perfect environment for recording Buckwheat's six-piece band.

The band hit the studio like a string of exploding firecrackers, possibly fueled by the nearly full case of brown liquor I discovered in the studio's kitchen area (even more surprising, as I would later learn, because several band members did not drink). Buckwheat was determined to take advantage of this opportunity, and he gave the recording everything he had. We had not talked in detail about the songs we would record, but Buckwheat assured me that he would have everything ready, and he did—road-tested and tight. The Tyrone Davis song "Turning Point" (the album's title cut) became a zydeco tour de force, with the rhythm section of Lee Allen Zeno and drummer Nat Jolivette locking into a groove that never let up. Buckwheat put a humorous spin on his arrangement of the popular John

Delafose song "Joe Pitre a Deux Femmes" (Joe Pitre has two women) as "Madame Pitre a Deux Hommes" (Mrs. Pitre has two men), while stream-lining the song's old-time feel into a breezy bounce.

We finished the basic tracks in two days, then began adding Buckwheat's piano and organ parts. We overdubbed harmony backing vocals to the soul ballad "Help Me Understand You" and stacked Calvin Landry's trumpet to create a fat brass section on several songs.

For the front cover photo, Buckwheat contemplated something that many in Louisiana would consider audacious, and I encouraged him to do so. In 1983, Clifton Chenier remained the acknowledged King of Zydeco. In fact, the Lafayette area was rife with royalty. It was not uncommon to see advertisements and billboards with photos of various crowned kings of used car sales and real estate, and my favorite, Junior Lagneaux, the King of Seafood (I still dine there sometimes). Buckwheat had brought with him a crown and a purple cape with faux ermine trim, and he decided to use this outfit for the album's cover photo. After his brother Harold had carefully styled his hair, he posed in front of the pine trees in back of the studio. Zydeco artists could be like professional wrestlers in their rivalries, and this was a statement that the champ had a new challenger.

During this tour, the band was booked at Sandy's Jazz Revival in Beverly, Massachusetts, but only a handful of people attended. It was embarrassing, given the publicity the record company had managed to raise, and because I knew Buckwheat was underwriting this tour with money he had made back home. Yet he played the show as if he were playing for ten thousand people, leaving the audience breathless.

"You know," he told me, "The next time I play here, the place will be packed, and the time after that, they won't be able to afford me." He was right. *Turning Point* won a Grammy nomination, and Buckwheat Zydeco was on his way.

We returned to Blue Jay in 1985, this time with new engineer Gragg Lunsford. For this session, we decided to experiment with a few new songs that the band had not been playing onstage. Usually, with a working band, I've found there is a great advantage to performing the songs on the road before a session, but this time I was not worried, as the Ils Sont Partis Band had become such a well-tuned machine.

Buckwheat's sound was coalescing as a unique Creole/Caribbean spin on rhythm and blues. He performed the Don Williams hit "Warm and

Club owner/entrepreneur Sid Williams and Stanley "Buckwheat" Dural (photograph © Rick Olivier)

Tender Love" with a gentle ska beat, and his update of Tony Troutman's "Your Man Is Home Tonight" was as funky as anything to ever come out of New Orleans, with Lee Allen Zeno's bass part carving out a huge pocket. Lee Allen was Buckwheat's groove maker, contributing arranging ideas and bass lines that lifted every song. He stayed with Buckwheat for the duration of the band's existence.

On our next-to-last day, I felt that we were still lacking a song or two, so I stayed up late looking for possibilities. When I stumbled upon Lee Dorsey's "Ya Ya," I thought I might have something, and I was sure that Buckwheat was familiar with it. When I brought him the song the next morning, he smiled and said, "OK. I've got it." He then went to the piano and almost immediately started playing the syncopated reggae motif that is the heart of the performance. Within two hours, we had the whole track together, with its easygoing accordion solo and Calvin's one-man brass section.

In keeping with the Caribbean feel of the session, Gragg and I began to think about mixing the music in the manor of a reggae record, with Lee Allen's melodic bass parts pushed up front. Gragg suggested that we experiment with using no reverb, so we settled on a dry, in-your-face sound that used only delay effects to create sonic space. A few reviewers did not like it (*DownBeat* magazine responded negatively to Nat's timbale-like, dry snare sound), but it was also something new for zydeco. I began to realize how crucial the mix was to the way in which a listener would respond to the music—that making records was not only the art of capturing an exceptional performance—because the tools of the studio gave us the possibility of drawing out aspects of the music that allowed it to be heard in a new way.

"Ya Ya" was a sensation in south Louisiana. Rounder licensed the track to local record man Floyd Soileau for release on his Maison de Soul label as a 45-rpm single. He had it mastered (the final stage before manufacturing) with even more low end, and it was soon receiving airplay on both R&B and Top 40 stations. It became one of Buckwheat's signature songs, and he often closed his show with it, even thirty years after the sessions. *Waitin' for My Ya Ya* won Buckwheat a second Grammy nomination.

As Buckwheat's career began to soar, many people in the music business took notice, so when he asked me to lunch one day, I had a premonition of what the conversation might be.

Buckwheat and his wife, Bernite, lived in a spacious new home on the rural north side of Lafayette. He was an animal lover, and the property gave him room to indulge his hobby, with a collection of exotic birds and other small creatures who lived in cages and pens behind the house. This time, though, he invited me to his smaller family home, where he had grown up. We were greeted by the meanest dog I have ever met, who appeared ready to tear both of us to pieces, but he calmed down once Buckwheat spoke to him and led him away. Buckwheat had brought beer and *boudin*—spicy rice and pork sausage—for our lunch.

If many people associate Creole and Cajun food with well-known dishes such as jambalaya or gumbo, the dominant food specialty of the area may be its charcuterie—sausages, tasso (spicy cured pork or turkey), turducken (a boneless chicken with crawfish stuffing placed inside a boneless duck, both of which are then tucked into a boneless turkey), and cracklins (fried pork skin). After a few days of eating in southwest Louisiana, away from my usual vegetable-based diet, my stomach sometimes rebels, but I have a weakness for good *boudin*, whether sourced from a local gas station or a well-known butcher such as the Best Stop Supermarket in Scott, Louisiana. I enjoyed my meal with Buckwheat.

"Scott, what would you think about managing me?" he asked.

It did not take me long to answer.

"I'm not sure I would be especially good at doing that, but I'm honored that you would ask."

"You know," he said, "There's a manager named Ted Fox who has approached me. He says can line up a session with Island Records. Do you know him?"

I knew of Ted, but only through the book he had written about New York's Apollo Theatre. I also knew about Chris Blackwell at Island Records. As I would later learn, Chris heard the same potential in Buckwheat's zydeco music that he had heard in Bob Marley's reggae.

"I don't know Ted personally, but this sounds like a step forward," I said. At the time, Rounder's distribution and promotional reach was growing, but certainly not in the same league as Island.

"Well, I wanted to give you the first chance to say yes or no. You and Rounder Records have been good to me."

I was flattered, but I declined without hesitation, because I did not believe I had the kind of aggressive personality that would make for a good manager, nor did I want to forsake the musically creative side of the record business for the business side (which, to be fair, can have its own creativity, at least at its best).

Ted and Buckwheat made a formidable team, and when I look back at what they accomplished together (performing at both Clinton inaugurations, appearing on the major late-night talk shows, playing on national television for the New Year's Eve ceremonies at the turn of the century), it is clear the Buckwheat made the right decision. In fact, I have observed few musician/management relationships that worked so well. They stuck together for the remainder of Buckwheat's life.

I liked the records they made, and Ted was adept at finding cover songs for Buckwheat, such as the Rolling Stones' "Beast of Burden" and Bob Dylan's "On a Night Like This" that would appeal to a broad audience. But I missed the promise of the *Waitin' for My Ya Ya* record, with its boldly Creolized, Caribbean-leaning hybrid of funk, R&B, and zydeco. If Buckwheat and Ted took a slightly safer musical route, they were both shrewd in positioning Buckwheat as the standard-bearer of Louisiana Creole music, always careful to distinguish it from its cousin, Cajun music. In fact, both could be militant about making sure Buckwheat was never advertised as a Cajun artist.

Buckwheat and I remained friends until his death in 2016, at the age of sixty-eight. He lived hard, never letting up, which may have led to the health problems he endured during the final decade of his life. If he achieved a level of success that no other south Louisiana Creole musician had attained, he worked for it. Many of the songs we recorded together remained in his show until the very end, and I think our two records were career highlights for both of us. He was my entrée into the zydeco world—my introduction to this beautiful south Louisiana Creole manifestation of American musical culture, and to many people who became lifelong friends. Long live the new king!

RECOMMENDED LISTENING:

"Turning Point" from *Turning Point*
"Ya Ya" from *Waitin' for My Ya Ya*

Chapter 6

SOLOMON BURKE

SOLOMON BURKE SAT BACKSTAGE ON AN EQUIPMENT CASE. THE LEGENDARY vocalist and extravagant entertainer had just performed his headlining set at the 2003 Porretta Soul Festival, which is located, improbably, in the foothills of the Apennine Mountains in Italy. Preaching, crooning, shouting, and teasing, Solomon had tapped the full emotional and theatrical scope of his material, living up to his reputation as the world's greatest soul singer.

The show had been spectacular in every way. Foremost was Solomon sitting on his throne in his crown and ermine-lined robe. Surrounding him were a blond and statuesque classical harpist in a scarlet gown, a wildly gesticulating blind church organist, and a Superfly look-alike in a red fedora who ran about the stage waving his trumpet over his head. Over the course of the show, Solomon emptied the bucket of red roses that sat by his side, handing them out, one by one, to female fans who approached the stage. His latest comeback tour was on a roll, and the audience of locals and soul music fans from around the world loved every minute.

I had been at least partially responsible for his previous comeback in the mid-1980s, but we had not parted on good terms. In fact, our relationship had imploded with the force of Hurricane Elena as she bore down on New Orleans during our last recording session together in 1985.

Born in 1940 in Philadelphia, Solomon Burke was one of the most powerful and archetypal soul singers of the 1960s. He began his stage career as a boy preacher and spiritual leader, fulfilling a prophecy made by his grandmother, who was a link to the hegemony of the vastly influential Pentecostal preacher Charles M. "Sweet Daddy" Grace and his United

Solomon Burke (photograph © Rick Oliver)

House of Prayer for All People. Solomon began his recording career as a teenager, singing in the clean-voiced style of his idol Roy Hamilton. He also devoted considerable energy to cultivating his network of churches and to obtaining a mortician's license (earning him his sobriquet of "Doctor").

When he joined the Atlantic Records roster, under the aegis of producers Jerry Wexler and Bert Berns, his career blossomed with such hit records as "Just Out of Reach," "Cry to Me," and "Everybody Needs Somebody to Love," which was later covered by the Rolling Stones. Atlantic had marketed Joe Tex, Don Covay, Wilson Pickett, and Solomon as "the Soul Clan," and Burke may have possessed the greatest voice of all of them. When it came to articulating the link between country music and R&B, he was neck and neck with Ray Charles. While his later Atlantic recordings left no doubt about his roots in the Black church, his first Atlantic hit, "Just Out of Reach," was so convincing as a country song that he was mistakenly booked at a Klan rally in Mississippi. At the height of his initial popularity, he commanded large flocks in both secular and religious worlds.

After our final recording sessions, I had seen Solomon only once, at a sold-out show at the Municipal Auditorium in New Orleans. At the time, Solomon was still riding high on a wave of renewed popularity driven by his hit live album *Soul Alive!* and our subsequent studio album, *A Change Is Gonna Come.* The live album was immensely successful with African American audiences at a time when traditional soul music had faded as a commercial force. Solomon had tapped a yearning for the real thing, particularly with his pro-feminist sermon called "The Women of Today" ("The women of today are rising, my brothers!"), delivered as an interlude in a medley of classic soul songs. In fact, the women of the day threw themselves at his majestic bulk as he walked among them with his offering of roses, with his son Selassie at his side to wipe his father's perspiring brow. After the show, with a crowd of people around him, Solomon had asked me, "So, when are we going to make another album, baby?" It was an absurd question (as I will later explain), although I did not know for sure whether it was conciliatory or mocking. Nonetheless, we had not had further contact until now.

I was looking forward to seeing him, and I waited until he was alone. Solomon looked weary, his face wan, and his shaven head still wet with perspiration. The maroon three-piece suit that had contributed mightily to his regal stage presence now hung damply on his ample frame. ("There are three hundred pounds of me, and you can have any part you want," he often told the women in his audience.) We had once been friends, and I remained in awe of his talent—his power to tap into a realm of feeling that few human beings can achieve. He knew I was at the festival, because earlier in the day I had seen Selassie, who told me his dad would be glad to see me. My daughter, Meredith, and I had once shared ice cream with then-teenaged Selassie, his siblings Queen Victoria and Queen Elizabeth, and Solomon in Boston. Now, I was ready make peace, and I approached him backstage with enthusiasm.

"Solomon, how you doin'? It's me, Scott."

He slowly turned toward me, his tired countenance quickly composing itself into a focused glare.

"You ripped me off," he said flatly.

Solomon Burke poster (from the collection of Scott Billington)

I responded immediately that I had done no such thing. He had been paid a good advance for his second Rounder album, and he had been receiving royalties. He reiterated that I had indeed cheated him, adding that I had completed work on our final record together without his participation or approval. Well, that much was true. He had not left me much choice.

"You're about to hear from our attorney."

My pulse quickened and I was dumbstruck—stricken by a feeling, somewhere between panic and incredulity, that had been the undercurrent of our stubborn war of wits twenty years earlier. I hoped that no one, not even an Italian stagehand, was overhearing our conversation, because I believed that what Solomon was saying just was not true.

Then, when it was clear that I had no idea what to say next, he asked cordially, "So, how's your daughter?"

I met Solomon Burke for the first time at the mixing sessions for his live album *Soul Alive!* He had personally arranged to record his 1981 show at the Phoenix I Club in Washington, DC, on which he was ably supported by the New York–based Realtones, who had served the same function for him in gigs at Manhattan's Lone Star Cafe. Our mutual friend Peter Guralnick, the renowned writer and champion of American music, heard the tapes and had facilitated a deal with Rounder Records to release them.

On our final mixing day, I had stayed up all night to plot the final edit of Solomon's raw concert tapes into a coherent two-album set before he was scheduled to go home. We had spent the prior week mixing the record—combining the instrumental sounds and vocals that had been recorded on separate tracks. Solomon was appreciative enough to slip a hundred-dollar bill into our farewell handshake, telling me to take my girlfriend out for a good dinner. He compared the Rounder Records owners in a complimentary way to their early Atlantic records counterparts, the family-like team responsible for his initial success as a soul music star in the 1960s. Rounder co-owner Marian Leighton-Levy was the latter-day Miriam Abramson (Solomon gave Marian a dozen red roses when he visited our offices); Bill Nowlin the new Ahmet Ertegun; and Ken Irwin and me stand-ins for producer Jerry Wexler. (Marian later commented, when she saw me on a ladder as I scraped peeling paint from my home, that Jerry Wexler would never have painted his own house.)

The sessions had not been without drama. Recording engineer Glenn Berger and I had toiled for days over the set of two-inch, twenty-four-track tapes (each with room for twenty-four discrete and parallel vocal or instrumental sounds that can later be mixed down to stereo) that Solomon had first given us. He told us that he had copied the original half-inch, eight-track tapes (each with room for only eight discrete sounds) onto these new reels in order to make room for the additional voices and instruments. Even after we turned off the distracting overdubs, the sound was not good, because the band tracks had been transferred out of phase. Finally, after my stream of pleas for the original tapes, Solomon walked out to his Lincoln town car, chauffeured for the occasion by a sister from his church in Philadelphia, and came back with a set of eight-track reels.

We had to scramble to rent a machine that would play them, but from the moment we threaded the first tape onto the deck and pushed the play button, Peter and I saw that the potential he had heard on the cassettes that Solomon had sent him would be realized—that this might be one of the greatest live albums of soul music ever released. They were masterfully recorded (although the recording engineer remains unknown). The inter-action between Solomon and the audience makes his spoken "sermons" as powerful as the songs, and the band follows him without ever missing a cue. Solomon revels in the full range of his vocal powers. To celebrate, Solomon, Peter, Ken, and I went to a bar at the suburban Colonial Sheraton in Wakefield, Massachusetts, where we heard the rockabilly piano player and singer Preacher Jack.

Later, it turned out that Solomon had not paid the musicians who played on the album, as he had represented, a situation remedied by paying them union scale. We also were not able to obtain a cover photograph from Solomon or book a photo session.

When Solomon was booked to perform at a small nightclub in a crime-ridden neighborhood in Dorchester, Massachusetts, I made arrangements with local photographer Stanley Rowin attend to the show with me. The club owner, standing by a "no weapons or drugs allowed" sign at the door, had little patience for us. So Stanley and I waited in the street with his expensive gear for almost three hours, until Solomon showed up in a lim-ousine at midnight, for his 10 p.m. show. The club owner was furious, and there was a further delay while they brokered an agreement. When Solomon finally took the stage, it quickly became apparent that the house band had no idea who he was or what songs they would play. "Keep it in the key of G," he told them, but to no avail. When it was clear that their musical worlds were never to meet, he grabbed a guitar and sent the band away, accompanying himself for a sublime solo set that satisfied those patrons who had weathered the wait. We got our cover image.

Soul Alive! was a big success for Rounder, best known at the time for traditional folk music, bluegrass, and the roots rocker George Thorogood. Legendary names in the world of traditional African American radio—DJs such as E. Rodney Jones in Baton Rouge, Harvey Holiday in Philadelphia, and tip sheet publisher Jack the Rapper—were soon touting Solomon's record. We hired independent radio promoter Charles Adell, a sincere man with a prosthetic right arm that looked as if it had been borrowed from a large doll, who had worked Solomon's records during the heyday of soul music. In his road-worn automobile, he hit the road with a trunk full of promotional copies and a modest expense account, glad to be back in the game. Initially, we were not able to keep up with orders, and we were never able to figure out exactly what favors to grant to whom to keep the record going, but the orders and the airplay kept coming. The popular press was no less enthusiastic, primed by Peter's liner notes that chronicled both Solomon's unimpeachable musical legacy and his penchant for a quick hustle, such as selling pork chops backstage, or showing up at the Apollo Theatre in New York with a sixteen-wheeler full of popcorn, because he had a concessions clause in his contract.

Nonetheless, everyone was making money, and we liked Solomon enough to be forgiving of his loose business ends. We decided that we should keep the ball rolling with another record, and we made a new deal. Because I had established my recording base in New Orleans, along with relationships with musicians who would be perfect accompanists for Solomon, he was enthusiastic about coproducing the album with me there. A near fatal flaw, as I would soon discover, is that Solomon had convinced Bill Nowlin to pay him his advance up front (demonstrating that he may not have been Rounder's Ahmet Ertegun, after all).

Everything went well enough at first. Solomon and his brother Elec traveled to Boston to go over song ideas. I still have the cassette tape we made in Solomon's hotel room in June 1985, with Solomon brilliantly extemporizing song ideas as Elec tried to keep up with him on guitar. The songs included a version of Hank Williams's "Your Cheatin' Heart" (which, in retrospect, I wish we had recorded) and a promising groove called "Don't Put No Chains on Me." Solomon pledged to take time over the next month to develop his new ideas into full-fledged songs. This was going to be fun, I thought. Nevertheless, I knew it would not hurt to cover our bet by soliciting songs from such likely sympathetic writers such as Dan Penn, Doc Pomus, Jimmy Lewis, Sarah Brown, Paul Kelly, and Johnny Copeland, each of whom was quick to respond with a cassette tape of song demos to present to Solomon.

I arrived in New Orleans on a steamy August day. I had sent Solomon air tickets for himself, his keyboard player, and his guitarist/musical director Sam Mayfield. The rhythm section would be the best that New Orleans had to offer. Bassist David Barard and drummer Herman Ernest III had played for producer Allen Toussaint on such hits as LaBelle's "Lady Marmalade," and they remained the core of New Orleans pianist Dr. John's band for many years. Keyboard player Craig Wroten and guitarist Renard Poché were talented young musicians with whom I had previously worked on albums by guitarist Clarence "Gatemouth" Brown and singers Irma Thomas and Johnny Adams. We were set to rendezvous at the small Studio Solo in Slidell, Louisiana, about twenty miles east of New Orleans.

On the first day of our scheduled sessions, the musicians, recording engineer David Farrell, and I assembled to await the arrival of Solomon and his crew.

They did not show. I called all the phone numbers I had for Solomon, and I desperately called his mother in Philadelphia before sending the musicians home. The same scenario was reprised the next day, when I received a call from his friend Ed Davis in New Orleans, who told me to be patient. Solomon was on the way.

A Checker cab pulled up in front of the studio, a boxy and nondescript brick building surrounded by medical offices. It was a dank, drizzly day, and a sour smell had drifted in from the paper mills north of Slidell. Solomon emerged from the cab, dressed in a crisp, white three-piece suit. I rushed outside to greet him, withholding my anger at his tardiness and the dollars spent on the running studio clock.

Solomon danced into the mist and grabbed me in his arms. We twirled around.

He said something like, "I'm so happy to be here, baby. Did you finish the album yet?"

"No, Solomon. We've been waiting for you. This is about you, you know, not us. But I'm glad you made it. Come on in and meet the guys." Solomon was alone, with no keyboard player and no guitarist.

We went inside and everyone got acquainted. Herman, in particular, was up to meeting Solomon's panache. He was a quick and muscular musician, with a sharp sense of humor that cut no one any slack. Solomon knew right away not to mess with him. David, the engineer, remains one of the most patient people I know, with ears that keep every one of his recording sessions on track. The other players may have been quiet, but Solomon knew right away that he was in the presence of a team that could make great music.

We joked nervously about Hurricane Elena, which had crossed Florida into the Gulf of Mexico, on a beeline path for New Orleans. Solomon looked at me with the serious scowl that I'd come to know as his preface to saying something funny. "Don't worry about the hurricane," he said, his face now barely hinting of a smile. "We'll take care of that." Considering this thought for a moment, he put forward the idea that if each person in

New Orleans would send him fifty dollars, he could pray the hurricane away for good.

We got down to work. The studio was basic and functional, nothing like the big LA or New York studios with fancy lounge areas and elaborate decor. The control room, with the recording console, the tape machines, and the sound processing gear, was separated from the recording room by a large glass window. The room itself had formerly been a dance studio, and it was more or less unchanged except for the addition of a drum booth, to keep the loud drum sounds from "leaking" into microphones of the other instruments.

Selecting the first song in a session is an important decision. If a song proves too difficult to learn, the session can bog down, and the confidence of even the best musicians can be shaken. I thought his idea for a song called "Got to Get Myself Some Money," a Little Richard–style rocker loosely built on archetypal themes ("romance without finance is a nuisance") might be a good place to start. Solomon seemed amused that I knew the material on the hotel room tape well enough to ask him about this song, which he had now plainly forgotten. I think he was impressed, however, with the seriousness with which we were considering his idea. We worked on an arrangement while Solomon got his lyrics together, and the track soon coalesced into a coherent song, enough so that Solomon could call live solos from the musicians. His vocal, with its screams and forced rasp, was a keeper. We were off to a good start.

Next, Solomon suggested that we work on Sam Cooke's magnificent civil rights–era anthem, "A Change Is Gonna Come." Craig used MIDI technology to link together several keyboard sounds, creating a moody and ethereal sonic bed, while Solomon directed Herman to play the snare sidestick style, against a syncopated, reggae-like kick drum pattern. It is an outstanding performance. Solomon made up several new verses on the fly, before improvising a rap at the end of the song that was a fair summation of the world's ills. This was exactly what I hoped we would be able to do—to capture the feeling of authentic soul music, but without resorting to musical cliché, or the sound of the 1960s.

Yet the feeling of a session on a roll was short lived. We referred back to the cassette tape that we had made in Boston. Solomon furtively tried to improvise another song from his "Don't Put No Chains on Me" idea, but this time it did not work. He kept changing verse lengths, chords, and lyrics, and we could never pin down a musical structure to allow us to record a track. Next, Solomon directed the band to play a repeating riff over which he ad-libbed about ten minutes of an on-the-spot composition called "For You" ("I'd buy the White House and paint it pink for you"). He sent the band to the control room while he overdubbed female and male lovemaking sounds, à la Barry White. "Oh brother," I thought. This low-rent *Bolero* would float neither with Solomon's older fans, nor with Rounder's younger roots music audience. Mostly, though, I thought Solomon was faking it. I decided to call the session for the day, which, after all, had been long and productive.

We needed to figure out what to do next. I did not want to spend our week in the studio fumbling through Solomon's unformed ideas, especially if the resulting songs were not going to amount to anything. We needed songs that would be worthy of the greatness that resided in Solomon Burke. On the other hand, I did not want to sell him short. After the musicians had left, I told Solomon that when songwriters had gotten wind of our session, they had sent songs, and that I had brought a few that he might like to hear. Would he listen to them? He looked at me with skepticism, but he agreed. We began playing the song demos.

Solomon smiled. "That's Dan Penn. I've always liked the way he sings. That's one soulful country boy."

Dan and Spooner Oldham are writers of such classic songs as "Dark End of the Street" and "Cry Like a Baby," and we were listening to their new song, "It Don't Get No Better Than This." Solomon said quietly, "We'll cut that one."

We went through the remaining cassettes, until Solomon had selected six songs he wanted to record. He may have been relieved to be off the hook, because we now had our material. I had the feeling that we were back on track. Before I drove Solomon back to New Orleans to his suite at the Holiday Inn Crowne Plaza, I asked if he might consider revamping his rap at the end of "A Change Is Gonna Come" to specifically address the timely issue of South African apartheid, which he had touched upon briefly in his improvisation. In my mind, this would bring a new dimension of relevance to the song, showing its timelessness. Solomon looked at me as if I had suggested painting a mustache on the Mona Lisa.

We established a routine over the next few days. I would pick up Solomon at the hotel, usually after waiting an hour or so past our agreed meeting time. The band would be waiting for us when we arrived at the studio, and we would work on cutting tracks for the songs he had chosen. As before, Solomon contributed arranging ideas that helped shape each track. After finding the right key and tempo, the musicians would run through each song a few times to work on a groove and the fine points of the arrangement, or to find the right keyboard and guitar sounds. We would then roll tape, with Solomon singing from the lyric sheets I had made for him.

After we went through the new songs, we recorded one more of Solomon's "down from the sky" tunes, a funky jam called "Here We Go Again." Solomon taught Herman the unorthodox drum part, which Herman quickly turned into pure New Orleans funk, commenting, "That's a new one on me!" When Solomon jokingly sang a verse from Percy Sledge's "When a Man Loves a Woman" we cut that too, with Solomon improvising new verses. Finally, we had our tracks, the basic skeletons of the songs, with each instrument recorded separately on multitrack tape, ready for the recording of final vocals and other instrumental parts.

All along, we had been anxiously watching the weather forecast on the control room television. We were astonished to see that Hurricane Elena had made a 180-degree turn, and was heading back toward Florida, away from New Orleans. Solomon nodded smugly. "I told you we'd take care of that."

I had become accustomed to working with singers in two different ways. When a band knows the songs well, having rehearsed them or played them onstage, it is often possible to nail the entire track at once, with the singer delivering his or her final performance live. Alternately, as I assumed we were working here, we would record the basic musical accompaniment, then work with the singer to capture a final vocal performance. This can take a few days, while the singer gets comfortable with the material. It was with this agenda that I asked Solomon if he was ready to start work on his vocals.

He turned and faced me with the same steely-eyed glare that I would see again, two decades later, in Porretta. "You want to do what?"

I told him that I wanted to work on the vocals, now that he did not have to worry about the music, so he could focus on getting the best interpretation of each song.

"You want me to sing those songs again?"

"Yes, Solomon. I think you can do better."

"You want soul, right?" he asked.

"That's what this is about."

"Well, what you have on tape is soul, baby. That's inspiration. That's pure soul."

I replied, "Well, you could look at it that way, but you don't know the songs."

He focused his glare and told me that if a song was a hit, then he would learn it.

Here was an unforeseen development, to say the least, quickly compounded when Solomon revealed a new concern. He asked me when he was going to receive the rest of his money.

The way his recording agreement was written, Solomon would be paid any money left over from the recording budget once we had delivered the final recording, after the musicians, the recording studio, and expenses such as meals and travel had been paid. I had not given this much thought, because he had already received his advance (along with the extra plane tickets). Generally, the recording fund goes toward making the best possible record, and any money left over is lagniappe for the artist.

I told him that he would receive more money only if we brought the album in under budget, and that we had better get to work if that was going to happen.

Thus began three stressful days. I was relieved that Solomon continued to show up, but we spent most of our time engaged in a skirmish of words—the verbally gifted preacher and the earnest Yankee arguing about the nature of what constituted "soul."

Our dialogue went something like this:

"Solomon, how can you be soulful with a song if you don't know it? How can you make love to a woman if you don't know her first?"

"Oh, I can just picture you in the love act. I'll bet you keep a glass of ice water by your bed so you can pour it on your head if you get too excited."

And so it went. We never raised our voices. While Solomon and I droned on in quiet disagreement, David sat patiently off to the side, looking slightly bemused and playing the demo recording of each song. Finally, Solomon would acquiesce to my request to sing the song again. He would walk out to the microphone and give us another take or two, each one inevitably better than the time before. It was a maddening process. I was afraid to truly confront him, to tell him to cut the bullshit, for fear that he would pack up and go home, leaving me with no record at all.

I did not understand his holding back, except that he may have enjoyed my polite squirming under his large thumb. If we succeeded with this album, Solomon stood to gain more than anyone. He had seen a resurgence in his career and substantial royalties from *Soul Alive!*, maybe more than from any previous record. Ultimately, though, I knew I was in this for a different reason than Solomon, for I wanted to make a first-rate record, and that was what mattered the most to me—not how much Solomon got paid, or even whether the record would sell. If I backed off and settled for his off-the-cuff first readings of the songs, what was the point of doing this at all?

Solomon had a different take on the proceedings. For him, I began to think, the game of putting something over and getting his money anyway had assumed far greater importance than making a great album. I did not know what to do. Sometimes, I had learned, the best approach to record production could be to shut up and let it happen on its own, but I did not believe that was the case here. I resolved to slug it out and try to get what I thought Solomon truly wanted anyway, no matter how difficult the process.

Peter Guralnick had a personal investment in the project, having been the link that led to this session in the first place, and a great friend to both Solomon and me. As it turned out, Solomon and I were both phoning Peter each night with a blow-by-blow of the day's work. Solomon complained that I was stifling his spirit. I lamented Solomon's lack of preparation and his willingness to jive his way through the sessions.

We eventually captured credible vocal performances on all the songs. When Solomon suggested that he add his own harmony and background vocal parts, I was happy to comply. In contrast to the belabored process of recording his primary vocals, he sang the background parts with abandon and fire, embellishing the main story lines with his effortless preaching and unerring ear for harmony. When we broke for dinner at Vera's Crab Shack on Lake Ponchartrain, he was in high spirits, joking about my taskmaster regimen and hoping we would have a hit. The New Orleans writer Jeff Hannusch, who was a friend of Solomon's and perennially a great source of support for my New Orleans recording endeavors, became the session's peacemaker, urging us to put our differences aside and to keep our eyes on what was going to be a great record. For now, the pressure was off.

Yet, the worst was yet to some. Knowing that we had the core of our album in place, I reluctantly agreed to Solomon's ideas for instrumental overdubs, which I perceived as haphazard. This is the phase of the recording process when additional sounds can be added to those already on tape, to flesh out the arrangements. Solomon's brother Elec, who had since arrived in New Orleans, was a fair enough player, but Renard had more or less filled the space available for guitar, and Elec's new parts seemed superfluous.

Over the weekend, horn arranger Bill Samuel arrived from Texas. With his bearlike presence and workingman's cap, Bill is one of the most gifted arrangers with whom I have worked, and a veteran of numerous rhythm and blues recording sessions. The idea was for him to familiarize himself with the tracks and to get overall guidance from Solomon before writing charts for a four-piece horn section, to be recorded later. But the proceedings took a mystical turn when Solomon directed Bill to follow him into the recording room. While David played the tracks, Solomon hovered over Bill, directing him to play whatever came to mind whenever Solomon touched his shoulder. Bill was flustered by this approach, but he genially complied.

On the meteorological front, Hurricane Elena was still at bay, holding itself away from New Orleans.

Sunday came, and Solomon announced that he would bring in a "sissy" keyboard player from church, after services, to put the final touch on our tapes. He showed up with Raymond Myles, the brilliant gospel keyboardist and arranger who was later murdered in New Orleans by an acquaintance, ostensibly when he refused to turn over the keys to his new SUV. Solomon had us set up the studio's synthesizers on a rack, directing Raymond to hit a different preset sound on the keyboards each time he gave a hand signal from the control room. Thus, as the majestic "A Change Is Gonna Come" played, Raymond might hit the "Polynesian log drum #2" or "Earthquake" sound from his keyboard array, and then frantically try to play something to fit the track. He was neither familiar with the keyboards, nor with Solomon's approach. Again, he cheerfully complied. Solomon danced in the control room, miming an action to suggest that he was pulling dollar bills from the air that were sure to be realized by the new sounds he was adding to the record.

In fact, quite the opposite was happening, for the only dollars involved here were those being squandered—money that might have remained in the budget for Solomon. In my estimation, we were accumulating a jumble of nonsensical sounds over our crisply played tracks. At the end of the day, after another of our discussions over money that Solomon felt was now imminently due, he called me aside.

He asked me how much money Rounder had invested in this project.

I told him that I did not know exactly—that I would have to add it up.

He offered to write a check on the spot, and to take the tapes with him. The idea was preposterous to me, even as I suspected that a check from Solomon, based on legend, was a risky proposition. I responded that I was not going to give up at this stage, after all the progress we had made.

He responded with a threat along the lines of, "Look, we have other ways to settle this. Do you know about my acquaintances in New Orleans? We can come and get the tapes."

"No, Solomon, we're going to finish this album. We came here to make this record, and that's what we're going to do."

With that, Solomon gave me an ominous, over-the-shoulder look, and left the studio with his party. That was the end of our sessions with Solomon.

The studio owner got wind of our argument, and he was protective of his client . . . me. When I arrived at the studio the next day, he was ready, with his .30-06 rifle in tow. I could picture the headlines: "Legendary Soul Singer and Studio Crew Die in Gangland Shootout." But Solomon never returned. He had, I assumed, returned to Los Angeles. What did return was Hurricane Elena, which now had regained its momentum and taken another 180-degree turn, heading straight for New Orleans.

The next day, as the skies darkened, I boarded my flight for Boston, one of the last flights to leave New Orleans before the airport was shut down. As we took off, we were caught in the kind of wind shear that had smacked another airliner into the Metairie suburbs only a year before. "Damn," I thought, "We're all gonna die!" Yet, the plane recovered, and I made it home. I joked with Peter that Solomon had just taken a year off my life.

Later, I returned to New Orleans to finish work on the album. To complete the instrumental tracks, Craig and Renard refined their keyboard and guitar parts, and Bill returned with his horn section. David and I edited together Solomon's vocals, choosing the best of his lines from our multiple takes, to make what we considered to be the best composite vocal performance of each song. I mixed the album with engineer Gragg Lunsford in Massachusetts, processing and balancing each sound from our twenty-four-track master to make the final stereo mix.

The album was a modest success. In Germany, the track "A Change Is Gonna Come" scored big when it was released as a twelve-inch vinyl single. Some critics thought this was the best album—recorded as a whole, as opposed to a collection of singles—that Solomon had ever made. Again, we had no cover photo, and we settled for a computer-generated graphic (in the early days of computer graphics) that should have been vetoed, but the music sounded good, as if Solomon was truly at the top of his game.

In a way, Solomon had been right about Rounder ripping him off, for it emerged years later that he had not been paid the mechanical royalties on his original songs. Solomon had not registered his publishing company with the Harry Fox Agency, upon which Rounder depended for collecting the royalties that must be paid to publishers for each reproduction of a copyrighted work (at the time, about seven cents per song, per record). It was ultimately not his attorneys who called Rounder, but Solomon himself. When the error was identified, he was paid a considerable lump sum—far more than his initial advance—and he continued to receive his overall artist royalties for the album.

The session left me puzzled by the nature of the freedom possible in recorded music. There is clearly something to be gained in mastering the rudiments of any musical situation in order set the stage for uninhibited and clear expression, something along the lines of what Duke Ellington said about writing within the confines of what his musicians could do best, so each could express his or her true genius. It is a delicate balance that, for me, will forever tip between staged precision and joyous accident. Listening to *A Change Is Gonna Come* thirty-five years after it was recorded, you might even think that's what we achieved.

In 2008, I saw Solomon for the last time at a party for Grammy nominees. As I tentatively approached his wheelchair, he spotted me and exclaimed, "Come over here and give me a hug, baby." He was a giant of American music, and his passing in 2010 left the world devoid of the greatest voice that soul music may ever know.

RECOMMENDED LISTENING:

"Monologue (The Women of Today), Hold What You've Got, He'll Have to Go" from *Soul Alive!*
"A Change Is Gonna Come" from *A Change Is Gonna Come*

Chapter 7

THE DIRTY DOZEN BRASS BAND

MY INTRODUCTION TO NEW ORLEANS BRASS BAND MUSIC CAME NOT ON the streets of the city, but in the 1973 James Bond movie, *Live and Let Die.* The Olympia Brass Band moves solemnly through the streets of the French Quarter, playing "Just a Closer Walk with Thee" and walking with a slow and exaggerated cadence. The hitch is that the funeral is for one of the film's characters, who is murdered in plain sight as the band marches by. The pallbearers deftly pick up his body, using a tricked-out coffin. Then, the trumpet player sounds the call to "cut the body loose," and the band breaks into a second line. Sporting early 1970s Afros and wearing the hippest clothes of the era, everyone dances. Looking back, it was not a culturally inaccurate portrayal, except that the body had not been put into its tomb before the partying started.

Brass band music in New Orleans is performed not only for entertainment, but as an essential part of the fabric of life, often present at important social, political, and family events, and as a cultural affirmation that becomes the birthright of everyone who grows up in the city and participates in a second line. The term "second line," for the dancers who follow a band through the streets, has become the name given to any parade, whether it is the celebration of a wedding, or a funeral. During the cool months of the year, there is a second line in the city nearly every Sunday afternoon, sponsored by one of the city's many social aid and pleasure clubs—the Money Wasters, the Black Men of Labor, the Devastating Ladies, the Pigeon Town Steppers. These organizations grew out of African American benevolent associations in the 1800s, which guaranteed their members, among other benefits, a proper funeral and send-off. Today, the Sunday afternoon parades remain as important community rituals. Each year, club members create new matching costumes to show off as they dance down the street in *front* of the band, while everyone else follows behind.

Brass bands were likely introduced to the city by German and Italian immigrants, who employed musicians at picnics, political rallies, and other social gatherings. The city's Creoles of color—people of mixed European and African descent, as opposed to Spanish and French Creoles and their American-born descendants (the use of the word *Creole* can mean different things to different people in Louisiana)—soon embraced the format of horns and drums. This new generation of reading musicians performed written compositions, for there was an established tradition of formal musical training, perhaps due to the institution of the city's French Opera House. When ragtime became a fad in the late 1800s, New Orleans bands were at the forefront, and when nonreading musicians, especially blues-based Creole/African Americans and their Sicilian neighbors, began playing the tunes by ear (they were often called "fakers" by reading musicians), the foundations of jazz may have been laid, especially when fused with the city's rich African-derived rhythmic traditions.

Or something like that! The history of improvising brass bands and jazz in New Orleans is complicated, and there are few firsthand accounts. In *Pops Foster: The Autobiography of a New Orleans Jazzman*, the renowned bassist observed, "The bands that couldn't read made the most money and were the biggest talk of the town." The musician and author Danny Barker, in *My Life in Jazz*, commented, "The New Orleans brass band and jazz band business was a very serious one." His grandfather, Isidore Barbarin, was part of a family musical legacy that extends to the present time, and a member of the Onward Brass Band, which was founded in the 1870s. According to Barker, Barbarin disparaged nonreading players as "routine" musicians, who learned the pattern of playing a melody with the ensemble, then improvising around it and creating variations over the chord changes. "Routine" was a slur.

Danny Barker left New Orleans for New York, at the instigation of his uncle, the renowned drummer Paul Barbarin. For many years, Barker played guitar in Cab Calloway's orchestra and recorded extensively with the cream of New York jazz musicians, including a date with the bebop saxophonist Charlie Parker. In the late 1930s, he made a series of semi-risqué records with his wife, Louise "Blue Lu" Barker, including his well-known composition "Don't You Make Me High" (popularly known as "Don't You Feel My Leg"), which was later a hit for Maria Muldaur. In 1965, he retired and returned to New Orleans, where he took a job at the New Orleans Jazz Museum and began playing local gigs.

Danny and Blue Lu attended the Fairview Baptist Church, where he and the Reverend Andrew Darby Jr. hatched a plan. Darby had noted the aging population of musicians in the city's brass bands, and the lack of interest in the tradition among younger players. He asked Barker to help him recruit young people from the neighborhood to form a brass band that could play for church functions. The Fairview Baptist Church Christian Marching Band quickly became a magnet for aspiring and talented young players, with Barker as its mentor and chief instructor. In its short history, the ensemble came to include future New Orleans jazz stars such as trumpeter Wynton Marsalis, saxophonist Branford Marsalis, drummer Herlin Riley, trumpeter Leroy Jones, trombonist Lucien Barbarin, and clarinetist Dr. Michael White, along with future Dirty Dozen Brass Band members Charles Joseph, Kirk Joseph, Kevin Harris, and Anthony "Tuba Fats" Lacen.

When Barker got in trouble with the musicians union for performing professionally with his underage, nonunion players, Jones responded by joining the union and founding the Hurricane Brass Band, which included several Fairview bandmates, along with his friend Gregory Davis, with whom he had played in the St. Augustine High School Marching Band. "Edwin Hampton, the band director at St. Augustine, decided to create a breakout brass band in 1974, which led to the Hurricane Brass Band," recalled Gregory, whose interest at the time was in the funk and R&B he was performing in the backup bands of artists such as Johnny Adams and Jean Knight.

When Leroy Jones began taking other gigs of his own, the Hurricane Brass Band morphed into the Tornado Brass Band. Organized by alto saxophonist and Fairview member Darryl Adams, also a St. Augustine graduate, the band included future Dirty Dozen members Charles Joseph on trombone, Efrem Towns on trumpet, and Kevin Harris on tenor saxophone, along with Anthony "Tuba Fats" Lacen on sousaphone. Baritone and soprano saxophonist Roger Lewis, who played in Fats Domino's band, would sometimes sit in.

Concurrently, Charles began jamming with the Sixth Ward Dirty Dozen Kazoo Band, an offshoot of the informally organized Dirty Dozen Social and Pleasure Club. This loose-knit group of revelers played kazoos, drums, buckets, Coke bottles, and whatever else would make noise. They would "roam the neighborhood," according to Gregory Davis, on Mardi Gras Day, Halloween, and other occasions, raising a racket. As Charles recounted in *OffBeat* magazine, Kazoo Band drummers Benny Jones and Jenell "Chi-Lite" Marshall began reaching out to horn players, and a more serious "musical" version of the band began to take shape. "It was really Benny Jones who put the band together," asserts Roger Lewis. "It all started with him."

A third influence on the formation of the Dirty Dozen Brass Band was the evening rehearsals that Charles and Kirk Joseph held at their parents' home. Charles was studying at Southern University New Orleans with the jazz saxophonist Edward "Kidd" Jordan. Gregory Davis remarked, "It was the height of the disco era, and there weren't many gigs for horn players. I was studying at Loyola, and the rehearsals were an outlet for the music we were learning. It was not necessarily brass band music." Charles invited Roger Lewis, another SUNO student, to the rehearsals.

Eventually, all these threads came together as the Dirty Dozen Brass Band, with an evolving cast of musicians eventually coalescing as a committed group. The band began accepting gigs at picnics, parties, and funerals, eliciting interest in some of the nontraditional material they played. Gregory Davis and Roger Lewis were the last to sign on. "I was often asked to play with them at the last minute, just before a gig," recalls Gregory. "Finally, I said 'enough,' and I joined the band."

"The brass bands weren't really dying out," observes Roger. Older groups such as the Tuxedo Brass Band and the Olympia Brass Band, with whom he occasionally played, were performing both internationally and for local functions. "The Dirty Dozen just put a new twist on it, and that brought more young people into the music."

A brass band revolution was in the making, partly fomented by a jazz musician who had come home to plant the seeds for the rejuvenation of a cultural tradition.

I first heard the Dirty Dozen Brass Band in early 1980s, at their Monday night gig at the Glass House, a tiny, nondescript bar on Saratoga Street at the edge of the Central City area of New Orleans. The low ceilings, Christmas lights, and lack of windows made the place feel claustrophobic

Buckjumpers at the Glass House (photograph © Rick Olivier)

even when it was empty. Every city occupancy code must have been broken by the shoulder-to-shoulder crowds that gathered there each week. The Dozen had been hired for the gig by happenstance, when they ended up at the bar after a second-line parade, and then played for half the night. The owner sold so much alcohol that the weekly residency was started. "We really didn't make any money, but it gave us a place to play what we were rehearsing," commented Gregory.

The place crackled with energy, not only from the band, whose members stood on the floor with their backs against the wall, but also from the "buckjumpers" directly in front of them. The perspiration flew as these young male dancers executed extremely physical jumps and spins in a tiny amount of floor space, elbow to elbow with club patrons. I had seen this kind of dancing on the street, at Sunday afternoon second lines, but this was more intense.

The band was playing Charlie Parker's "Bongo Beep," Jimmy Forrest's (via James Brown) "Night Train," Thelonious Monk's "Blue Monk," and its own "Blackbird Special" and "My Feet Can't Fail Me Now," along with revved-up versions of a few traditional tunes such as "Lil' Liza Jane." Kirk Joseph—who would influence the sound of the sousaphone not only in New Orleans but also around the world—was delivering the funkiest possible bass lines, with an adept touch that suggested a fretless electric bass, but with a fatter sound. Roger Lewis and Kevin Harris played as a harmonized unit on reeds, while Gregory Davis and Efrem Townes countered them with intricate top-line parts on trumpets. Gregory took his time with solos, enunciating clearly formed melodies and ideas, while Efrem reached for the stratosphere. Charles Joseph's trombone was the glue between the other parts, an inheritance from his father, the traditional jazz trombonist Waldren "Frog" Joseph. At times, the band suggested the free jazz of, say, the Art Ensemble of Chicago, but the deep and almost ancient groove of drummers Benny Jones and Jenell "Chi-Lite" Marshall kept the music grounded, with its feet in the street. The music was precise and loose at the same time, and it made my head spin.

A few older musicians may have found the sound discomfiting, because the Dozen did not sound like a traditional brass band, but many, such as Edward "Kidd" Jordan, found reason to celebrate the discipline of these young musicians—reading horn players who were executing imaginatively conceived and sometimes complicated arrangements. And they connected with the people who came out onto the streets on Sunday afternoon to dance and party, because the second-line community kept hiring them. In 1983, the band released two 45-rpm singles on its own Mad Musicians label that were played constantly on the local community radio station, WWOZ, and they were soon no secret to New Orleans music fans at large.

I decided to approach them with a proposal to make an album (as did, I would later learn, several others), so Rounder founder Ken Irwin and I arranged a meeting with Gregory, who was the band's spokesperson at the time. The record might have happened, except that jazz impresario George Wein, founder of the New Orleans Jazz and Heritage Festival, had just made a deal with Concord Jazz Records to start his own label imprint, to be marketed as the George Wein Collection. Quint Davis, his associate and the producer of the New Orleans Jazz and Heritage Festival, had become the band's informal manager. Quint accompanied them to Studio in the Country in Bogalusa, where they cut their debut album, *My Feet Can't Fail Me Now*, in three days. It was a major event in New Orleans music.

Their initial success came at a furious pace. When they returned from their first two-week tour of Europe, they were immediately booked for a week at the New York jazz club the Village Gate. More New York engagements followed, at Sweet Basil and the Lone Star Cafe. It would be seven weeks before they returned to New Orleans.

Then, serendipity brought the band to Rounder. Founder Marian Leighton-Levy had become acquainted with Quint, and George Wein's deal with Concord Jazz Records was now over. Quint suggested that Rounder release the recording of their concert from the 1985 Montreux Jazz Festival. Thus, one record later, the band was signed to Rounder, and it was my task to edit and mix the record with Gragg Lunsford at Blue Jay Studio in Massachusetts. It was an exciting set, but Gragg and I both felt the groove was lacking because the Swiss engineers had not done a particularly good job of recording the bass drum. We decided to find a suitable bass drum sample to mix in with the undefined sound on the twenty-four-track tape. The technology to do this is vastly better today, but we eventually figured out how to use a gated trigger to fire off the sample, and we recorded a new bass drum track, sometimes one hit at a time, doing our best to preserve the dynamics of Lionel Batiste's performance (Lionel, the son of iconic drummer Uncle Lionel Batiste, had replaced Benny Jones, who had not been able to leave his job to travel with the band). It was not a perfect solution, but I believe it helped to get the excitement across.

Soon, it was time to begin work on a new record, and the band and the Rounder founders selected me be the producer. The resulting album, *Voodoo*, was one of the highlights of my career. The Dirty Dozen's new brass band sound was resonating throughout New Orleans, especially with an even younger generation of players such as the brothers Phillip and Keith Frazier, who would cofound the Rebirth Brass Band and take over the Glass House gig. But the Dirty Dozen was just hitting its first creative peak.

In August 1987, we convened at Southlake Studio in suburban Metairie, Louisiana, where David Farrell had been hired as chief engineer. David and I had become a team, and we knew what we were after, both in terms of sound and in capturing a moment of genuine and spontaneous feeling.

It took a day or two for us to get to that point, as everyone became acclimated to the studio.

The band had yet to record several of the songs they had "workshopped"
at the Glass House and on the streets, when they had the luxury of letting
songs evolve gradually, as new ideas were incorporated. We recorded several of these, including "Santa Cruz" and the album's title track, which was
a variation on a tune that several band members had played in high school.
"Voodoo" is a spooky tour de force, with breathtaking ensemble work and
solos from Gregory and Roger. At a live show, I had seen Roger play both
of his saxophones at once, putting them both in his mouth and playing in
harmony, like the jazz genius Rahsaan Roland Kirk, and I suggested that he
could finish his solo that way. When you hear the saxes talking in tongues,
that is how Roger made the sound.

Roger is the band's elder, about a decade older than the others, who
had played in the bands of Fats Domino, Irma Thomas, and others. He is
a stylish man who wears his clothes well, and one of the purest musicians
I know. He never misses an opportunity to make music, even if that might
mean taking a gig with the Tremé Brass Band the day after coming home
from a six-week tour. Several years ago, the Selmer company gave him a
tour of their factory in Mantes-la-Ville, France, and presented him with a
custom-made baritone saxophone.

We recorded musical guest Dr. John live with the band at Southlake.
The Valentinos song "It's All Over Now" had been the first number-one
hit for the Rolling Stones, but now was the perfect time to restore it to the
New Orleans songbook, because the original recording had been cut, in
Los Angeles, with a sousaphone bass and with John Boudreaux's ferocious
New Orleans drumming. I went to Jim Russell's Rare Records on Magazine
Street to buy a copy of the vinyl 45, for ten dollars, so we could get the
lyrics right, but drummer Jenell "Chi-Lite" Marshall and Mac "Dr. John"
Rebennack quickly deconstructed them into something of their own. As
the performance went to tape, I had to pinch myself to affirm that it was
actually happening, because it was thrilling. We worked on a solo or two,
then added backing vocals and percussion, and the track was done. The
recording has become a perennial New Orleans favorite.

We traveled to New York to record with Dizzy Gillespie and Branford
Marsalis at the Hit Factory, where former Blue Jay Studio engineer Rob
Feaster was now working. On our first day, the session with Branford was

The Dirty Dozen at Southlake Studio, Metairie, Louisiana, 1987. *Back row, left to right:* Roger Lewis, David Farrell, Kevin Harris, Kirk Joseph, Scott Billington; *middle row, left to right:* Jenell "Chi-Lite" Marshall, Mac "Dr. John" Rebennack, Charles Joseph; *front row, left to right:* Gregory Davis, Efrem Towns, Lionel Batiste (photograph © Scott Billington).

a dream. He was the same age as the musicians in the Dozen, and the chemistry was immediate. We did four takes of Charlie Parker's "Moose the Mooche," each one a keeper.

Things with Dizzy did not go so well, at least at first. He had been to the Glass House to hear the band and had subsequently played a gig with them (the Dizzy Dozen!). But when we began working on an arrangement of his bop blues standard "Ooh-Pop-A-Dah," it never gelled. We eventually ended up with a long string of solos over the rhythm section, and Dizzy seemed tired. I kept trying to guide the session back to something more concise. It was not easy, on so many levels, to give direction to Dizzy Gillespie, although Roger still jokes with me that I might have been the only man ever to ask Dizzy to do it again . . . and again. At the end of the session, we were crestfallen. We did not have a usable track.

Dizzy had left his cologne-saturated terry cloth towel, which he had used to cradle his trumpet in its case for what may have been years, behind in the studio. I decided to take it home with me so I could mail it to back to him. My back hall smelled of *eau-de-Diz* for weeks.

In New Orleans, we regrouped, and decided that we might cut a track to which Dizzy could later add his vocal and trumpet parts. When I called him to ask if he was game, he said yes. We went to Southlake and cut the song, with Charles's dragging "tailgate" trombone a key part of the arrangement.

Back in New York, I was ready for Dizzy. I hired a car pick to him up at his home in Englewood, New Jersey, to take him to Sorcerer Sound in SoHo—one of the great recording spaces in Manhattan that was forced to close a few years ago, when it could not keep up with escalating rents. Dizzy played and sang beautifully, then entertained us with a story about how he could be an ideal spokesperson for Armstrong Tires, carrying the jazz legacy of the Armstrong name forward. He winked as he showed us a small, high-tech pipe that recaptured its own smoke, rendering detection in airplane restrooms difficult. The great musician and entertainer remained a rascal, even in his later years.

Just as the album was finished, a business wrinkle emerged. Joe McEwen, an acquaintance from Boston who was now an A&R (artists and repertoire) person at Columbia Records, approached the band to ask if they would sign with him. Of course, this was not possible, as they were already committed to Rounder. But, as with Buckwheat Zydeco, this seemed like a big opportunity for the band—a major label ready to put a major push behind them. There were several awkward moments between Rounder, the band, and me, as I acted as a go-between, but ultimately a deal was worked out, and the album was released by Columbia in 1989. I still believe it was the right thing to have done, although Rounder was growing in its marketing ability. I did not know it then, but the band would choose to have me stay on as their producer for their next three albums.

Joe conceived of a concept for the follow-up record to *Voodoo*. He proposed that *The New Orleans Album* be a sort of history of New Orleans music filtered through the Dirty Dozen, with guests who might include Dave Bartholomew, Fats Domino, and Danny Barker, alongside the band's new compositions. Gregory Davis's "Hannibal" was a standout, and a hint of things to come from him. I am not sure the record coalesced in the way that Joe wanted it to, but there are some very special tracks that remain highlights of the Dirty Dozen discography. We recorded at Ultrasonic Studio in New Orleans, where David Farrell now worked. He would eventually become the studio's co-owner, with Steve Reynolds, and we made dozens of records together there.

We asked Danny Barker to cut his best-known song, "Don't You Make Me High (Don't You Feel My Leg)," with the gender roles necessarily reversed. Pianist Eddie Bo was added to the band, giving the track an easy, bluesy roll. Danny was a remarkable storyteller—the word *raconteur* might as well have been invented for him—and he introduced a few of his best characters in the preamble of the song: Pork Chop Willie, Wide Open Annie, and Juicy Lucy. It is a wonderful track, as the band pays homage to one of its mentors. Danny's vocal perfectly conveys his sage-like and humorous take on a few of the foibles of human beings.

Linda Ronstadt was in town that day, and Quint Davis called to ask if they could sit in on the session. And they did, literally, sitting on the floor of the control room, out of sight. A few days later, they attended a second line in Mid-City, with Ronstadt clearly enjoying the energy and the ambience. I bought a pork-chop sandwich—two slices of white bread surrounding a grilled pork chop—and a beer from the vendors who followed the parade, setting up shop each time the band and the costumed dancers took their periodic breaks at barrooms along the way.

The producer and songwriter Dave Bartholomew arrived the next day to record his humorous song "The Monkey." He was a whir of energy in the studio as he arranged the song, singing lines for each musician to play, demonstrating the bass drum pattern, and finally putting the parts together to create an interlocking groove that was perfect for the song. We cut the track live, with Dave delivering a blistering trumpet solo. His chops were in astonishingly good shape—precise and loud. Legend has it that the pre-recording-era trumpet player and jazz pioneer Buddy Bolden could be heard miles away, and I believe Dave could have been, too.

When he first entered the studio, I had made a gesture for him to take my chair—the producer's seat—next to David's. Now that the basic track was on tape, there were backing vocals to overdub, and a few horn ensemble parts to punch in (replacing the parts with mistakes with new performances). He motioned for me to take my chair back.

When we were finished, I asked him, "Were musicians so much better back in the fifties, when you cut all those great records live in mono, with no overdubs?"

He chuckled. "No. You don't know the half of it. We might play a song thirty or forty times, and get it perfect, only to have the tenor player squeak a note in the solo. I'd go home with that song playing over and over in my head. It would drive me crazy."

He had a theory about multiple takes. Things would go downhill after three or four takes, as the band lost energy. I could vouch for that. However, he theorized that there was a point in time when it would come back, if you stuck with it long enough. I would seldom push any group of musicians to repeat the same song long enough for that to happen, though. I realized the luxury that multitrack recording gave us, because almost anything except the drum tracks could be replaced (and even the drums, at times). Something can be lost in that process, though, because constructing a song piece by piece seldom gives you the feeling of something that actually happened in real time, with everyone unified in groove.

The intended track with Fats Domino did not come to pass. He had asked for $10,000 in cash for the performance, which Joe had arranged to be delivered, and we had chosen a song on which Fats owned the full copyright, "When I'm Walking (Let Me Walk)." All good, we thought.

Then, for several sessions in a row, over a period of a month or two, I would call his manager, Reggie Hall, to ask if he could choose a time for Fats to come to the studio. We would agree on the date. Inevitably, the day before the session, Reggie would call and say, "Y'know, Fats ain't feelin' too good today. Can we pick another time?"

When we were down to our final week of sessions, I called Reggie and said, "Look, we'll be at Ultrasonic for five days next week. You can pick any time, midnight or noon, and we'll be ready for you. Do you think you can make it happen?"

"Well," he replied, "I don't think Fats is gonna be feelin' too good next week."

Since Roger Lewis had played in Domino's band for years (you can see him with the all-cylinders-firing Fats Domino band in the film *American Masters: Fats Domino and the Birth of Rock and Roll*), he decided we should take matters into our own hands. Each day, Fats would frequent a series of bars in his native Ninth Ward, saying hello to friends along the way, and Roger thought we could track him down there.

"Aw, man, Fats was here not more than an hour ago," was the typical response. We never found him. Finally, we decided to let it go, and we cut the track with Eddie Bo, who delivered a performance in which he found the gospel soul in Fats's tune.

Our last guest was Elvis Costello. The band had just been featured heavily on his *Spike* album, and he wanted to return the favor. We decided to approach his song the same way we had recorded Dizzy, by making a track in New Orleans that I would take to New York. Elvis chose the Dave Bartholomew song "That's How You Got Killed Before." We recorded a basic track, an up-tempo version of the song based on Dave Bartholomew's original arrangement, to which we could add Elvis's voice.

Back at Sorcerer Sound in New York, working with engineer Judy Kirschner, we set up the session for Elvis's vocal, using a vintage Neumann U-47 tube microphone. I did the sound check, singing into the microphone while Judy adjusted levels. Elvis arrived, listened to the track, and was ready to go. He squared his shoulders, stepped up to the mic, and delivered a no-holds-barred vocal performance that was perfect for the song—a frenetic scream. The problem was that the distortion on his voice was massive—the microphone, the preamplifier, and the tape itself were all pushed past their limits, and it sounded awful—a blur of fuzzed-out overload. He came back into the control room.

"I'm so sorry, man," I apologized, "I did the mic check myself, and I should have asked you to do it."

"Wait a minute," he said, "Let me hear that."

We played the tape back.

"That's fucking brilliant! I love it!" was his evaluation.

To be fair, it was the kind of analog distortion that was often heard on old rhythm and blues records, when the vocal goes into overdrive, and it had a vibe, but there was just too much of it. I asked him if he would cut the part again, after we turned everything down, but he was now determined to make his vocal distort at all the right moments, and it did. In retrospect, I can appreciate where he was coming from, because analog vocal distortion can be an emotional sound (you can hear it used that way on several of Prince's records), but I was not entirely ready for it then.

The next record we made, 1992's *Open Up: Whatcha Gonna Do for the Rest of Your Life*, is one of my favorite Dirty Dozen records. With the exception of one composition by the South African bassist Johnny Dyani, which

I had brought to the band, this was the first Dirty Dozen record to feature all original compositions. It was different, because instead of developing material as a unit, as they had with, say, *Voodoo*, individual band members brought finished compositions for the ensemble to learn to play. We did not use the full band on every cut, opting to try to create a listening experience that was more of a tapestry of sonic colors. For instance, Roger's "Song for Lady M" is a solo baritone saxophone performance that follows the frenetic free-jazz playing of Charles's "Charlie Dozen."

This was also the first Dirty Dozen record to incorporate a drummer who used a full kit, when gifted Raymond Weber played on several songs. While the classic brass band percussion section of two parade drummers, one each on bass drum and snare, had given the band its propulsive street groove, the horn players began at times to feel constricted by this format. With Raymond on drums, Roger's "Use Your Brain" became pure New Orleans funk. It was a new direction, and it worked.

The most ambitious part of the record is Gregory's fourteen-and-a-half minute, three-part suite, "The Lost Souls (of Southern Louisiana)." Sometimes, it is reminiscent of Duke Ellington's writing, with its dissonant voicings, tonal shifts, and varying rhythms. We cut it one section at a time, like a classical record. "Even though it isn't a second-line or brass band piece, I wanted it to have motion," Gregory told me. The idea of the composition as a springboard for movement was realized when the Dayton Contemporary Dance Company created choreography for the suite, which was performed in Atlanta, New York, and New Orleans.

For many years, Gregory was the band's business manager. When he joined the Dozen, he was a student in the music program at Loyola University, but the band's nonstop travel meant that he would not complete his degree until twenty years later, when he stepped away for a time as a full-time touring member. Back in New Orleans, he began working for Festival Productions, where he booked the contemporary jazz artists, brass bands, Mardi Gras Indians, and social aid and pleasure clubs for the New Orleans Jazz and Heritage Festival, as well as booking the "Superlounges" at the Essence Festival. Additionally, he became the talent buyer for the Storyville District club, which was owned by George Wein, Quint Davis, newsman Ed Bradley, restauranteur Ralph Brennan, and others. If that was not enough, he began teaching at Loyola (including the Introduction to Music Business class that I would teach for one semester a few years later), so if he was able to spend time at home with his family, his schedule was even more demanding. "It was a jigsaw puzzle," he said.

We submitted *Open Up* to our new A&R rep at Columbia, as Joe McEwen had left the company for a position at Warner Bros. He seemed happy enough with the record we delivered, but then came back with the idea that we overdub additional musicians such as P-Funk keyboardist Bernie Worrell and guitarist Marc Ribot. Well, I thought, that would have been cool if we had started that way, but to add them now? New manager Mike Kappus stepped in and nixed the idea, but I could tell that by rejecting the A&R rep's suggestions, we were perhaps demotivating any initiative he might have taken as the band's advocate at the label, especially considering that the Dozen was not his signing.

We made one more record for Columbia, when the band was moved to the label's jazz division, which at the time was under the direction of the veteran jazz executive Dr. George Butler, who had given Blue Note Records its string of crossover hits in the 1970s.

The Broadway musical *Jelly's Last Jam*, written around the music and the last years in the life of the New Orleans jazz pioneer and composer Jelly Roll Morton, was a hit in 1992, and Dr. Butler wanted the Dirty Dozen to record a full album of his compositions. On the surface, it seemed like a good idea. However, aside from a few Morton compositions such as "Milenberg Joys" and "The Pearls," his music was not widely played in contemporary New Orleans. This would be a learning process for all of us.

We decided to take a different approach with *Jelly*, augmenting the band's skills by hiring outside arrangers to work with Jelly Roll's material. We chose the best: Wardell Quezergue, who had produced and arranged hits such as King Floyd's "Groove Me"; Edward Frank, the jazz pianist who had also played on classic rhythm and blues records such as Big Joe Turner's "Honey Hush" and arranged a part of Dr. John's album *Goin' Back to New Orleans*; Fred Kemp, the jazz tenor saxophonist who was Roger's best friend and Fats Domino's bandmate; and Tom McDermott, the young pianist who would soon be instrumental in founding the New Orleans Nightcrawlers brass band.

There had been two crucial personnel changes in the band, with both Joseph brothers gone and two younger musicians taking their place. Keith Anderson was the new sousaphone player, and Revert Andrews joined on trombone. In spite of the challenging nature of the material, Lionel and

The Dirty Dozen Brass Band (photograph © Rick Olivier)

Chi-Lite made the parade-drum setup work, pushing themselves as they explored new grooves. We also added percussionists Kenyatta Simon and Big Chief Smiley Ricks on a few tracks. Danny Barker was our spiritual guide, because he had worked with Jelly Roll in New York in the 1930s. He provided several spoken pieces for the record that put Jelly Roll and his music into historical perspective, in his inimitable New Orleans/Brooklyn-esque accent. Gregory and I had often talked about coproducing a new Danny Barker record, and it is one of the regrets of my career that we waited too long.

I cannot say that making the Jelly Roll record was easy, because instead of recording music that had evolved organically into a signature sound, we were starting from scratch with compositions that might have been more suited to a classic traditional jazz ensemble—or even Broadway—than to an edgy brass band. The challenge was in walking the line between honoring Jelly Roll's compositions and maintaining the integrity of the Dirty Dozen.

We approached the songs a few at a time, with long rehearsals at the musicians' union hall on Esplanade Avenue. Each arranger would hand out charts, and we would work through them until everyone could feel the songs. Only then would we go to Ultrasonic to record. There are some standout moments. George French sings on Wardell's masterful reworking of "Milenberg Joys," while "Georgia Swing" is an effective melding of a traditional jazz stomp and a modern jazz big-band sensibility. I think we were all proud that we pulled the record off, but I also began to understand how the wrong A&R direction, no matter how well intentioned, could get in the way of what an artist might do best.

For the next twenty years, I stayed in touch with Gregory, Roger, and Kirk. After any confusion about the band's heart and soul that might have been created with *Jelly*, producer John Medeski got them back on track with *Buck Jump*. The band now had a full-time trap-kit drummer and a keyboardist, having made complete the transition from street band to concert ensemble. It was during this time that Gregory stopped touring with the band, although he continued to appear on their recordings. *Medicated Magic* featured guest artists, including Norah Jones and Widespread Panic's John Bell, while their post-Katrina *What's Going On* imaginatively and successfully reinterpreted Marvin Gaye's album, one of the most iconic recordings of all time.

In 2011, Roger (who was now the band's business manager) called to ask if I would like to work with them on a new record. The idea was to pick up where *Open Up* had left off, with mostly new compositions by the band members. There would be no celebrity cameos. I was thrilled to accept the offer, because here was the chance to put everything we had learned about making records and music into play, and to make an album that truly reflected all the strengths of the Dirty Dozen.

Kirk had been back in the band for a while, now augmenting his sousaphone with electronic effects such as an octave divider that gave him an even lower low, and Gregory was now back full time. Former members, the guitarist Jake Eckert and the drummer Terence Higgins, would rejoin the band for these sessions. We recruited Hammond B-3 player Nigel Hall and trombonist Corey Henry for several songs each.

The writing on *Twenty Dozen* is superb, with a variety of grooves and approaches that honor New Orleans roots while often exploring influences from other ports on the Caribbean. "Best of All," written by Gregory, Kevin, Terence and Kirk, may be just that, with its joyful island lope. The band asked me to look for one cover tune, so we chose Rihanna's "Don't Stop the Music" and turned it into a sort of West African high life/New Orleans funk hybrid. Roger's bawdy "Dirty Old Man" closes the record. An aspect of New Orleans music that I have always appreciated is that most musicians, no matter how serious they are about their art, do not lose sight of the objective of entertaining their audience, and that's what the band does on this song. In New Orleans music, it is not uncommon to have high art, booty-shaking groove, virtuosic soloing, and tongue-in-cheek humor all rubbing shoulders in the same song. Gregory told me that he appreciated that about Danny Barker—that his music was meant to be enjoyed or played live for people, to help them to have a good time.

Forty years on, the Dirty Dozen still sets a standard that other brass bands emulate. I was fortunate to work with two of the ensembles most influenced by them: the Soul Rebels and the New Orleans Nightcrawlers. Both bands maintain a very high level of musicianship. The Soul Rebels often explore grooves that are further removed from the second-line foundation, adding elements of hip-hop. The Nightcrawlers, who boast several accomplished composers and the sousaphone of the gifted Kirk Joseph disciple Matt Perrine, adhere for the most part to the street groove. As with the Dirty Dozen, you can dance and buckjump and celebrate life to both bands, or you can get your ears involved and just listen, because the music happens in both spaces at once.

Today, there are more young brass bands in New Orleans than ever, and if some of them play music that can seem monochromatic, with grooves and chanted vocal lines that aspire only to enliven the party, they are part of a vigorous and vital tradition that no other city can match, because the street-level sharing of music and culture is the lifeblood of New Orleans identity. The legacy of the Dirty Dozen Brass Band—and of Danny Barker and the Fairview Baptist Church Christian Marching Band—is that the brass band sound in New Orleans is secure for a long time to come, and that we will undoubtedly be surprised by the next group of upstarts who come along and show us how it can be imagined anew.

RECOMMENDED LISTENING:

"Voodoo" and "It's All Over Now" from *Voodoo*

"Don't You Make Me High (Don't You Feel My Leg)" from *The New Orleans Album*

"The Lost Souls (of Southern Louisiana)" and "Use Your Brain" from *Open Up: Whatcha Gonna Do for the Rest of Your Life?*

Chapter 8

JOHNNY ADAMS

A YOUNG MAN WITH A CLIPBOARD CAME NEAR AS JOHNNY ADAMS AND I walked toward his black Cadillac, which was parked under the North Claiborne Avenue overpass in New Orleans, near the housing project where he shared an apartment with his mother.

"Excuse me, sirs," he said politely, and we nodded. Despite the stifling August humidity, he wore a frayed white shirt and tie, with a button-down collar. His Jheri curl locks were drooping in the heat.

"You guys need work? Do you know that truck drivers can make over fifteen dollars an hour?" He was attempting to sign up recruits for a truck-driving school, and he held out a brochure.

"Work?" asked Johnny, suggesting both surprise and feigned horror at the idea. He wore a crisp yellow golf shirt tucked into pleated pants, a thin tan belt with matching leather shoes, and a white visor that shaded his dark glasses. "I don't want no work. I'm a musician." He spoke with the New Orleans/Brooklyn-esque accent that made "work" come out like "woik."

The recruiter turned toward me. "You a musician too, I guess," he said as he looked downward and turned away.

We got into Johnny's car. As the engine rumbled to life, it was clear that his Cadillac had seen grander days. The air conditioner did not work, and there was an incessant beeping from the dashboard—the sound that tells you to fasten your seatbelt or close the door.

"Johnny, is there a way to stop that?"

"Naw, it's been like that for a while." And it was like that for a while longer. Actually, for as long as he owned the car.

Johnny Adams may have been the most accomplished, versatile, and soulful singer to emerge from the New Orleans rhythm and blues scene of the 1960s and '70s. The pioneering producer and engineer Cosimo Matassa often said so, and Johnny's contemporaries such as Aaron Neville and Irma Thomas might tell you that today. Johnny's remarkable voice could effectively deliver everything from a baritone growl to a screeching falsetto, which became a reluctant trademark, earning him the sobriquet "the Tan Canary." His midrange crooning was seductive and smooth, and he could testify with the gruff authority of, say, Otis Redding. He was first and foremost a musician, with an ear for improvisation that could negotiate the trickiest chord changes. Yet, he could also be a reticent artist who may have failed to grasp the full potential impact of his talent.

I knew about Johnny Adams because I had bought his *Heart and Soul* album on SSS International Records in 1969, soon after it was released, when I was in high school in Massachusetts. He was one of the first artists I wanted to hear when I attended the New Orleans Jazz and Heritage Festival a decade later. I was personally introduced to him in 1982 by my friend Jeff Hannusch, the respected music writer. Johnny immediately agreed to make a new album for Rounder Records, and we began an artist/producer relationship that would last until his death in 1998.

At the time, Johnny's career had settled into a modest routine. On most weekends, he performed at Dorothy's Medallion Lounge on Orleans Avenue, backed by Walter "Wolfman" Washington and the Solar System Band. The gig started around one in the morning and often ended when the sun came up. Dorothy's could accommodate perhaps eighty patrons, who sat at tiny tables and ordered setups—a bottle of Coke, a pint of liquor, and a bucket of ice—along with a few food items such as hot sausage links. The thick cloud of cigarette smoke stung my eyes. Owner Dorothy Esteves, who wore a blond wig and, indeed, several gold medallions, presided from behind the bar, which was festooned with Christmas lights. Two amply proportioned and scantily dressed go-go dancers in cages were sometimes augmented by a shake dancer, whose skill in moving her derriere reflected the African American dance form that evolved into the New Orleans style called bounce (with its attendant music), and that today is manifested as twerking.

Yet, in spite of its cramped stage area and modest comforts, Dorothy's was not a dive. Rather, it was a throwback to an earlier era of aspired elegance at places like Prout's Alhambra Club on North Claiborne Avenue and the Dew Drop Inn on LaSalle Street, which often featured comedians, female impersonators, and dancers, in addition to the main act. Dorothy's attracted a well-dressed, middle-aged clientele, who came to escape their workaday travails. Throughout the night, men would arrive to sell roses, or to take souvenir Polaroid photos of the patrons of the club.

Once, when I played harmonica with Walter and the band during their warm-up set, I came back to a tabletop filled with enough drinks—gifts from the patrons—to put me away for good. A wiry woman sat down next to my friend Tom Smith and me. She put her arm around me and said, "It takes a white boy like you to come in here and [I leave it to the reader to imagine what she said, which was meant as a compliment]," then invited me to leave the club to party with her. While I appreciated the spirit of her offer, I declined what might have been the party experience of my life. Dorothy's was a friendly place, even for a visiting Yankee.

Johnny would arrive early, sitting at the bar as he smoked Kools and sipped Cokes. He was always "clean," immaculately dressed in a suit with a tie and pocket square, and freshly shined shoes. He wore dark glasses to hide his blind right eye, which may have been the result of a birth defect. Walter, on the other hand, would arrive just in time for the gig, sometimes looking disheveled. Yet, the two men were a perfect musical match. Walter's ability as a guitarist allowed him to play complex, jazzy harmonies while remaining deeply entrenched in the blues. The plucky, urgent sound he extracted from his Hohner Les Paul copy inspired Johnny, and their sets could reach ecstatic heights.

Laten John Adams Jr. was born on January 5, 1932, and reared in the Hollygrove neighborhood of New Orleans, which today retains a more laid-back and even countrified feel than much of the city. He dropped out of high school before graduating, but not before he mastered a beautiful cursive hand. According to Jeff Hannusch, Johnny had worked as a young man hauling sod out of the Barataria swamp, which Johnny reiterated by telling me he had worked as a landscaper, one of his few jobs outside of the music business.

He found his calling early, singing in church and with such groups as the Soul Revivers, and Bessie Griffin and Her Soul Consolators. In *I Hear You Knockin'*, he told Jeff Hannusch, "Oh I really enjoyed singing gospel.

There was this feeling of inner satisfaction that you don't always get from singing R&B. The people that come out to hear gospel are there to hear you sing. Most of the people at my gigs now are out to have a good time, not necessarily to listen to music."

Yet he decided to make the switch to rhythm and blues in 1958, after his neighbor, the songwriter Dorothy LaBostrie (who had famously cleaned up the lyrics to Little Richard's "Tutti Frutti") convinced him to record her song "I Won't Cry." Produced by the nineteen-year-old Mac Rebennack (who would later assume the persona of Dr. John) and released on the local Ric Records label, it was a modest hit. His follow-up, "A Losing Battle" (written by Rebennack), made number twenty-seven on the *Billboard* R&B charts.

In 1962, during his tenure with Ric Records, Johnny and fellow musicians Earl King, Joe Jones, Smokey Johnson, and George French drove to Detroit to audition for Motown Records. Owner Berry Gordy Jr. was impressed enough to offer Johnny a recording contract, but Ric Records owner Joe Ruffino threatened a lawsuit, and the deal was off. Ruffino died a year later, and Johnny's contract was assigned to the Watch label, which was owned by Ruffino's brother-in-law, Joe Assunto. Johnny did not recall that there ever had been a formal contract, but he went along with the label switch as a way to continue recording, hoping again for the kind of break he had just lost.

He settled into a routine and a period of modest success, as he played gigs across the Gulf Coast, booked by the hardworking agent Percy Stovall. He would eventually release singles on labels that included Ric, Ron, Gone, Watch, Pacemaker, Gamma, SSS International, Atlantic, PaID, JB's, Hep' Me, and Ariola Records America, garnering enough airplay, at least locally, to keep people coming to his shows. Johnny told Hannusch that he would often take a Greyhound bus to gigs, making just enough money to get by.

After he signed with Shelby Singleton's Nashville-based SSS International label in 1968, he enjoyed a string of modest national hits with the songs "Release Me," "Reconsider Me," and "I Can't Be All Bad," each of which charted in both R&B and pop. "Reconsider Me" is a tour de force, written by the Shreveport, Louisiana, team of Myra Smith and Margaret Lewis and produced in Nashville by Jerry Kennedy. Its juxtaposition of a slow-burn country music feel, complete with pedal steel guitar, and Johnny's clearly enunciated and soulful delivery reaches a thrilling peak when his falsetto takes over. These hits led to a booking relationship with Universal Attractions, and for a time he toured outside the South.

When I met Johnny, he was at the end of a business relationship with the producer Senator Jones, who had kept up a steady stream of releases on his Hep' Me label, and with a license to the Ariola Records America label. Actually, the partnership was not quite over yet, as the New Orleans music entrepreneur Marshall Sehorn emerged with a claim that Johnny was now under contract to him, the rights having been assigned to him by Senator Jones. Johnny was both frustrated and angered, but we nonetheless had to wait until this agreement, a copy of which Sehorn provided, had run its course. Finally, in late 1983, we were ready to move forward with his first Rounder album.

We would record with Walter and the band (bassist Darrel Francis Sr., drummer Wilbert "Junkyard Dog" Arnold, and percussionist George "Geeje" Jackson Jr.), along with keyboardist Craig Wroten, horn arranger/saxophonist Bill Samuel, saxophonist Alvin "Red" Tyler, and trumpet player Terry Tullos, most of whom who had worked with me on sessions for Gatemouth Brown's Grammy-winning *Alright Again!* and its follow-up, *One More Mile.* I wanted to capture the vibe of a performance on a good night at Dorothy's, but I also wanted to make an album that would show the breadth of what Johnny could do.

Johnny and I selected the songs together, tapping a few from his set ("I Feel Like Breaking Up Somebody's Home," "Your Love Is So Doggone Good"), along with little-known songs by Sam Cooke ("Laughin' and Clownin'") and Percy Mayfield ("We Don't See Eye to Eye"). Massachusetts-based Roger Ebacher contributed the jazzy "Why Do I." The producer Joel Dorn, who had been working on an Aaron Neville EP at Ultrasonic Studio in New Orleans, suggested that I reach out to the brilliant Brill Building songwriter Doc Pomus, who had recently written an album, with Mac Rebennack, for B. B. King. It turned out that Doc was a Johnny Adams fan, and he sent the beautiful ballad that became the album's title song, "From the Heart."

We rehearsed at Wilbert's apartment, which was off a courtyard on North Rampart Street where the buggy drivers in the French Quarter kept their horses and carriages at night. The music felt good, and it had to, because we had only three days to record the album.

The sessions at Ultrasonic Studios on Washington Avenue went well, with the best performances coming live on the floor with the rhythm section, especially the songs from Johnny's regular set. Engineer Jay Gallagher and I stayed up nearly all night on the third day, overdubbing the horn section. Still, a few of the vocals did not feel as engaged as they might have been. It was as if Johnny was feeling the responsibility of making the session succeed instead of connecting with the songs. I had returned to Massachusetts, so Johnny went back into the studio with Jeff Hannusch in support and worked on several of the songs. We now had a record that represented Johnny at his best, including the impassioned vocal on Janis W. Tyrone's blues "Scarred Knees." In the liner notes to *From the Heart*, Johnny said, "I didn't mind putting in the extra hours rehearsing and getting these tunes down right. This record is different."

The record was received with considerable enthusiasm, especially in Europe, where it was released on the Demon label. That part of my objective was realized, but Johnny became anxious. Rounder released "From the Heart" on a 45-rpm single, but the local mainstream stations seldom played classic rhythm and blues, and an outsider label from Boston was unlikely to convince them otherwise. Rounder was a roots/folk label, and if *From the Heart*, with its funky New Orleans rhythms and polished R&B sound, was something new for the label, Rounder's strength was in marketing music to an audience that listened to National Public Radio. Johnny wanted commercial airplay in New Orleans, which was out of Rounder's reach.

During this same period, I recorded a track with Johnny for the debut Rounder album of saxophonist Alvin "Red" Tyler, whom I had come to rely on as a seasoned studio pro, and as a balancing presence in any recording session. Red was also a top-tier jazz player and composer, and other musicians revered him. He composed most of the challenging and beautifully haunting original material for his Rounder debut in the few weeks before the sessions, but for Johnny, he chose a ballad, "I'll Only Miss Her When I Think of Her," which he had learned from a Tony Bennett record. Johnny's performance of the song is exquisite and heartbreaking, but when I sent him a few copies of the LP, his reaction was, "You know that coffee table I had that wobbled a little bit? It doesn't wobble anymore" (implying that he had put the LPs to use as shims for a table leg). It was difficult for Johnny to accept that something that was not a hit record would advance his career in any way.

Around the same time, producers Hal Willner and Paul M. Young came to New Orleans to record Johnny and Aaron Neville for their album *Lost in the Stars, The Music of Kurt Weill*. I brought Johnny to the studio

Alvin "Red" Tyler (photograph © Rick Olivier)

and watched as he performed his near-operatic duet with Aaron on "Oh Heavenly Salvation." Johnny sang with aplomb, but I think he was puzzled by the objective of recording such a dark and noncommercial song, which would never have made it in the gospel world.

Yet Johnny's career started to change for the better. He began getting bookings at places like the Club Lingerie in Los Angeles, and at Antone's in Austin, where he was backed by the wonderful house band.

The journalist, A&R person, and music entrepreneur Bill Bentley, who booked Johnny at the Club Lingerie, recalls:

In 1983 I heard Johnny Adams sing at his regular gig at Dorothy's Medallion Lounge and vowed to bring him to Los Angeles as soon as I could find a way. It took a year, and I had to start a New Orleans weekly series at Club Lingerie on Sunset Boulevard in Hollywood to do it. In early February 1984 Adams finally made it. We assembled a primo band for Adams at the Lingerie, led by Harold Battiste and including guitarist Leo Nocentelli from the Meters, Henry Butler, Johnny Boudreaux from Battiste's AFO Records studio band, Jerry Jumonville (from Delaney & Bonnie), Ivan Neville, Diz Williams, Hutch Hutchinson (from the Neville Brothers), and singer Tami Lynn. Going to rehearsal that afternoon of the show, Johnny decided he first needed to stroll up a couple blocks to Hollywood Boulevard and buy some shoes. But when we finally got to the Lingerie for the rehearsal it was like old home week between him and all the musicians. We'd dubbed the band the New Orleans Natives, because that's what they were, and all were thrilled about working together.

That night Johnny Adams totally destroyed the audience at Club Lingerie. It was full of hipsters, musicians, actors, and a large contingent of New Orleanians from Watts. Song after song, he just kept turning up the emotions until no one could believe what they were hearing. People were screaming between songs, just thrilled to hear Adams, most for the very first time. Bonnie Raitt had volunteered to deejay that night. Singer-songwriter John Hiatt came to hear Adams, and told me he had a song or two that might work for the singer's next album. He was right, too, because Hiatt's "She Said the Same Things to Me" and "Lovers Will" both made the 1985 release *After Dark*.

After the performance was over at 2 a.m., Raitt invited a dozen people, including Adams, up to her Hollywood Hills house for a small post-show party. Johnny was thrilled, as he sat on a white sofa in a room with white rugs and white walls. His black-on-black-on-black attire that night made him look like a king in a room of his subjects. It was a long way from the Claiborne Avenue projects where Johnny Adams lived. But that night in the Hollywood Hills, Adams owned the place, like he always did no matter where he went.

It was a new beginning for Johnny, and the first time in many years that he had been to Los Angeles. However, Johnny returned home to what eventually became a falling out with Walter, and they stopped playing together. The residency at Dorothy's ended, Walter took a gig at the Krazy Korner on Bourbon Street, and the band broke up. I never understood exactly what had happened. Johnny and Walter were like two brothers who would ultimately reconcile, although it would be a few years before they would again collaborate.

Soon after the split, I traveled with Johnny to a Saturday night gig in Diamond, Louisiana, an unincorporated community in Plaquemines Parish that does not appear on most maps. He put together a band that departed from New Orleans in the afternoon, in a caravan of marginally roadworthy vehicles. The equipment—instruments and amplifiers—was transported in the open bed of a pickup truck. We stopped several times for snacks and bathroom breaks. Then, the sky opened up in a spectacular thunderstorm, and there was no tarp to cover the gear. Fortunately, we found a gas station with a canopy, where we waited out the storm.

When we arrived, the club owner sheepishly explained that he had not been able to promote the show, and that no one was going to show up. The gig was off. We drove back to New Orleans. Under the surface of his cool and detached countenance, Johnny was embarrassed and exasperated. He took gigs as they came, one phone call at a time, seldom working with a booking agent, and this one had not worked out well.

Nonetheless, we got busy on a second record, *After Dark*. Encouraged by my new friendship with Doc Pomus, I started reaching out to other songwriters, including Paul Kelly, who had written the Angela Bofill hit "Personally." We had the two songs that John Hiatt had given Johnny through Bill Bentley, and Doc gave us the beautiful ballad "Give a Broken Heart a Break."

Hoping to recreate the feeling of the first album, I hired the same rhythm section, along with guitarist Wayne Bennett, who had played on many of Bobby "Blue" Bland's hits. Despite their falling out, Johnny and I decided to ask Walter to join us, so we went to his gig at the Krazy Korner. Johnny sat in, singing "Funny How Time Slips Away." Walter barely acknowledged us, but he agreed to do the sessions. He asked Johnny to pick him up at his mother's house the next morning at 11:30, to attend our rehearsal at the Maple Leaf Bar. Yet when Johnny arrived, Walter was not with him. Walter had not been at his mother's house.

We traveled to Studio Solo in Slidell to record with engineer David Farrell. Unfortunately, the sessions never caught fire. Without Walter as the bandleader, the tracks were unfocused, and the album was a near disaster. Almost every day, one or another of the musicians showed up very late, always with some sort of elaborate excuse ("I heard it might rain on Thursday, and my windshield wipers was broken"). Wilbert Arnold had a French Quarter gig that ended at five in the morning, and he kept falling asleep in the drum booth between takes. Wayne Bennett, for all his reputation and chops, had a difficult time with the chord changes on the new tunes, but he was not interested in playing the blues, either.

Further, many of the songs, in spite of their pedigree, were just not right for Johnny, for I had been attracted to the songs themselves rather than imagining Johnny's voice inhabiting them. For Johnny to give his best, the songs needed the right harmonic progressions—gospel-derived did not hurt—and a lot of space. After the band went home, I hired the gifted guitarist Renard Poché to replace many of the guitar parts. Johnny and I labored for several days over his vocals. He was willing, but the spirit was just not there.

Surprisingly, most critics did not hear it. The Hiatt and Pomus tunes were hip, and the horn-driven R&B version of Hiatt's "She Said the Same Things to Me," with Lisa Foster's guest vocal, had a tough swagger. We released "Give a Broken Heart a Break" as a single, and *Newsweek* gave the album a glowing review. The best song on the album may be the blues "Garbage Man," on which Johnny, for one of the only times on record, played lead guitar. He was a closet guitarist who would often play along with Kenny Burrell and Jimmy Smith records at home, and he played with feeling. Yet, when I saw Mac Rebennack after the record was released, he reproached me, "What the hell you doin' wit' Johnny?" He was right—I had let Johnny down, and I knew I could do better.

Our next record, *Room with a View of the Blues* (1987), put things back in the pocket. My first call was to Mac himself, who agreed to play keyboards. We used his rhythm section, bassist David Barard and drummer Herman Ernest III, along with guitarists Walter Washington and Duke Robillard. Walter had mended his friendship with Johnny and was enthusiastic about participating. Duke was the cofounder of the Rhode Island band Roomful of Blues. I had worked with him on his first few solo albums in New England and had grown to appreciate how he was able to move with ease from a myriad of blues styles to classic jazz. Bill Samuel returned to write horn charts for a few of the songs.

This time, the tracks exploded onto tape, and we had the right songs. The title song, newly written by Lowell Fulson and Billy Vera, became an underground hit on stations such as WBGO in Newark. "A World I Never Made," written by Doc Pomus and Mac, gave everyone the chills as Johnny laid down the live vocal. The Doc Pomus/Duke Robillard collaboration, "Body and Fender Man," was humorous and funky. Mac added a small percussion part to the tune, played on the Hammond B-3 organ, saying, "Every tune I ever played this on has been a hit." I came to appreciate that Mac was a master at playing seemingly inconsequential parts that lifted a record, and that he knew exactly the underlying harmonies that would inspire Johnny. At this time, Mac was struggling with a persistent drug habit, and he sometimes nodded off between takes, but he was fully present once the tape started rolling. Johnny dug the whole experience.

Johnny had recently married, after his mother passed away. His new wife, Judy, became a great source of support. They moved from New Orleans to Baton Rouge, into a pleasant house with a tree-filled yard. Johnny set up a putting green in the garage. He was an avid golfer, and he would sometimes retreat to the garage to read his golf magazines while he listened to records. In earlier years, Johnny and a group of musician friends often played on the course at City Park in New Orleans, and by all accounts he was an accomplished golfer. Johnny and Judy soon had a daughter, Alitalia, who was named for the Italian airline, just because Johnny loved the sound of the word.

My perspective on Johnny was shifting. Yes, he was versatile, but I began to believe that he was simply one of the great vocal artists of our time, capable of interpreting any song in the most soulful and musical way, at least when given the right support. I thought of the Ella Fitzgerald songbook records, on which she sang the compositions of the Gershwins or Cole Porter. With that in mind, I proposed to Johnny that we make an album of all Percy Mayfield songs. Mayfield, "the poet of the blues," had his own hits in the 1950s ("Please Send Me Someone to Love") and had worked for a time as a staff writer for Ray Charles ("Hit the Road, Jack"). We had recorded his songs before, both on *From the Heart* and *Room with a View of the Blues.*

I was able to contact Mayfield, who had continued to write new songs in spite of his debilitating struggle with alcoholism. Through the Chicago-based producer Dick Shurman, we obtained his demo of a new song, "My Heart Is Hanging Heavy." I again enlisted Duke Robillard and Walter Washington, along with the New Orleans rhythm section of acoustic bassist

James Singleton and drummer Johnny Vidacovich, and pianist Jon Cleary, the British R&B player whose immense talent has since made him a New Orleans institution. Bill Samuel came back to write horn arrangements. Tenor saxophonist Amadée Castenell, a veteran of many Allen Toussaint sessions, was added as a featured soloist. I realized the impact that the Percy Mayfield album *My Jug and I* had on me over the years, because I was making blues records with musicians who were not exclusively blues musicians.

Johnny's vocal performances on the record are perhaps understated in comparison with *Room with a View of the Blues*, but they are gorgeous, playful, and swinging in every way, and sound of the record is filled with depth, enough so that the masterful recording engineer George Massenburg contacted David Farrell to ask how he had recorded the bass.

The title track, "Walking on a Tightrope," taught me a lesson about patience in the recording studio. We had attempted to cut the song, one of Mayfield's best, on three successive days. We tried different tempos and grooves, but it never gelled, and I was ready to give up on it. Then, as we were taking a break on our last day, Jon sat down at the piano and began playing a syncopated motif. The other musicians heard it, and quickly joined him, just for fun. I nodded to engineer David Farrell, and he hit the record button on the tape machine.

Then, to everyone's surprise, Johnny got up from the couch in the control room and walked quietly into the studio, gently closing the vocal booth door behind him, where he delivered a powerful and focused interpretation of "Walking on a Tightrope" against the new groove. Of course, the musicians know the song well by then. Walter played the solo live, and the band did its own fade at the end of the song. Everyone broke out in laughter. Someone said, "Man, you should have recorded that one, because that's the shit."

"Well, we did," I said. "Come on into the control room and give it a listen."

We were all excited, but the sentiment was, "OK, we got that. Now let's go out and cut it for real." But this time, in spite of what might have been more precise playing, the feeling was gone. David and I edited the beginning of the accidental take to make a clean intro, and the rest of the improvised performance is what you hear on the record. It remains one of my favorite Johnny Adams recorded performances.

Johnny kept getting better jobs, including regular gigs at the Lone Star Cafe in New York. Doc Pomus was always in the audience. He and I were now talking every few weeks, and he became one of my most steadfast supporters (as he was for so many others), often telling me, "Scott, you know what you're doing. Stick with it." I attended his sixtieth birthday party, where his friends from seemingly every background—from punk rocker to old family acquaintance—had gathered, and I visited him in his apartment on the Upper West Side of Manhattan, where the world came to him by telephone as he lay in bed, surrounded by just about everything he needed—books, notebooks, and a cassette recorder. An assistant would help him into his wheelchair when it was time to go out.

A remarkable set from this era was taped at the Lone Star for the Japanese public broadcaster NHK, with Jon Cleary, bassist George Porter Jr., guitarist Danny Caron, and drummer Kenneth Blevins in support. Doc was especially excited about the live version of "A World I Never Made," which had attained a spiritual aspect that the studio cut might only have suggested. The concept for the next record was obvious. Why not continue the songbook concept and make a whole album of Doc Pomus songs?

Johnny loved the idea, and the resulting 1991 album, *The Real Me: Johnny Adams Sings Doc Pomus*, may be his greatest recorded achievement. Doc quickly got to work, combing through his catalog and writing a few new songs with Mac. We decided to stay away from his big hits such as "Save the Last Dance for Me" in favor of songs that Doc felt had the most depth, and that were best suited to Johnny. Mac agreed to coproduce the record, and to play keyboards on the sessions.

Then, when we were just about ready to go, Doc passed away. It was a heavy blow for me. As he aged, his lyrics had gained profundity, sadness, and subtlety, and he surely had many more songs in him. An entire community had formed around his largess and kindness, which we were all determined to honor.

We assembled a dream band. Duke, James, and Johnny returned, along with Mac and a horn section comprised of Red Tyler (who wrote the charts, and played baritone this time), trumpet player Charlie Miller, and tenor saxophonist Eric Traub. Impressively, Mac was now fully clean and sober, his only remaining addiction being to Nat Sherman cigarettes. The sessions were a producer's dream—almost effortless—and we tracked everything live with the horns. Johnny brought so much passion to his vocals that spirits kept lifting higher, and every track ended with laughter from the musicians, always a sign that something wonderful has happened. Once, on the song "My Baby's Quit Me," he asked if we could move the key of the tune a half step higher, to C sharp, which is not exactly a piano or saxophone player's favorite key. Yet, Mac and the horns adapted beautifully, and Mac delivered a virtuosic piano solo. The key change transformed Johnny's vocal, the key change making all the difference.

I could feel Johnny reaching into himself to find the best way to tell the story of each song, never falling back on the vocal acrobatics of which he was capable, but using them to great effect when the song called for it. He saw these songs as a gift, and he returned Doc's generosity with deep respect and feeling. Johnny always did his homework when he received a song he wanted to record, learning the melody exactly as the composer had written it, and he would always sing it straight the first time through, even if he took it somewhere else later in the song. His improvisations had a richness that went beyond the blues/gospel pentatonic scale, showing his thorough understanding of what made each song unique. We did a few vocal overdubs on *The Real Me*, but mostly because Johnny enjoyed singing the songs again, and looking for what else he might find in them.

The album was a slow-burn success, and it remains a cult favorite today. The song "There Is Always One More Time" (cowritten with Ken Hirsch) was used over the opening credits of the Eddie Murphy/Steve Martin film *Bowfinger*, while "The Real Me" (cowritten with Mac) was used on two episodes of the John Larroquette television show. As is the custom, the producers of the Larroquette show asked for an instrumental track. We did not exactly have one, because the song is a duet with Johnny and James— just bass and voice with a few subtle colors added by Mac and Johnny V. There was bass leaking into the vocal track, and vocals in the bass track. It is that intimacy that made it work, sounding at the same time as big as the sky. I never succeeded in explaining why we could not provide an instrumental track to the television producers, but Larroquette insisted on using it anyway.

Our next three albums veered into jazz territory. By this time, Johnny was ready to admit that his many of his new fans were truly listening to him as an artist, after all. Jazz was what he listened to at home. He was also an incisive improviser on "mouth trombone." He had the ability to perfectly mimic a trombone, by buzzing his lips close to the microphone and singing the notes, and he could negotiate the most challenging chord changes. I saw the jazz route as a way to stimulate interest among festivals

At the sessions for *Johnny Adams Sings Doc Pomus*, 1991. *Left to right:* Scott Billington, Johnny Vidacovich, James Singleton, Johnny Adams, Eric Traub, Charlie Miller, Mac "Dr. John" Rebennack, Duke Robillard, Alvin "Red" Tyler (photograph © Rick Olivier).

in Europe and Japan, for I believed that he was a peer of the greatest male jazz singers—Lou Rawls, Kevin Mahogany, or Tony Bennett. Some R&B fans might not have been happy with this direction, but I believed it was a side of Johnny that the world needed to hear. I was thankful that the Rounder Records owners continued to fund our projects, even as we went farther afield from roots music. They believed in Johnny.

1993's *Good Morning Heartache* uses two bands. The "large band" was arranged and conducted by Wardell Quezergue, who had produced sessions by Johnny for Watch Records back in the sixties. It featured the cream of New Orleans jazz horn players: trumpeters Jamil Sharif and Clyde Kerr Jr.; saxophonists Joe Saulsbury Jr., Tony Dagradi, and Edward "Kidd" Jordan; and trombonist Maynard Chatters. The rhythm section, which again featured James Singleton and Johnny Vidacovich, was led by pianist David Torkanowsky. Walter Washington played guitar on two tracks. The "small band," which was arranged by Torkanowsky, featured only the rhythm section and tenor saxophonist Ralph Johnson.

The Johnny Adams big band at the sessions for *Good Morning Heartache*, 1993. *Left to right:* Scott Billington, Joe Saulsbury Jr., Jamil Sharif, Clyde Kerr Jr., Johnny Adams, David Farrell, Maynard Chatters, Wardell Quezergue, David Torkanowsky, James Singleton, Walter "Wolfman" Washington, Edward "Kidd" Jordan, Johnny Vidacovich, Tony Dagradi (photograph © Rick Olivier).

Johnny and I prepared for the sessions by selecting a number of songs from the Great American Songbook, by writers such as Ray Noble, Johnny Mercer/Harold Arlen, and the Gershwins. We then got together with Wardell to find the best keys and tempos for Johnny. Wardell was a musical genius. With only a tuning fork in C, he would sit as his kitchen table and write the full score for each song, in pencil, imagining every note and hearing the harmonies in his head, after which he would copy the individual parts by hand (before computer software did this with the stroke of a key). He wrote parts for everyone, including the rhythm section, then conducted the band live in the studio, with his scores spread out over three music stands.

The album was a revelation to jazz radio programmers, after Rounder hired an independent jazz promoter, Doctor Jazz, to introduce Johnny to them. The music swings, and Johnny's vocals are elegant—a jazz player's ear with a gospel singer's soul. I noticed, however, that Johnny was having dental issues that occasionally got in his way of his enunciation. Outwardly, he was a fit and spry man, but he demurred whenever I brought up the topic of a dentist or doctor. I wondered if he had ever seen either. He told me, with a typically understated wink, "I know I should quit smoking and eat more vegetables, but I really can't stand carrots."

Our next album, 1995's *The Verdict*, was more adventurous, with David Torkanowsky serving as musical director. Along with a few jazz standards, we added three unrecorded songs from Doc Pomus and Mac Rebennack, including the exquisite "Dreams Must Be Going Out of Style," an unrecorded song from drummer James Black that David Torkanowsky had discovered, and a new song from Ken Hirsch and Hal David called "Come Home to Love." We chose musicians to suit each song, including drummers Shannon Powell and Billy Kilson, bassists Chris Severin and James Singleton, guitarists Steve Masakowski and Carl LeBlanc, percussionist Michael Skinkus, and the legendary tenor saxophonist Houston Person. My favorite tracks, though, are the two duets with pianist Harry Connick Jr. On "A Lot of Living to Do," from the musical *Bye Bye Birdie*, Harry and Johnny come out of the second bridge by adding two measures to the opening of the final verse while Johnny holds a note—a stroke of telepathic brilliance.

Johnny's sense of humor is exemplified in the track we called "D Jam Blues." While we were waiting for our catered dinner from the Bennachin African restaurant, James began playing a riff that caught Johnny's ear. Johnny headed for the vocal booth and began improvising lyrics, including, "We have to wait till 7 p.m., to get some African food."

"That's the best thing on the record," he commented with a grin, because he was at his most relaxed and creative in that moment. As it turned out, he was not a fan of "Come Home to Love," even though he had been firm about recording it. As we labored with overdubs of the vocal, he said, "It's not that I despise the song, I just don't like it worth a damn." We eventually recorded a good enough vocal performance for release.

On the title track, we employed Pro Tools software for the first time, even though we were recording to twenty-four-track analog tape. I had learned that it was never a good idea for Johnny to sing while the band was getting the arrangement of a song together, because he often gave his best performance on the first or second take. On this song, though, I was unsuccessful, and Johnny nailed his vocal on a less-than-perfect instrumental first take. I asked engineer Steve Reynolds if we could copy Johnny's vocal from the first take and paste it into the final instrumental version. The early two-track Pro Tools enabled us to use one track for Johnny's vocal, and the second for a rough mix of the new track. Steve lined everything up, moving the vocal around until it matched the tempo of the final instrumental, and then recorded the vocal back to tape.

The same year, Rounder Records celebrated its twenty-fifth anniversary at the Austin, Texas, music festival South by Southwest. After a second line down Sixth Street with the Rebirth Brass Band, the entire block at Sixth and Brazos Streets, in front of the Driskill Hotel, was cordoned off for a free show with Irma Thomas, Johnny Adams, and Beau Jocque and the Zydeco Hi-Rollers. I asked the Austin bass player Sarah Brown to put together a band for Johnny, a variation of the Antone's house band, and we spent the afternoon at Antone's rehearsing for the show. Johnny delivered a spectacular set of his Rounder songs, fully commanding the stage in a black velvet suit and black-and-white striped shoes. The audience was captivated by the range of the material, the range of his voice, and the mix of elegance and rough soul that he presented.

Later, I asked him about the shoes, because I had never seen anything like them.

"I bought those in Italy," he said, and then more quietly, "They were four hundred bucks a pair."

"Well, they looked really good onstage," I replied.

"That ain't the worst of it, though—I bought three pair," he confided. "Just don't tell Judy."

Judy Adams had been encouraging me to manage Johnny, and I thought this might be the time to give it a try. I had the idea that Johnny could play three successive "sit down" gigs of three or four days each at Blues Alley in Washington, DC, Sweet Basil in New York, and the Regattabar in Cambridge, Massachusetts. We would invite jazz promoters and press, who would be knocked out by Johnny and a band made up of some of the musicians who played on *The Verdict*. I found a booking agent who would work with us. This would be the springboard that Johnny needed to graduate to jazz festivals around the world.

But there was a problem. The gross for each week would have been about $10,000, out of which Johnny would have received about $1500, after paying the musicians, airfare, and hotels.

"Do you mean to tell me that out of a $10,000 gig, I'm only going to make fifteen hundred bucks?" he asked me.

"Don't worry about that, Johnny." I replied. "This is a step toward something much bigger. Plus, you're not going to make that much by staying home."

Sometimes, on gigs in New Orleans, Johnny would employ musicians who would work for little money, but who also could not adequately perform his repertoire, which would have required chord charts and rehearsals. The result could be a twenty-five-minute version of "Stand by Me," or something else with standard and repetitive chords. It was still Johnny Adams, but he needed musicians who were as good as he was, and who would have the dedication to rehearse, if he were going to make any kind of breakthrough.

Johnny and Judy conferred, and decided to decline. It was disheartening. I had come to care about Johnny as a person, and I had complete belief in his artistry. I could not believe his short-sightedness. I vowed to stay out of the managing business, and to concentrate on making records.

So, we kept making records. I had noticed that many of Johnny's favorite albums were of the classic organ combo sound of artists like Jimmy Smith, Jimmy McGriff, and Brother Jack McDuff. I asked Johnny about making a record in this style, and we set about looking for the right organ player. My friend Bob Porter, a DJ at WBGO in Newark, suggested that I check out Dr. Lonnie Smith. Bob was right, because Dr. Smith the perfect choice for the gig and, as it turned out, an engaging and willing participant. We booked sessions in New Orleans with Dr. Smith and his longtime collaborator, the guitarist Jimmy Ponder, along with New Orleans drummer Shannon Powell, trumpet player Jamil Sharif, and tenor saxophonist Ed Petersen.

Dr. Smith, whose mischievous eyes, turban, and white goatee make him look like a wizard, is indeed the magician of the Hammond organ. We did not need a bass player, because he plays bass on the instrument's pedals, while creating a blur of motion as he manipulates the keys, organ stops, and Leslie speaker. Engineers David Farrell and Steve Reynolds had the idea to remove the back plate from the Leslie cabinet, and to insert an RE20 microphone (along with an external stereo pair to capture the whirling speaker), which gave us a huge bass sound.

We chose a repertoire of bluesy tunes from Percy Mayfield, Buddy Johnson, and others. When I called the songwriter Dan Penn, who had become a dedicated Johnny Adams fan, and told him we were making a new record, he asked me what the concept would be.

"Well," I responded, "It's kind of one foot in the blues and one foot in jazz."

A couple of weeks later, a cassette tape arrived in the mail with the new song, "One Foot in the Blues," and a note saying, "Well, I got half of it for you!" It became our title cut.

Johnny responded to this setting and to the repertoire with great enthusiasm, and I think the album comes close to the Doc Pomus collection in terms of capturing Johnny at his best. One day, alto saxophonist Donald Harrison Jr. dropped by the studio, having heard that Dr. Smith was in town, and he joined the band, adding an extra sparkle. *One Foot in the Blues* is a sly album that is filled with whisper-to-a-scream dynamics. Hearing Johnny sing Buddy Johnson's "I Wonder Where Our Love Has Gone" (with its wonderful tight-harmony Ed Petersen horn arrangement) lets you know that there was no better singer of classic ballads. The chemistry between Dr. Smith and Shannon Powell made them sound like a full band, even though Shannon often played deceptively simple parts, always completely in the pocket and with a look of total delight.

Rounder founder Bill Nowlin came up with the humorous cover concept. Johnny would wear a suit and tie, but on one foot would be a funky boot, held together with duct tape. Photographer Rick Olivier owned a bright yellow backdrop, so I called Johnny to ask if he had a red suit. "Well, what shade of red would you like? I have maroon, fire engine red and hot pink." We chose fire engine red.

Following the release of *One Foot in the Blues*, Donald Harrison Jr. booked a six-week tour of Europe with Johnny and Dr. Smith. So, in a sense, my plan for Johnny was starting to come true. He returned with enough money to buy a new car and a new set of golf clubs, and his disposition seemed sunnier than I had generally known it to be. When we were walking to lunch one day, he said, "You know what my problem is, Scott? I'm just too damn lazy," but he said it with the wink of someone who had seen his fortune turn for the better.

About the same time, David Torkanowsky and the New Orleans Contemporary Arts Center pulled together a package of grants to produce a big-band concert, for which David commissioned new arrangements of standards to be written. He assembled a band of the best players in the city, including drummer Herlin Riley, trumpet player Nicholas Payton, and pianist Peter Martin, along with featured vocalists Germaine Bazzle, George French, and Johnny Adams. The recording of the event, *Mood Indigo* by the New Orleans CAC Orchestra, was released by Rounder.

Things seemed to be looking up for Johnny. Yet the optimism did not last long. His car was repossessed, and then he received a diagnosis of stage 4 prostate cancer. He told me that he had had symptoms for some time before he finally got the courage to go to a doctor. But the cancer was found too late, and he became sicker.

Support for Johnny within the New Orleans community was strong, with three benefit concerts given for him. John Blancher staged one at the Rock 'n' Bowl, which had become a steady venue for Johnny. Nina Buck gave a benefit at the Palm Court Cafe, and I organized another at Tipitina's, which featured performances by Red Tyler and the jazz band (with James Singleton and Johnny Vidacovich), Walter "Wolfman" Washington and the Roadmasters, Irma Thomas, Marva Wright, Jon Cleary, Aaron Neville, and many others. Tipitina's owner Roland von Kurnatowski was so impressed that he donated the proceeds from the bar as well. At the end of the night, I handed Johnny a check for $11,000. Further, the Rhythm and Blues Foundation, following a recommendation from founders Ruth Brown and Howell Begle, picked up Johnny's mortgage and utility bills.

Even without insurance, Johnny received excellent care at the Mary Bird Perkins Cancer Center in Baton Rouge, and his cancer went into remission. Before he became ill, we had talked about making a full-bore, Memphis-inspired R&B album, and Johnny soon felt well enough to ask me if we could go forward. Of course, I was delighted that he was up for a new recording. I started reaching out to writers—Dan Penn, Jonnie Barnett, Bobby Charles, Carson Whitsett, David Egan, and others—and we accumulated a great batch of songs. To get the feel we were looking for, I hired Memphis horn players Jim Spake and Scott Thompson, and guitarist Michael Toles. The remaining musicians would be from New Orleans—Walter Washington, David Torkanowsky, and bassist George Porter Jr.—with the exception of the young Philadelphia drummer Donnell Spencer Jr., who had just completed a tour with David.

To prepare for the sessions, David and I drove to Baton Rouge to go over the songs with Johnny. I wanted to cut everything live, horns and all, to give Johnny the best possible inspiration, which meant agreeing on song keys and tempos so Jim Spake and Scott Thompson could prepare horn arrangements. Our rehearsal was successful, and Johnny looked surprisingly good. At the end of the day, he said, "Come and let me show you something." When he opened the door to his garage, the putting green was gone, and in its place was a white Lincoln town car. On the drive back to New Orleans, David and I considered this unforeseen benefit of the benefit concerts. At least, we decided, he would ride through his health struggles in style.

Johnny worked hard on the vocals for *Man of My Word*. It was not easy for him, and he tired quickly. Yet, his performances on David Egan's "Even

Now" and Bobby Charles's "I Don't Want to Know" stand with the very best of his work, with beautiful falsetto and emotional control. A lagniappe session produced the poignant "Never Alone," an a cappella performance with Aaron Neville, Charles Elam III, Nick Daniels and Earl Smith Jr. When John Blancher attended a vocal overdub session, he had his name inserted into the Jonnie Barnett, Carson Whitsett, and Dan Penn song, "It Ain't the Same Thing."

Unfortunately, Johnny's remission was short lived, and it became clear that there was no going back. I visited him a few days before he died. It was not easy to see a man who had taken so much care in his clothes and carriage looking so diminished, unkempt, and small. He lived to see the release of his final record, and to be told that he would be receiving the Rhythm and Blues Foundation's Pioneer Award. On September 14, 1998, he passed away. I was one of his pallbearers, and I spoke at his funeral at the Rhodes Funeral Home on Washington Avenue, which was followed by a small second line led by the popular grand marshal Wanda Rouzan. It was a difficult death for me on many levels, as it seemed that we could have gone on making records forever. To me, our partnership was special and unique in my career, reflecting many shared ideals, in spite of our different backgrounds. I also learned the responsibility that comes with supporting such an awesome and limitless talent.

At the Rhythm and Blues Awards in Los Angeles the next year, Judy accepted his award. I sat at a table with Texas musicians Delbert McClinton and Marcia Ball, filled with pride that Johnny was being recognized. The prize also came with a $15,000 payment, which I knew Judy could use.

Then, Judy began to speak. To great applause, she railed against the record companies and managers that had ripped off her husband; against the exploitation of African American artists by conniving Anglo-American record executives; and about the roadblocks that had been thrown up before Johnny. She claimed that Johnny had never received payment from any record company. I kept waiting for "except," but it never came. I was fuming. Johnny had been paid well for his Rounder sessions, and he had received his royalties. Maybe, I considered for a moment, Johnny had kept his advances a secret, but anger was my first response.

I found her after the ceremony and confronted her. "Judy, what the hell were you saying?"

"Well, I wasn't talking about you," was her response as she turned her shoulder and walked away.

I wrote to the Rhythm and Blues Foundation, to go on record to repudiate the accusations that, in their scope, included Rounder and me. A few days later, I received a call from board member and Atlantic Records founder Ahmet Ertegun (who had provided considerable funding for the organization and the awards, while forgiving all unrecouped expenses and initiating royalties for the Atlantic Records roster of legacy R&B artists). He consoled me by telling me that accusations like this just went with the territory, and to let it go.

Judy believed that Johnny's records were selling in large quantities. With a talent as big as Johnny's, how could that not be? When the *Bowfinger* use of Johnny's recording gave her a big payday, she hired an unscrupulous attorney who took a share of the proceeds for making just one phone call, to ascertain that the album, *The Real Me*, was not cross-collateralized with his other Rounder releases. Still, it was more money than Johnny had ever made from his recordings while he was living. In 2008, she self-published a book, *The Johnny Adams Story: New Orleans Famous Blues Legend*. At the end of the day, we both cared deeply about Johnny, and did not want the world to forget him.

In Johnny's *OffBeat* obituary, Dan Penn said, "Maybe more than any singer I know, he stayed true to the writer, and really captured the meaning and emotion of the song. A lot of singers will change melody lines, or mess with the lyrics, and it doesn't always work. He respected the songwriter. And what a voice." It was a sentiment expressed by many songwriters, and that is why they sent him their best songs.

Johnny Adams never achieved his commercial potential. He was a world-class artist in a provincial town. He came up in a world in which music attorneys and other professionals seemed beyond his reach, and where scuffling for the next gig was the day-to-day objective. He was also capable of jeopardizing his own opportunities, and sometimes culpable for failing to accept responsibility for his own career. He was a kind and serious man who carried himself with class and dignity. I believe that during our years together, he began to appreciate how highly regarded he was by fans around the world, not as an oldies act or a novelty falsetto singer, but as an artist, and as one of the greatest singers of our time. His recorded legacy proves exactly that.

RECOMMENDED LISTENING:

"I Feel Like Breaking Up Somebody's Home" from *From the Heart*
"I'll Only Miss Her When I Think of Her" from *Heritage* by Alvin "Red" Tyler
"There Is Always One More Time" from *The Real Me: Johnny Adams Sings Doc Pomus*
"I Wonder Where Our Love Has Gone" from *One Foot in the Blues*
"I Don't Want to Know" from *Man of My Word*

Chapter 9

IRMA THOMAS

IN DECEMBER 2005, LESS THAN FOUR MONTHS AFTER HURRICANE KATRINA and the ensuing flood that devastated New Orleans and spun most of its residents off to far corners of the country, a dedicated group of musicians was making its way back to Louisiana, to Dockside Studio in rural Maurice. In September, we had been scheduled to record Irma Thomas's new album at Ultrasonic Studio on Washington Avenue in New Orleans, and everything had been ready to go. Now, Ultrasonic was destroyed. Its guitar amplifiers, Hammond organ, and grand piano were left floating in dirty water, and the integrity of the building was so compromised that it had to be torn down.

Irma Thomas had been gigging in Austin, Texas, when the storm left her home underwater, and was now living in her husband's hometown of Gonzalez, Louisiana. Pianist David Torkanowsky, bassist James Singleton, and drummer Stanton Moore had all been displaced and were now gradually putting the lives they had left behind back together. Guitarist Corey Harris had left New Orleans a few years earlier and was traveling from Charlottesville. Engineer David Farrell was back home, while engineer Steve Reynolds had decamped to Dockside until he could return to his apartment. The Rounder Records apartment on Camp Street in New Orleans that was my second home had been spared flooding, but a big part of the roof had blown off, and it was uninhabitable. This would be the first recording sessions for any of us since the storm.

Dockside is a comfortable place along the Bayou Vermillion, with huge live oak trees and a pond on the grounds. The studio is in a barnlike structure outfitted with a vintage Neve console and a selection of excellent microphones. The property also has accommodations for musicians, a kitchen,

Irma Thomas at the Grand Ole Opry for the fortieth anniversary of Rounder Records, 2009 (photograph © Rick Olivier)

and a dining area, all overlooking the river. The setting recalls an older, more isolated and more languid south Louisiana, sequestered by water and geography. Owners Steve and Cezanne "Wish" Nails have created an ideal spot for getting away from routine and doing nothing other than making a record. Passing through the gate onto the studio driveway had always given me an immediate sense of serenity, and now it felt like going home.

When we began planning these sessions, Irma and I had been working together for over twenty years, and we had cultivated a fair degree of mutual respect and trust (as well as a friendship that endures to the present day). I do not think our record *After the Rain* would have happened any other way.

Most of the music we had made together followed a sort of template based on the rhythm and blues of the 1960s and '70s, with a few contemporary sounds mixed in. It was what felt natural. I loved working with a horn section and building big soundscapes around Irma's voice. Yet, the more I got to know her as an artist, the more confining I felt that format had become. More than any other singer I had worked with, Irma could get to the heart of a song, and could make each listener believe that she was singing their own story. Her warmth, her unadorned delivery, and her ability to tap her own emotional well place her among the rarest of singers—a storyteller who can stop you in your tracks and make you feel what she is singing on the deepest level.

I started imagining a different kind of Irma Thomas record, with acoustic instruments, with her voice front and center, and with songs chosen only because they would come to life when she sang them—songs that would sound good when inhabited by her voice. The producer and composer Allen Toussaint once told me that he often heard Irma's voice when he wrote, and now I was hearing Irma's voice singing new songs by Eleni Mandell and Kevin Gordon, and old songs by Blind Willie Johnson and Mississippi John Hurt. I called Irma and told her what I was thinking.

"Well, that sounds interesting," she said. "Why don't you send me some of the songs?"

"I'll overnight them to you tomorrow," I replied. "You may think I'm crazy, but I can hear this so clearly."

A few days after she received the compact disc I had sent, she called.

"Scott, have you lost your mind? What am I going to do with this material?" she laughed.

Then, she changed her tone to something more serious and said, "But you know me pretty well, and I guess you really are hearing something, so I'll give it a shot."

Now, we were at Dockside Studio, and it felt good to be back in action. To start the sessions, we chose the gentle and sad Arthur Alexander song "In the Middle of It All." Stanton began playing a lyrical, beautifully subdivided groove. As the drummer for the band Galactic, he is one of the young standard-bearers of the New Orleans drum tradition, and I could see Irma turn her head. James, who is both a first-call jazz bassist and playful musical innovator, emphasized fat whole tones on his bass, with only the subtlest of grace notes. David Torkanowsky, one of the most versatile keyboardists in New Orleans, kept everything moving with a sparse and delicate Wurlitzer piano part. Everyone was leaving space for Irma to fill. Then, she started to sing. It was if she had discovered in that moment that the song was about exactly what everyone was feeling—the displacement, uncertainty, and melancholy—with the only comfort to be found in the power and embrace of her voice. After the first full take and the silence that followed, most of us began to cry. There it was—the essence of what Irma can do with a song. We had captured something that was undeniable. After a few minutes, she turned to me and said, "OK, I get it now."

The sessions were a dream in a quiet place that seemed a refuge from what everyone had been through, and we fell into our self-contained world with focus and gratitude. The Lafayette-based songwriter David Egan joined us, with the intention of playing piano on the songs he had written. We started to run down his song "If You Knew How Much." The track sounded good, but Irma was not getting it, so she asked, "David, I'm not quite feeling what this song is about. What were you thinking when you wrote it?"

"Well, imagine that you're in love with someone you never could be with, a love that could not happen," he said. "You see that person every day, and you exchange smiles. Now, if that person knew how you felt, he might shun you entirely, robbing you of that bright spot in your life. You keep it a secret, holding your passion inside."

She nodded and said "OK. Now let's give it a try." Then, she delivered the vocal you hear on the album, breaking into tears as she reached the second chorus. You can hear her voice crack. Rather than going for a more perfect take, we left it as it was.

The only song that did not work as I hoped was Jack White's "My Doorbell." Groove-wise, it was in the pocket, and the chorus is a sing-along winner, but she never could put her finger on the story, and her performance seemed emotionally empty in comparison to the other tracks. Irma is tough on songs, but it is for good reason. It is like expecting a great actor to play a convincing character in a script to which she cannot relate. Irma has always done her best to find the meaning and the story in every song I have brought her, with the understanding that we will let the song go if the connection is not there.

Irma approached David Egan with a song idea. Earlier in the day, she had been on the phone with Emile, giving him her "honey do" list of chores that had to be done and errands to be run. A good idea for a song, she thought, and gave David the "honey do this, honey do that" line. He returned the next day with the humorous "These Honey Dos," which the trio played with a jazzy swing.

Corey accompanied Irma on the Blind Willie Johnson song "Soul of a Man." Irma chose not to sing the last verse, as not to cross into gospel territory on an R&B record. Stanton overdubbed percussion parts, yielding a simple and powerful track.

We wrapped up our sessions in less than a week. Eerily, it now seemed that all the songs we had chosen before the hurricane were all about the storm. I was satisfied that we had created a spacious aural landscape, with plenty of room for Irma. We knew we had something precious in spirit.

A few weeks later, we returned to Dockside for overdub sessions. Sonny Landreth added slide guitar to "In the Middle of It All" and several other songs. Dirk Powell played his soulful old-time fiddle and fretless banjo on "Flowers" and "Another Lonely Heart," as well as electric guitar parts on "In the Middle of It All" and "Another Man Done Gone." Irma resang a couple of vocals on songs that she now knew better, and that we both felt might be improved.

On our last overdub day, we were joined by singers Juanita Brooks, Marc Broussard, and Charles "Chucky C" Elam III. After adding their backing parts to existing tracks, I asked if they would sing an a cappella performance with Irma, the Doc Pomus/Mort Shuman song "I Count the Tears." Actually, we cheated a little bit, because David Egan came by to play a guide track, on piano, for the singers (which we did not use in the final mix). Steve Reynolds and I then took the track to James Singleton's house along Bayou St. John in New Orleans, just after he had moved back, and recorded the bass part in his living room.

We were almost finished recording when I heard the recent Stevie Wonder song "Shelter in the Rain" and proposed to Irma that we cut it as a piano and vocal duet with David Torkanowsky. We went to his small studio on Camp Street in New Orleans and captured their live performance on the second take. It is the only song on the album that was not chosen before Katrina. Later, she told me, "You know that's a gospel song, don't you?" But she sang it anyway, breaking her rule of not mixing secular and religious material on the same album.

The album mix was done in Cambridge with Paul Q. Kolderie, the producer and engineer who had worked with Radiohead, the Pixies, and the Go-Go's. He had a studio full of vintage gear, including the LA-3A audio leveler that seemed tailor-made for Irma's voice. It was always fun to experiment with Paul's equipment, running sounds through different tube compressors and equalizers, sometimes without touching a knob, just to see what they would sound like. But his standout piece of equipment was the recording console, custom-made by Tweed Audio in Kelso, Scotland.

According to Paul, "Tweed was a short-lived company founded by Kirsh Mustapha, who was reputedly a bit of an audio swashbuckler! He took over the Neve factory in Kelso [after Neve had gone out of business] and hired the workers who had just been laid off." I am not an over-the-top gearhead, but I appreciate anything that enhances the listening experience and emotional impact for the listener. This console did exactly that, adding a fat, warm sound that I have never heard anywhere else. The console is still in service, now in Chicago.

I mastered the album with Adam Ayan at Gateway Studios in Portland, Maine, where he made the final artistic contribution: adjustments in frequency response and overall presence. The record was done.

A little more than a year later, Irma, Emile, and I were seated together at the 2006 Grammy Awards, along with David Egan, where *After the Rain* had been nominated for Best Contemporary Blues Album. When Irma's name was read as the winner, she at first did not react, staring in seeming disbelief at the large video monitor above the stage. Finally, Emile said, "Baby, you have to go up there." Then, we all stood up and screamed. Emile took her arm and walked her to the podium.

In the whirlwind of post-win backstage activity, Irma stood before a roomful of journalists, fielding questions. One of them asked, "Do you think you won this Grammy because of hurricane Katrina?"

I looked at her eyes and could see her start to boil on the inside. After her nearly fifty years in the business, was her accomplishment going to be written off by some writer as an adjunct to a natural disaster? Irma seldom gets angry, but when she does . . .

Then, she took a deep breath and composed herself. She looked the writer straight in the eye.

"Well, if that's the reason I have won my first Grammy award, then I accept it on behalf of all the people of New Orleans."

Her triumph was all the greater.

While I had received only a Grammy certificate for Gatemouth Brown's album, this time David, Steve, and I received statues of our own. It was a long time coming for Irma and for all of us—the product of twenty years of working together. It sure felt good.

Irma Lee was born in Ponchatoula, Louisiana, an hour north of New Orleans, on February 18, 1941. In the 1960s, after taking the name of her first husband, she enjoyed a string of regional hit records, and one national hit with her own composition "Wish Someone Would Care." Her records with producer and songwriter Allen Toussaint, including "I Done Got Over It," "It's Raining," and "Ruler of My Heart," are a beloved part of the New Orleans musical firmament. Allen considered Irma to be one of his muses, and the songs he wrote for her have endured.

She became a popular Gulf Coast attraction, booked by agent Percy Stovall in venues that ranged from nightclubs to Uptown New Orleans society balls and high school proms. Many of her Louisiana fans today remember her from this era. Her band, the Toronados, included guitarist Walter "Wolfman" Washington and saxophonist Roger Lewis, who would become one of the founders of the Dirty Dozen Brass Band.

When Hurricane Camille devastated the Gulf Coast—along with most of Irma's gigs—in 1969, she relocated to Los Angeles, where, as a single mother with four children to raise, she took a job at Montgomery Ward. She continued performing, and made an album there with producer Jerry "Swamp Dogg" Williams. In 1974, she began returning to New Orleans to perform at the Jazz and Heritage Festival, backed by her friend Tommy Ridgley and his band. After she met and married Emile Jackson, she moved back to New Orleans for good. The Soul Queen of New Orleans had come home.

Emile Jackson, an immaculately dressed, handsome man with a thick New Orleans accent, has been Irma's manager since I have known them. He is a tough negotiator who refuses to let Irma perform for less than his asking price, and he runs the band, the Professionals, as a well-disciplined unit, with a dress code and no leeway for tardiness. While his no-nonsense approach has sometimes made musicians or promoters grumble, and while his refusal to relinquish authority to booking agents or outside managers may have at times curtailed opportunity, he is a fair-minded person who always has Irma's back. I grew to like and respect him.

I was introduced to Irma and Emile in 1984 by the writer Jeff Hannusch, whose book *I Hear You Knockin': The Sound of New Orleans Rhythm and Blues* (Swallow Books) includes a chapter on Irma, as well as his original research on many of the key musical figures in New Orleans R&B. He opened many doors for me.

When I asked Irma if she would like to make a record for Rounder, she was happy to sign on. In fact, New Orleans was in the midst of a recording hiatus in the early 1980s. Allen Toussaint's run of hits with artists such as Patti LaBelle and Dr. John was over, and interest in New Orleans roots music in general was just beginning to grow again, due, in great part, to the popularity of the New Orleans Jazz and Heritage Festival. Really, I could not believe my luck at being able to work with such a legendary artist as Irma, or with many of the other artists I produced in those years. Rounder had a simple, four-page recording contract that covered most of the bases (it has held up to this day), and Irma and I were quickly in business together.

We both started looking for songs. I had begun a long correspondence with the talented R&B songwriter Paul Kelly, who sent the title track, "The New Rules," while Doc Pomus sent his new song, "There Is Always One More Time," written with Ken Hirsch (which I would later record again with Johnny Adams). Irma chose a few of her lesser-known older songs to rerecord, and we decided to cover the Bette Midler hit (written by Larry Hensley and Jeff Silbar) "The Wind Beneath My Wings," as well as Etta James's "The Love of My Man" (written by Ed Townsend), which may be the most emotionally raw Irma Thomas performance on record. I hired arranger Bill Samuel, whom I had met at my earlier sessions with Gatemouth Brown, to write horn arrangements. We would record with Irma's live band, the Professionals.

I arrived in New Orleans in time for a final rehearsal in Irma's garage before heading to Southlake Studio in Metairie, just outside New Orleans. To my surprise, Irma and the band had every song ready and down tight, with horns arranged by her alto saxophonist, Joe Saulsbury Jr., leaving little for Bill to do other than join the horn section on baritone and tenor saxes. The only hitch, when we got to the studio, was that the intonation on Leroy Aych's guitar was so far off that the instrument was not usable. That taught me a lesson about making sure that everyone's equipment was in good shape before beginning a session. For backing vocals, I hired the outstanding vocal group ELS (Elaine, Lisa, and Sharon Foster), who would also become a part of many future sessions.

We recorded everything in just a few days. I was thirty-four years old at the time, and Irma was just forty-four. It seemed impossible to me that the woman who had recorded "Time Is on My Side," and whose records had left such an indelible impression on both American and British musicians, was still so young. She was proud of the preparation she had done for the record, and she will still joke about how little I had to do when I arrived for the sessions. She also knew, as both an artist and businesswoman, that the album was another step forward in relaunching her career. *The New Rules* was enthusiastically received, especially in Europe, where it was released by UK-based Demon Records.

For her next release, *The Way I Feel*, I tried to kick everything up a notch, partly by using a studio band on six of the tracks and by casting a wider net for songs. Jerry Ragovoy, who had cowritten Irma's hit "Time Is on My Side" (as Norman Meade), sent "Sorry, Wrong Number" and "The Way I Feel." Allen Toussaint gave us "Old Records," and Paul Kelly supplied us "I'm Gonna Hold You to Your Promise." Louisiana-via-Nashville songwriters Michael Garvin and Walter Klocko provided the gently loping "You Can Think Twice." The rhythm section was the best: bassist David Barard and drummer Herman Ernest III, who were then in Dr. John's band and who had been stalwarts of Allen Toussaint's later productions. Keyboard player Craig Wroten, whom I had met through Gatemouth Brown, and guitarist Renard Poché rounded out the band.

Looking back, these sessions got closer to a pop sensibility than anything Irma and I did before or after, with full orchestration on several of the songs. On "Old Records," we used Craig's keyboards to create a big MIDI string sound, along with Terry Tullos playing a real French horn, in addition to Bill Samuel's horn section. I played the solo on a harmonica that I retuned for the occasion (filing the fifth reed up a half step, so I could play the major seventh). ELS added background vocals. Irma's gentle lead vocal, which she had recorded with the track, was the keeper, even though we had tried a couple of different approaches in later overdub sessions. "Sorry, Wrong Number" is a magnificent performance, with one of Irma's most powerful vocals on record. In fact, her voice could be so strong that, in spite of her excellent microphone technique, engineer David Farrell had to keep one hand on the knob of a limiter, watching for when she would lean back and open her full voice.

We were pleased with the album, and I think some of the songs are among our best work, but I also could see that if I was aiming for a pop hit, our record was not at all like what was being played on mainstream radio, especially as emerging sound technologies such as sampling and programmed drums were beginning to permeate pop music production.

Irma Thomas and Scott Billington (photograph © Barbara Roberds)

Still, I was gaining an appreciation for an architectural approach to making records—capturing an exciting live performance and then building a bigger soundscape around it.

The album also featured two iconic cover tunes that we probably should have left alone—Aretha Franklin's "Baby I Love You" and the Martha and the Vandellas Motown hit "Dancing in the Street." The arrangements are tight and certainly different from the originals, but I began to realize that setting an artist up to compete with the past—either their own or someone else's—was not a recipe for success. I resolved, especially with singers like Irma and Johnny Adams, to try to look for what the artist had not done yet, rather than to recapitulate past sounds and songs.

Well, almost! Our next record was *Live! Simply the Best*, which we recorded using the Phil Edwards mobile truck at Slim's in San Francisco, with Irma's own band. She had two very good nights in front of a packed house, and the band was tight. The live album was the perfect vehicle for

Irma to perform her older material, before we got on with making new
music, and her fans loved the recording of her second-line medley, and of
hits such as "It's Raining." As an entertainer, Irma felt that her fans always
deserved to hear what they wanted to hear, so she faithfully performed her
sixties classics, but she always opened her sets with her new material. To
our surprise, the record won Irma's first Grammy nomination.

By the time of 1992's *True Believer*, my network of publishers and songwriters came through in a big way, with new songs from exceptional writers
such as Dan Penn, Jonnie Barnett, Tony Joe White, Doc Pomus, Dr. John,
Johnny Neel, Ken Hirsch, and Daryl Burgess. With drummer Herman
Ernest III, bassist Chris Severin, guitarist Cranston Clements, and the
dual keyboards of Sammy Berfect and David Torkanowsky, we had a New
Orleans band that could balance a roots sensibility with an up-to-the-
minute attitude. Most of the horns were again arranged by Bill Samuel,
but Alvin "Red" Tyler contributed the jazzy arrangement for "Heart Full
of Rain." Sammy Berfect, "the Bishop," was one of the top church organists
and choral directors in New Orleans. The deep gospel feeling in his playing
provided sure footing for Irma.

On "Smoke Filled Room," Irma became so engaged with the song's story
that she began to cry as she sang the second chorus. She finished the song
with tears streaming down her face. When she came to the control room
to listen, she was still caught up in the hurt felt by the song's protagonist.
Herman went into the bathroom to splash water on his face, then came
back bawling. He broke the tension, and everyone had a good laugh. I
used that vocal on the final mix, but writer Dan Penn thought it was a
mistake—that I should have used the overdub in which she did not cry. I
loved the emotion.

Gospel music and the church have been a central part of Irma's life. She
can be found each week singing in the choir at the First African Baptist
Church in New Orleans, and each year at a special Jazz Fest show, when
she presents a gospel set in addition to her big stage appearance. She had
always wanted to make a gospel record, so we enlisted Sammy as well as
arranger/keyboardist Dwight Franklin as associate producers on *Walk
Around Heaven: The Gospel Soul of Irma Thomas* in 1993. The resulting
album is focused on Irma's vocal interplay with the vocal quartet of Tara
Darnell, Charles Elam III, Pamela Landrum, and Earl Smith, beautifully
arranged by Dwight and Sammy.

The sessions made me think about how so much of the best music in New Orleans is not made for commerce, and how many of the greatest singers and players in the city can be heard only on Sunday morning. Music in New Orleans often has a function beyond entertainment, whether in a sacred setting or, in the case of the second-line brass bands and Indian gangs, on the street. The genius of producers such as Allen Toussaint and Dave Bartholomew was to combine the inherent musicality of New Orleans—the way of walking, dancing, and talking—with great songs, an aesthetic that I aspired to continue with Irma, even if I did not often participate in the actual songwriting process.

During this period, the filmmaker Robert Mugge made the documentary *True Believers: The Musical Family of Rounder Records* (not related to our album of the same title) as part of the activity surrounding the label's twenty-fifth anniversary. Bob filmed Irma's set at the Lion's Den, the nightclub located near the New Orleans Municipal Court that she and Emile ran as a side venture, and he interviewed the three of us. The Lion's Den was a comfortable place for Irma's fans to hear her during Jazz Fest, where she performed a multi-night run, in addition to personally preparing the red beans and rice that were served to patrons as lagniappe. On most nights, though, it was a place for Emile to hang out with his friends. After Hurricane Katrina, the flooded club did not reopen.

I had become a regular correspondent with the songwriter Dan Penn, who cowrote such songs as "Dark End of the Street" for James Carr, "Cry Like a Baby" for the Box Tops, "I'm Your Puppet" for James and Bobby Purify, and "Do Right Man, Do Right Woman" for Aretha Franklin. He made Irma and me an offer that was difficult to turn down: Dan and his cowriters Jonnie Barnett and Carson Whitsett would travel to New Orleans from Nashville to write songs for our next album, *The Story of My Life*, in 1997.

I booked them a suite at a guest house on Audubon Park, and each day, after breakfast, they would get to work. Our samurai songwriters would arrive at Ultrasonic Studio, generally at about the time of our dinner break, with a new song demo in hand, sometimes based on an idea or story line from Irma. It was a magical process, because we would immediately start rehearsing the song and cut it that night, sometimes with Dan playing acoustic guitar or Carson playing keyboards. Once, while listening to a playback of "I Count the Tear Drops," drummer Raymond Weber started

Left to right: songwriter Bucky Lindsey, engineer David Farrell, songwriter Dan Penn, Irma Thomas, and Scott Billington at Ultrasonic Studio (photograph © Barbara Roberds)

playing along on the five-gallon water jug on the cooler just outside the control room door.

"Don't anyone take a drink!" I exclaimed, because the musical pitch of the water bottle was just right. David Farrell quickly set up a mic, and we added the sound to the track.

It was an easygoing session with a top-notch team. For the first time, bassist George Porter Jr. from the Meters joined us, along with keyboardist David Torkanowsky and the Memphis guitarist Michael Toles, who was a veteran of the Isaac Hayes band and innumerable sessions at Stax Records in Memphis and Malaco Records in Jackson, Mississippi (I had met him at my sessions with Charlie Rich in Memphis). When thinking about casting the players for a recording session, dependability and ability are always the first mandate, but it's also a matter of bringing together people that will enjoy being with one another, and who are secure enough in their abilities to play the simplest parts if that is what the session calls for. The musicians on this team could play almost anything, and the brilliance of their ideas can be heard on every track, for they played only what was needed.

That summer, I traveled to Italy with Irma and Emile to the 1998 Porretta Soul Festival, where she appeared with the Memphis All Star

Band, assembled each year by artistic director Graziano Uliani. She gave a spine-tingling performance, especially on Otis Redding's "I've Been Loving You Too Long." It inspired both of us to think about making a record in Memphis.

I enjoyed traveling with Irma. One day during the 1997 Porretta Festival, we took a hike together with my girlfriend, the photographer Jean Hangarter, along a wooded path that was marked with the Stations of the Cross. At the end of the mile-long trail was a small white chapel that was filled with bouquets of fresh flowers and sunlight, with no one in sight—a magical place. Emile had waited for us at the trailhead, and when we told him about the chapel, it seemed like a dream. I'm not sure I could ever find that place again, but Irma was always up for an adventure.

And a new musical adventure soon materialized. In 1998, the promotion director at Rounder Records, Brad Paul, had the idea to bring Irma together with fellow Rounder artists and singers Marcia Ball and Tracy Nelson for a show during the New Orleans Jazz and Heritage Festival. The trio discovered how well their voices blended, as well as how much fun it was to sing together. The album that followed, *Sing It!*, became one the most popular albums that any of the singers had released. While Marcia and Tracy are quick to cite Irma as an influence, this was a true collaboration, with each singer taking her turn in the spotlight, with the others in support.

I had worked with Austin-based pianist and singer Marcia Ball before, as the producer of her *Hot Tamale Baby* album, which we recorded at Studio Solo in Slidell, augmenting her band with Bill Samuel's horn section. She had spent several days with Jeff Hannusch, listening to soul songs from his extensive record collection, so we covered songs such as O. V. Wright's "I'm Gonna Forget About You" and the William Bell Stax classic "Never Like This Before." I was proud of both the big-band rhythm and blues sound we achieved, as well as the rollicking New Orleans groove of Marcia's own "That's Enough of That Stuff."

Tracy Nelson, originally from Madison, Wisconsin, became a major player in the insurgent San Francisco music scene of the late 1960s with the band Mother Earth, whose debut album featured two Irma Thomas covers. Tracy's big, majestic voice may have been one of the most grounding sounds of that heady era. After moving to Nashville and buying a small farm with the royalties from her popular song "Down So Low," she maintained a steady recording schedule and a loyal fan base.

The majority of the songs for *Sing It!* were new or were written just for these sessions. Dan Penn, working with Irma and Carson Whitsett contributed "Woman on the Move," while David Egan wrote the street-beat anthem "Sing It!," as well as the brooding "Please No More." Tracy brought the remarkable Mike Reid/Rory Michael Bourke song "In Tears." The rhythm section from *The Story of My Life* was back, with the substitution of Lee Allen Zeno, from the Buckwheat Zydeco band, on bass, and with Marcia playing her rollicking Texas roadhouse piano on many tracks. The horn arrangements were written by Wardell Quezergue.

The sessions at Ultrasonic were fun, and I think we got the best out of each singer. We were not dealing with a vocal group, per se, but three strong and assertive voices, so casting songs with the right singer was important. Nonetheless, the mutual support they gave each other, and their lighthearted repartee (when it turned a bit salty, Tracy proposed that they could be stand-ins for the soundtrack of a women's prison movie) made everything work. Among the highlights are Irma and Tracy's pyrotechnic version of the Jerry Ragovoy classic "You Don't Know Nothing About Love," while Marcia brings a tongue-in-cheek take to the Steve Cropper/Gary Nicholson tune "Love Maker."

After the album's release, the three singers embarked on a national tour, with Irma's band in support. On another occasion, they performed on *Austin City Limits*, with a band of hired hands and Wardell conducting. A unique and waggish honor in 1998 was Irma's coronation as queen of Krewe du Vieux, along with co-duchesses Marcia and Tracy. This infamous, satirical, and mildly obscene Mardi Gras walking parade is one of the few that makes its way through the French Quarter.

That year, I joined Krewe du Vieux as a member of the Mystic Krewe of Comatose (each sub-krewe prepares its own costumes and accoutrements, based on the year's theme). For "Souled Down the River," we masked as the zombies of laid-off workers from K&B (a local drugstore chain that had been purchased by Rite Aid), with white face paint, purple lipstick, and black circles around our eyes, dressed in official K&B uniforms. I also wore a disheveled black wig. We had constructed a small float with a statue of Our Lady of K&B, who was crying purple tears, in honor of the K&B signature color. At the ball afterward, in the recently vacated Krauss Department Store on Canal Street, Irma and Emile did not recognize me until I spoke to them.

Sing It! won a Grammy nomination, and we all traveled to Los Angeles for the ceremony. The album had been a significant event in the roots music world, but we did not win.

The idea of Irma recording with a Memphis band, inspired by the all-star ensemble at the Porretta Soul Festival, came to fruition with our next project, in 2000. I asked Dan Penn if he would coproduce an album of his own songs, either newly written or from his impressive catalog. Like the two previous songbook albums I had made with Johnny Adams, this seemed like a perfect story and opportunity—the combination of singer, songwriter, and the right musicians. In many ways, we were making records in an old-fashioned way, bringing together a team of specialists, all in support of the singer. In an era when many musicians make their records mostly in isolation, sitting in front of a computer, there is a lot to be said for the chemistry and surprises that can result when a talented group of people comes together in an environment that fosters collaboration.

Dan and his songwriting partners got to work, and the cassette tapes started to arrive. I was knocked out by "My Heart's in Memphis," cowritten with Buddy Emmons; "Not Enough Time to Change," written with Hoy Lindsey and Carson Whitsett; and "Life at the End of the Road," written with Carson. These were songs that only a mature artist could sing, wistful and melancholy, and they demanded a reflective frame of mind that might have at first made Irma hesitant. There were also exuberant songs such as "If You Want It, Come and Get It," written with Marvell Thomas, and the gentle "Irma's Song," written with Irma and Spooner Oldham.

The musicians were Memphis royalty, all veterans of sessions at Stax, Royal, and Malaco studios: Marvell, Spooner, and Carson on keyboards; Michael Toles on guitar; James Kinard on bass; Steve Potts or James Robertson on drums; and a horn section led by Jim Spake and trumpeter Scott Thompson. Dan's cowriters often joined on keyboards, on their own songs. We recorded at Sounds Unreel in Midtown, with engineers David Farrell from New Orleans and Dawn Hopkins from Memphis.

It all went well, and the level of playing was impeccable. Yet, in spite of my high expectations, I seldom felt the joy of hearing the team congeal into something greater than the whole, or of knowing that we had captured something miraculous (the exceptions being "If You Want It, Come and Get It" and "I'm Your Puppet"). We were crafting a record that would meet high standards, but I was not so sure about the elusive spark.

We completed Irma's vocals in New Orleans, at Ultrasonic, while also adding background parts sung by ELS. Dan was particular about wanting to hear the songs sung as he had imagined them, which I respected immensely, but sometimes I felt we were fencing Irma in by being too specific with regard to phrasing and attitude. She had lived with the songs for several weeks, and she knew what she wanted to say with them. Ultimately, we completed several of her vocal performances after Dan had returned to Nashville, and I believe we got close to what he wanted, while giving Irma enough leeway to fully inhabit the songs. I'm proud of the collaboration with two of my heroes, and we had made a bold step into something new for Irma.

Following the post-Katrina *After the Rain*, Irma and I made one more complete album together, in 2008. For *Simply Grand*, I thought about recording her with a different pianist on each track, because New Orleans is a piano town. We lined up our pianists. Marcia Ball, Henry Butler, Jon Cleary, Davell Crawford, David Egan, Dr. John, Norah Jones, Ellis Marsalis, John Medeski, Randy Newman, and David Torkanowsky, and we assembled a wide-ranging set of songs, from standards such as Rose McCoy's song written for Louis Jordan, "If I Had Any Sense I'd Go Back Home," to a new song by Burt Bacharach, "What Can I Do." It gave Irma a broad palette, again with plenty of space. Some of the songs are duets with Irma and the pianist, while others add acoustic bass, drums, and backing vocals.

The session with Ellis Marsalis was especially moving, as Irma sang a tender, jazz-inflected vocal, a style that few of her fans might have previously heard, on "This Bitter Earth." We recorded with Mac "Dr. John" Rebennack on the morning of Mardi Gras Day 2008, at Piety Street Studio in New Orleans. "Be You," a previously unrecorded song written by Mac and Doc Pomus, has a particular New Orleans bounce that perhaps only Irma and Mac could have conjured so spontaneously.

Sitting at an outdoor café in New York City, where Irma and I had traveled to record with Norah Jones and John Medeski at Sear Sound Studio, I decided to ask Irma a personal question. I had long admired her marriage to Emile, even if, as individuals, they seemed at times to be so different. At the age of sixty-one, she had completed her associate's degree at Delgado University, and, in 2007, she had founded the Irma Thomas Center for W.I.S.E. Women at Delgado, with the mission of helping women attain their education goals. She was always up for something new, from our walk

Scott Billington, Irma Thomas, and Mac "Dr. John" Rebennack at Piety Street Studio, New Orleans, Mardi Gras Day 2008 (photograph © Rick Olivier)

in the Italian mountains to trying Middle Eastern food for the first time. Emile was certainly supportive, but perhaps not as adventurous as his wife.

"Irma, I may be way off base to ask you this question, and forgive me if I am, but I have often wondered about the secret to your marriage. Sometimes you and Emile seem so different. What makes you tick as a couple?" I asked.

She chuckled and said, "Well, I can see why you might ask that, and I'll tell you. First, Emile is always a gentleman. Second, when we got together, we made a pact. We did not want to grow old and be broke, so we decided to save our money, to invest it well [in real estate], and to ensure that we would be comfortable as we aged. That was our goal."

If Irma never achieved the over-the-top stardom of, say, Aretha Franklin, she has taken the long view, and has sustained a steady career over the course of fifty years that would be the envy of almost anyone in the music business. Her success, however hard-won, never sacrificed family or well-being. She has taken care of herself on many levels. It is an accomplishment that few musicians can match.

RECOMMENDED LISTENING:

"The New Rules" from *The New Rules*
"Sorry, Wrong Number" from *The Way I Feel*
"In the Middle of It All" from *After the Rain*
"River Is Waiting" from *Simply Grand*

Chapter 10

NATHAN AND THE ZYDECO CHA CHAS

NATHAN AND THE ZYDECO CHA CHAS WERE ABOUT TO TAKE THE STAGE for the first of several performances at the 1993 Efes Pilsen Blues Festival in Istanbul, where we were opening for Texas bluesman Johnny Copeland. I was coaching Nathan Williams on how to say "hello" in Turkish, even if I was unsure of my own pronunciation.

"I think it goes like this, Nathan. *Merhaba*, Istanbul!"

"I don't know, Scott," he said. "I don't want to say it wrong."

"Aw, I don't think it will matter. They'll get it."

"OK," he replied, and then tentatively repeated, "Merhaba. Merhaba."

Promoter Ahmet Ülug gave us our signal, and we rushed into the lights. Nathan plugged in his accordion and stepped up to the mic.

"Merhaba, Istanbul!"

The crowd of perhaps two thousand people rose to its feet and screamed with delight as we launched into Nathan's song "Outside People," with its upbeat, ska-based groove. If Nathan may have been the first American musician at the festival to address the audience in Turkish, he may also have realized in that moment the power that he possessed as a cultural ambassador. At our show the next day, he proclaimed "merhaba" as if it was his native language.

If anyone had told me, when I was starting my career in the music business, that twenty years later I would be performing as a harmonica player in Turkey with a Louisiana zydeco band, I would have said they were crazy. Nathan himself may have been almost as surprised at how far his music had taken him.

Nathan and the Zydeco Cha Chas at the Pera Palas hotel, Istanbul, 1993. *Left to right:* James Benoit, Scott Billington, Dennis Paul Williams, Allen "Cat Roy" Broussard, Johnny Batiste, Nathan Williams, Bobby Matthews, Mark "Chuck" Williams (photograph © Scott Billington).

We were staying at the luxurious Pera Palas hotel, which was constructed in 1892 as the eastern terminus for passengers on the Orient Express train. Guitarist Dennis Paul Williams and I were roommates, and we spent much of our week in Istanbul exploring the mosques, the bazaar, and the alleyways where clusters of shops, selling anything from hardware to spices, might be found. We were a novelty wherever we went. For some reason, people thought I resembled Eric Clapton, while Dennis Paul, in his black beret and overcoat, might have been a young Dizzy Gillespie.

Dennis Paul, who has become a close friend (as has Nathan), is also a renowned visual artist, and a devout Catholic who has studied spiritual traditions from around the world. We were excited to find a traditional Sufi music ensemble playing for whirling dervishes. At an antiquarian Islamic book store, we were first greeted with disdain as errant Americans by the bearded young proprietors, but after an hour of conversation in which Dennis showed his understanding of Islamic principles, and how they related to Christianity, we were all laughing and sharing tea (for there was a constant shuttle of vendors across the city delivering tea in clear, tulip-shaped glasses). Dennis and I both bought ancient, hand-illuminated bookplates.

I was introduced to Nathan Williams in 1987 by Stanley "Buckwheat" Dural, who was a close friend of Nathan's oldest brother, Sid, the entrepreneur whose grocery store, gas station, and nightclub had revitalized a block along Martin Luther King Boulevard in Lafayette. Buckwheat had lived for a time in the apartment complex across the street from the grocery, Sid's One Stop. For many years, until his death in 2016, he performed a yearly Thanksgiving benefit, providing meals for dozens of seniors and families, at El Sid O's Zydeco and Blues Club.

Buckwheat had signed with Island Records after his two breakthrough albums on Rounder, and he saw the potential of a partnership between Nathan and Rounder. Nathan had released a couple of 45-rpm discs on the El Sid O's label and was managed by Sid, so Buckwheat was also doing a favor for his friend. At the same time, I had begun planning a weekend of live recording at Richard's Club in Lawtell, so I asked Nathan if he would like to be one of the featured bands. I was immediately impressed with his ambition and work ethic, as I had been with Buckwheat's, because he volunteered to set up at the club the day before, not only so I could hear his songs, but so we could give our equipment a test run. For his first release on Rounder, which comprised one side of a vinyl LP, Nathan and I chose the subsequent live recordings of three of the songs from his 45s, along with covers of Clifton Chenier's "Hungry Man Blues" and Major Handy's "Come on Home."

Born in St. Martinville in 1963, Nathan and his six siblings grew up in a Creole-speaking home. As a child, Nathan heard zydeco music close to home. He recounts:

There was this club called the Casino—an old club like Slim's or Double D's Club. All the time Clifton Chenier was playing, I'd go with my cousin Earl and Cleveland—little friends of mine—we'd get up on the washing machine in the back and peep through the window. "Oh yeah, baby, we're gonna have a good time tonight. You got the old hog here," he would say, and when he started playing, the floor would be rocking, I mean rocking. I liked that. There was a big, old time fan in the window, and I leaned in so far that it clipped the bill off my cap. There was this old lady, and we had to pass through her yard [to get to the window]. She didn't want us to be there. So next thing you know she came out with a big old purse, and she started whipping us with her purse, and ran us out of there. We had to go back with the police to get our bikes.

When Nathan was seven years old, his father died, and the family fell on hard times, with three generations living together in a small shotgun house. Sid was sixteen years old, so he quit high school and went to work. "First, I washed dishes in Lafayette," Sid told me.

Then, I decided to go to Venice, Louisiana, to work as a roustabout pusher for the Penrod drilling company, fifty miles offshore. I left St. Martinville with eighty cents, two pair of blues jeans, and three T-shirts. [I was] crying pure water, hitchhiking. I got there two days early, but the man let me stay in the Penrod shed. When I brought home $1800, my mother said to me, "You're not selling no dope, are you?" Finally, I got hurt on the job, and with the settlement, I bought property [for the store].

Mrs. Florita Williams had instilled in her children a sense of faith, determination, and courage. Sid enjoys telling the story of how he built the store, starting with pouring the slab, then going back to work until he had saved enough money to erect the walls. Finally, after many months, the roof and refrigerated cases were added. Stocking the shelves was another challenge, because no bank or vendor would give him credit. So he paid cash until they did.

Sid's One Stop became a central part of the community, while bringing Sid great success. "God and the dollar—that's my motto," he says, sometimes displaying the revolver he keeps in his waistband. He has never had to use it, but law and order is the rule at Sid's. He eventually built the nightclub on land near the store that he feared would be purchased by a competing convenience store, but only after promising his wife, Suzanne, that he would only open on weekends. He also built a large new home, with an accordion sculpture on the wrought iron gates to the driveway, within sight of the Interstate 10 exit ramp at University Drive. "When the tour bus comes by, I want the driver to say, 'And there on your right, ladies and gentlemen, is the home of the famous El Sid O.'" Sid has a flair for promotion. For many years, he continued to manage Nathan, while providing a home base at the club for the band to perform.

Nathan became serious about playing the accordion when he was a teenager, after suffering a near-fatal bout with thyroid disease. Dennis Paul prayed with him every day in the hospital. During his convalescence, Sid

At Sids's One Stop, Lafayette. *In foreground:* Nathan Williams Jr.; *in the doorway:* Sid Williams and Nathan Williams Sr. (photograph © Rick Olivier).

bought Nathan his first accordion, which he practiced rigorously, learn-ing the styles of his idols Clifton Chenier and Buckwheat Zydeco. While Nathan played the large piano accordion, and while he became adept at the intricate chords that many of his songs demanded, he developed a style that also let him play a down-home stomp that was every bit as exciting as those played on the smaller button accordion. He called his band the Zydeco Cha Chas, after Clifton Chenier's song of the same name (which is not a cha-cha). In later years, he also mastered the triple-row button accordion, which added variety to his sets.

In 1988, we made plans to record Nathan's first full album. He had a keen ear for the old Creole sayings and the conversations he had heard growing up or at Sid's store, which he often used as the basis for his new songs, such as "Everything on the Hog" and "If You Got a Problem." He also looked back to the advice that his mother had given her seven children, such as "Ain't Nobody Gonna Help You" (if you don't try to help yourself). It was a more personal approach to songwriting than anything heard before in zydeco. I looked for outside songs, as well, and brought a new Paul Kelly composition, "Steady Rock."

The sessions at Southlake Studio in Metairie went smoothly, in part because Nathan had rehearsed all the songs with the band ahead of time. With his cousin Chuck on rubboard and the powerhouse Kevin Menard on drums (who would soon leave to play with Buckwheat), the grooves were rock solid. I could see right away that Nathan was an artist who understood that the studio could be used for more than capturing a live performance, because he was focused on songs. Sometimes, after we had completed a basic track, we would recut his accordion and vocal performances, eliminating microphone leakage between the two sounds, so we could edit together the strongest possible vocal.

When it came time to name the album, we could not decide between *Steady Rock* and *Everything on the Hog*, from Nathan's song that celebrates the pig-derived culinary specialties of southwest Louisiana ("Everything on the hog is good, 'cept the eye"). One afternoon, at the store, Sid approached me with a snapshot and a question.

"Scott, how many people do you think have ever seen a six-hundred-pound hog?" he asked.

"Well, I suppose not many. That wouldn't be me, for sure," I replied.

He then showed me a photograph of Nathan standing behind the stainless-steel butcher table in the back of the shop, holding his accordion. On the table was the very large hog in question, eviscerated, with its hooves removed, lying on its back. Sid was proposing this image for the album cover. The Beatles' gory *Yesterday and Today* cover flashed to mind.

I did not know what to say, but I quickly rattled out, "That's amazing, Sid." I paused. "But you know, there are zydeco fans in the world who do not eat pork—Jewish fans and Muslim fans. We wouldn't want to offend them."

"You're right," he replied, with his usual business pragmatism. "I hadn't thought of that. We want everyone to buy this record."

We settled on *Steady Rock*. The song itself became enough of a local hit that several other zydeco bands covered the song onstage at the 1990 New Orleans Jazz and Heritage Festival. It was also played by the local zydeco disc jockeys, such as Lou Collins on KSLO in Opelousas, and Big Ed Poullard, the Zydeco Kid (who is also one of the few active Creole fiddlers), on KEUN in Eunice. And everyone listened to the KRVS Saturday morning zydeco show. The Lafayette High School Marching Band made an arrangement of "Steady Rock" that was played for the next few years at parades and football games.

Nathan signed on with Buckwheat's booking agency, Concerted Efforts, and began touring. He kept his truck and equipment in tip-top shape, and he was always on time. He quickly developed a reputation as an easy-to-work-with professional.

In 1990, we returned to the studio to make what soon became one of my favorite zydeco albums, *Your Mama Don't Know*. Again, the title track was written by the rhythm and blues songwriter Paul Kelly, who was now sending me his new compositions on a regular basis. However, Nathan was blossoming as writer himself, with his Creole parables such as "Outside People," "Slow Horses and Fast Women," and "You Got Me Baby Now You Don't." There had also been a near complete turnover in band personnel, with the notable addition of guitarists Dennis Paul Williams and James Benoit, the latter an alumnus of Clifton Chenier's band. I brought in Bill Samuel to play baritone saxophone on section parts with Nathan's new tenor player, "Doctor" John Wilson.

With his mastery of jazz harmony and music theory, Dennis Paul has since been the band's ace in the hole, adding melodic motifs and chords that often lift the songs into a wholly original place. His art is not confined to music, because his paintings and occasional sculptures have been shown in galleries around the world. Many were collected for the book *Soul Exchange: The Paintings of Dennis Paul Williams* (UL Press). He began painting as a child, when he pounded sticks to make brushes and used soot to make black ink. He also followed a local *traiteur*, a spiritual healer who ministered to anyone who needed help, a practice that Dennis Paul maintains today. He is one of the most accomplished and caring people I have known.

As we got to know one another, Nathan began asking me to sit in with the band. With John Wilson, and later with alto saxophonist Allen "Cat Roy" Broussard, I developed harmony-section parts that were great fun to play. When performing in Louisiana, I learned how grueling a traditional zydeco gig could be, because we often went on at nine o'clock and did not stop until one in the morning. To take a bathroom break, I had to quickly sneak offstage between songs. As is common at a zydeco dance, there was little or no applause, because the dancers showed their appreciation by filling the dance floor. At the end of the dance, I would be happily exhausted, with a sore back. I could not imagine how Nathan felt after holding his fifty-pound accordion for four hours.

I occasionally went on the road as an honorary Cha Cha. One of my favorite travel memories was a thirty-five-kilometer bicycle ride that Nathan, Dennis Paul, our tour manager, and I took after a festival gig in Austria. I had noticed bicycles at our hotel. As it turned out, there was an extensive network of bicycle-only trails through the vineyards and small villages along the Hungarian border. Our tour manager found us a map. We stopped at vineyards along the way, watching for the "weingut" signs, where we drank red wine and ate sausages and cheese. We eventually brushed against the Neusiedler See, a large lake where storks come to roost each summer. We felt like twelve-year-olds as we zigzagged through the sunny, flat landscape that was punctuated only by church spires. The opportunity to travel has been one of the greatest benefits of my work.

Back home, we started work on a new album. *Follow Me Chicken* delved into new territory for Nathan and perhaps for zydeco in general. On the songs "Zydeco Road" and "Zydeco Is Alright" we added New Orleans djembe player Kenyatta Simon, whose African-derived polyrhythms were a natural fit. On the new Dan Penn/Jon Tiven/Sally Tiven song, "Mama's Tired," we employed a ska beat, while Nathan worked up a novel arrangement of the Stevie Wonder song "Isn't She Lovely," sung in Creole. The title track was from another local proverb: "Follow me, chicken, I'm full of corn." Nathan and I wrote "Zydeco Road" together, after I had seen that street sign in Plaisance, on the site of the annual zydeco festival. I had been listening to James Brown records that week, so we added a Brown-like modulation to the sixth chord for the bridge. If the music we were recording was not always the au courant style for the local dance halls, I felt we were making records that were listenable for their song content. Perhaps this is the direction I would have gone with Buckwheat, had we continued to work together.

The idea for our next record came from an unexpected source. During breakfast at the Pera Palas hotel in Istanbul, during the 1993 tour, Nathan and I sat with the Louisiana-born bluesman Johnny Copeland, who was neither a stranger to zydeco music nor to the mélange of Gulf Coast sounds on the Texas-Louisiana border. Over bountiful plates of dates, olives, yogurt, pistachio pastries, and strong Turkish coffee, he said, "You know, the time might be right for you to make a record with a Cajun artist. It could be a good time to bring those two styles together—to build a bridge."

It was a perfect idea. When we returned home, we reached out to the Cajun fiddler Michael Doucet, the leader of the band BeauSoleil, which was the hottest touring Cajun band in the land. Michael had been one of the key figures in the revival of Cajun music in the 1980s, when he began making records that made the world aware of the wealth of traditional music in southwest Louisiana. Many Cajuns in his parents' generation had actively discouraged their children from speaking French. In their haste to become mainstream Americans, their language and musical traditions were often relegated to the poor and the elderly. Michael sought out senior musicians as his teachers and, in a few instances, may have rescued tunes that were by then being played only at home. Michael was also well versed in Creole fiddle styles, having learned directly from Canray Fontenot, with whom BeauSoleil made an album in 1989.

We recorded *Creole Crossroads* in 1995 with engineer Tony Daigle at Dockside Studio in Maurice, which allowed everyone but me to sleep in their own beds. Nathan wrote several new songs for the album, including his popular "Zydeco Hog." The highlights for me are the three Clifton Chenier tracks, including a version of "Black Gal" with only accordion, fiddle, and percussion. We stripped it down further for Nathan's "Ma Femme Nancy," written for his wife, with only Nathan's accordion and vocal, and Michael's fiddle. The old-time performance and the traditional two-step feel make the track seem like a modern incarnation of Amédé Ardoin and Dennis McGee, even if Nathan is playing the piano accordion. Michael brought his song "La Nuit de Clifton Chenier," a remembrance of the great musician that Nathan sings in French and English.

We followed up with a live record, *I'm a Zydeco Hog*, made at the Rock 'n' Bowl in New Orleans in 1998 before a packed house. The Rock 'n' Bowl remains a unique combination of bowling alley and dance hall, and one of the most important regular gigs for bands who make the trip from southwest Louisiana for zydeco night, each Thursday. In addition, proprietor John Blancher worked with me to license, from Rounder, a compact disc of the bands that played there regularly, and he sold thousands.

In 2000, we made a new studio album, *Let's Go!* Before those sessions, I had introduced Nathan to the Lafayette songwriter David Egan, and the duo came up with the humorous "Can't Get Nuthin' Sucka." I loved hearing a new song like this one, built with a deep understanding of its roots music foundation, because it could speak to people in a way that pure groove could not. And we kept experimenting with new sounds. On the ska-driven "Everything Happens for the Best," based on my mother's frequent adage, we added a chorus effect to Dennis's overdubbed guitar, approximating the style and sound I had learned from working with African soukous star Tabu Ley Rochereau.

At the 2003 Montreal International Jazz Festival, I joined the band for a high-energy set before an audience of ten thousand. If the lyrics of Nathan's songs may have gotten lost in the overall atmosphere of the good-time Louisiana music that the crowd expected, he had become an experienced entertainer with a repertoire that he could draw upon to suit any situation.

But the biggest surprise of the festival may have been the short opening set performed by Nathan's then-'tweenaged son. Lil' Nathan, as he is called, had often attended our recording sessions, and he had mastered both the rubboard and the drums at an early age, but now he was playing triple-row accordion. His confidence and energy quickly won the audience over. He went on to major in music at the University of Louisiana at Lafayette, where he is currently an adjunct professor. More importantly, Lil' Nathan and the Zydeco Big Timers became one of the top-drawing zydeco bands in southwest Louisiana (along with Keith Frank, Chris Ardoin, and J. Paul Jr.). He also excelled in the recording studio, making his own records and eventually producing a new album by his father. Nathan Sr. had built a small studio space in his home that had languished unused, which Nathan Jr. has transformed into a fully outfitted production suite.

Nathan Williams remained with Rounder Records longer than any other zydeco artist. As the national spotlight on zydeco began to dim in the early 2000s, he was a "steady rock" who at times could be his own best distributor. We recorded our final album together, *Hang It High, Hang It Low*, in 2005 at Ultrasonic in New Orleans, with Steve Reynolds and me coproducing. My favorite song is "Don't Worry 'Bout the Mule," from an old Creole adage, "Don't worry 'bout the mule, just load the wagon." The song and the groove happened spontaneously, from conception to final track, in a period of a couple of hours, with everyone laughing and feeling the

Dennis Paul Williams and Scott Billington at the Grand Ole Opry for the fortieth anniversary of Rounder Records, 2009 (photograph © Rick Olivier)

spirit. This album was more of a family affair than ever, because Lil' Nathan joined the band on keyboards and Dennis Paul provided a painting for the album cover. This would be the last album I would make at Ultrasonic, which was destroyed by Hurricane Katrina a month later.

In 2009, Rounder staged a concert at Nashville's Grand Ole Opry to celebrate its fortieth anniversary, in conjunction with Country Music Television. Nathan and Irma Thomas were the two Louisiana representatives, sharing the stage with Minnie Driver, Alison Krauss, Béla Fleck, Mary Chapin Carpenter, and others. I was proud to take the stage with Nathan and the band, along with our guests, pianist Henry Butler and lap steel player Jerry Douglas.

I have stayed close with the Williams family. Like many of the musicians I have recorded, Nathan, Dennis Paul, Sid, and I became lifelong friends. As of this writing, Sid is still running the store and presiding over the neighborhood. In addition to his work as an artist and musician, Dennis Paul has served several terms as a city council member in St. Martinville. And perhaps more than any living, touring musician, Nathan Williams is a standard-bearer of a traditional Louisiana culture that sustained itself with hard work, music, and more than a few incisive aphorisms that helped each person get from one day to the next. Altogether, the legacy of this extraordinary family continues to enrich the Louisiana Creole community, and the world at large.

RECOMMENDED LISTENING:

"Your Mama Don't Know" and "Outside People" from *Your Mama Don't Know*
"Don't Worry 'Bout the Mule" from *Hang It High, Hang It Low*

Chapter 11

CHARLIE RICH

IT WAS LATE IN THE SUMMER OF 1991, AND WE WERE NEAR THE END OF our first round of recording sessions at the Sam Phillips Studio in Memphis, having finished work at about five o'clock in the afternoon. As he had on several previous occasions, Charlie Rich invited me that evening to hang out with him at his own studio, located in a separate building behind his tree-shaded home, "out east" in Memphis. We used these evening get-togethers to listen to the tracks we had recorded that day, or to talk about music in general.

I had sent him a few songs to listen to before the sessions, but we had not yet attempted to record any of them. This evening seemed like the right time to listen together. One song I was particularly keen on was "Pictures and Paintings," which the songwriter Doc Pomus had sent me not long before his death that same year. The demo was crude and murky, recorded on a cheap cassette deck in Doc's apartment and performed on an electric keyboard by his cowriter, Mac "Dr. John" Rebennack.

Charlie passed me a joint as he listened intently, because the words were not always easy to decipher. He shook his head in approval at Doc's wistful story of a love that was never realized.

"I could hear this with a little swing put to it," he said. The demo was almost plodding, which was uncharacteristic for Mac.

The next day, we got together for one last time with our acoustic "jazz band." I had brought bassist James Singleton and drummer Johnny Vidacovich in from New Orleans. On baritone saxophone, we had Fred Ford, our senior band member who had toured widely with rhythm and blues artists such as the Johnny Otis Band and with jazz artists like Benny

Carter. As a studio musician, he had played on Clarence "Gatemouth" Brown's "Okie Dokie Stomp" in 1954. Our second cult legend was the guitarist Calvin Newborn, who was a vital part of the Memphis R&B scene and who toured with jazz artists such as Lionel Hampton and Earl Hines.

It was wrap-up time, as much for saying goodbye as for accomplishing anything new. To celebrate, Charlie lit a joint and passed it around, and everyone was suddenly in the mood to play. He called his old hit "Every Time You Touch Me (I Get High)," which he had written with producer Billy Sherrill during their reign at the top of the country charts in the mid-1970s. The band settled into a floating, bossa nova type of groove, to which Fred and Charlie contributed wonderful solos. It is a thoroughly cohesive track, with everything in just the right place, and it was effortless. It was an odd choice of song, considering our jazz- and blues-oriented direction, but it worked, and Charlie was happy with it. He shook everyone's hands and left the studio.

Before the musicians packed up, I asked if we could cut a quick new demo recording of "Pictures and Paintings," in 4/4 swing time. I knew this was a groove that Johnny and James could nail quickly. We listened to the original cassette, and James made a chord chart, then we did one take of the song, with me singing a scratch vocal. Calvin was having an issue with his guitar pickup, so it was more or less a bass, drum, and vocal performance, but it got the idea across. When I played it for Charlie that evening, asking him if this was what he was hearing, he smiled and said, "Yeah—you got it. That's it."

We resumed recording in the fall with a second round of sessions at Phillips, this time with an all-Memphis band that leaned toward rhythm and blues. Early on the second afternoon, Charlie surprised me by saying, "Why don't you put up that track of 'Pictures and Paintings.' I'd like to hear it again."

"What track, Charlie?" I replied.

"You know, the one you played for me."

"Well, sure, but that was just a demo."

We put the twenty-four-track reel on the tape deck and turned off my vocal. I could see Charlie mentally singing along with a track that, as it turned out, had a beautiful, relaxed groove. I wrote out a lyric sheet and handed it to him. The sad lyrics suited him well, because few other singers could evoke the feeling of loss and heartbreak like Charlie.

I thought we would work on the song with Charlie the next day, but he did not show up. Some days, as I had learned by now, the effort required to record was just was not in him. To make use of the time, I asked Michael Toles if he would work on a new rhythm guitar part and a solo for "Pictures and Paintings." Michael is one of the most versatile all-around musicians I have ever met. A frequent member of the Stax and Malaco Records house bands, he has recorded with rhythm and blues artists as diverse as Ann Peebles, Bobby "Blue" Band, O. V. Wright, B. B. King, and Albert King. He was a long-time member of the Isaac Hayes band (he was the second guitarist on the recording of "Shaft"). As I got to know him, I appreciated his wide-ranging musical tastes, from the Beatles to the classical organist E. Power Biggs. After the Charlie Rich sessions, we would become frequent collaborators.

The new parts did not take him long. Michael can be a sonic shape-shifter, presenting an array of sounds and ideas that can be a producer's dream, but which require a decisive response. For the rhythm guitar part, we chose an acoustic guitar. For the solo section, we chose a fat, dark electric guitar sound, with a touch of amp reverb. We now had the perfect bed for the vocal.

Charlie arrived late in the morning on the next day, and we played the track for him. I had learned to be patient with Charlie, and not to force an idea before its time, because the results were clearly better when Charlie felt like doing something. Peter Guralnick, the author and co-executive producer of the album, had come to town for the sessions, and we were both thrilled when Charlie said, "OK, let me take a pass at the vocal."

It was a breathtaking moment as he sang the song, perfectly evoking the loneliness and sad resignation of Doc's words. Peter was so overcome with Charlie's emotive vocal, and with the suspense of what was happening, that he had to leave the room. Charlie had clearly thought about the song, because he delivered the lyrics with confidence. I wondered if that was what he had been doing at home on the previous day.

I asked him for one more take, so we would have alternate lines from which to choose, and then he laid down two passes of piano which danced around his vocal and Michael's solo. When we listened back to a rough mix of the finished track, I felt that we had accomplished a miracle, following a path that I could not have intentionally chosen. It became the title track of our album. At times, I was reminded of my sessions with James Booker, because, more so than on most recordings, they were about the challenge of nurturing moments of beauty and collective spontaneity that were both fleeting and fragile. The difference with *Pictures and Paintings* was that we had the time to wait for them.

In years prior to our recording, Charlie had had hosted weekly jam sessions at the small recording studio behind his house, which was outfitted with a multitrack machine that was ably operated by his assistant, Big Al Holcomb. Local musicians such as baritone saxophonist Fred Ford and drummer Doug Garrison were regulars. They played standards such as "Green Dolphin Street" and "As Time Goes By," sometimes veering into spontaneous collective improvisation. The commonality of the material they rehearsed and recorded is that it revealed the breadth of Charlie's musical interests, crossing genres and showing off piano chops that hinted more of Erroll Garner than Floyd Cramer. Charlie had created a private forum to express something true and deep within him—something that his fans may only have glimpsed.

The idea of a Charlie Rich album of jazz, blues, and rhythm and blues songs was Peter Guralnick's, or maybe it was more like his vision of a recording on which Charlie was not bound by strictures of any kind—commercial, genre, or musical—like the music on the home studio recordings that Charlie had shared with him. Peter had written a chapter about Charlie in his book *Feel Like Going Home*, and they had become good friends, so much so that Charlie wrote the song "Feel Like Going Home," telling Peter that it was inspired by the *feeling* of his book. It was released as the B side of his 1973 Grammy-winning hit "The Most Beautiful Girl."

To present his idea, Peter made a "demo" tape consisting mostly of songs that had been recorded in Charlie's studio ("Am I Blue," "Go Ahead and Cry," "Somebody Broke into My Heart"), along with Charlie's original solo demo of "Feel Like Going Home" and a big-band version of "Don't Put No Headstone on My Grave." He circulated the tape for some five years, presenting it first to Jerry Wexler and then to Rounder Records, but no one would commit to the project. It was our mutual friend Joe McEwen, who was now vice president of A&R at Warner Bros. Records, who was finally able to make the record happen.

Joe's boss, Warner Bros. vice president and Sire Records founder Seymour Stein, had agreed to allow Joe to make one album per year that came with no commercial expectations, as a reward of sorts for Joe's exemplary work. Joe is a major-label A&R person who has always found a way to operate with musical integrity and who possesses a rare knack for fostering art within the confines of a job that is inherently sales driven. His grounding in American roots and soul music, which goes back to his days as a Boston disc jockey, when he called himself Mr. C., made him an asset as our second executive producer. Joe envisioned Charlie's record as the first in an ongoing series, but only one further record, by songwriter and singer Dan Penn, would be made under this arrangement.

In February 1991, Peter and Joe traveled to Memphis to attempt to convince Charlie that the time was right for the project, waiting for several days while Charlie drove back from a trip to Destin, Florida. They gathered around Charlie's kitchen table, where, Peter remembers, "I translated between two almost-silent (truly) conversationalists! I told each of them afterward, 'I've never seen Charlie/Joe so enthusiastic.'" I was thrilled to be asked help realize their vision when I was enlisted as producer.

If Charlie Rich had been present at the Sun Records studio for the famous Million Dollar Quartet photograph and informal gospel recording session, with Johnny Cash, Jerry Lee Lewis, Carl Perkins, and Elvis Presley, he would have completed the spontaneous gathering of major Sun artists, for, as Peter has written, Sun Records producer and visionary Sam Phillips said that Charlie was the most talented artist he had ever worked with. Yet, even though Charlie played piano and occasionally wrote songs for recording sessions by Sun rockabilly artists, it is a stretch to call him a rockabilly. His 1960 hit on Phillips International, "Lonely Weekends," is a gospel-derived pop song with only a faint reference to the wildness of rockabilly music in his vocal, which leans more toward post-rockabilly Elvis.

No one could have imagined, at that time, that Charlie Rich would become one of the biggest country music stars of the 1970s—the Silver Fox—fronting the "countrypolitan" sound built around him by producer Billy Sherrill. Charlie's hits such as "Behind Closed Doors" were centered by his disarming vocal performances, and the records were beautifully crafted. Charlie was also able to record songs such as the string-laden ballad "Nothing in the World (to Do With Me)" that were written by his wife, the talented Margaret Ann Rich. Charlie's records with Sherrill took a step away from established Nashville conventions, with a heavily orchestrated sound that sometimes crossed over into pop, a signal of the emergence of Nashville as a commercial power bigger than the country music niche. In a way, it was a parallel sound to the lush arrangements that producer and arranger Thom Bell was putting behind soul artists such as the Spinners and the Stylistics in Philadelphia during the same time.

Yet Charlie was little suited to be a star or a celebrity. He was a shy, introverted man who was the opposite of a gregarious entertainer like Sleepy LaBeef or Bobby Rush, and the trappings of the show business world that he was now compelled to enter made him uncomfortable. He told me that when it was suggested that he add dancers to his show in Las Vegas, he did not know how to respond. He was not a musician who thrived within the structure of a regular show, with the same sequence of events and banter each night. Then, at the 1975 Country Music Association Awards, he infamously took out his cigarette lighter and drunkenly burned the announcement telling him to present John Denver with the award as his successor as Entertainer of the Year. He would later say that he had no gripe with John Denver, but it was clear that Charlie was reaching the end of his rope with the mainstream country music entertainment business. If his substance abuse issues were a negative manifestation of his discomfiture, his refusal to be untrue to himself was a reflection of his integrity, no matter how contrary it was to sustained success. If he made very good pop-country music, the slickness of the country music business represented the antithesis of who he was.

He persevered for a while, making records in Nashville until the early 1980s, often overdubbing his vocals on tracks that had been produced for him. Then, he more or less retired to Memphis. Nashville and Memphis are only three hours apart by car, but the musical distance between them can seem immense. If Nashville attracts songwriters, singers, and musicians who are willing to commit to the discipline required by the city's industry hierarchy, and who aspire to be an archetypal kind of star, Memphis is its gritty, haphazard, and spontaneous alter ego, with success often emanating from entrepreneurs who simply steer talent in the right direction, and who let the music lead the way. It was iconoclasts such as Sam Phillips, Willie Mitchell, and the Stax Records stable of musicians and writers such as Isaac Hayes and Steve Cropper who each realized a different manifestation of the raw materials around them. Perhaps the only immediate commonality with Nashville was the appreciation of a good song.

If Memphis can sometimes seem to live in the past, with ghosts of records and musicians inhabiting many corners and conversations, its grit and its underlying bluesiness persevere. And that is how it felt when I entered Sam Phillips Recording Studio, where we would record Charlie's new record. Built in 1960, after Phillips had outgrown his original Sun Studio space, the building was a portal into that era, with its Sputnik-like decorative elements. When we made our record, the studio was managed by Sam's sons, Jerry and Knox, who maintained the facility just as it had been when it opened. Sam himself still came by every now and then. In 2019, I was able to visit the studio again, and this time was invited to see Sam's upstairs office and desk, with a Formica kidney-shaped top, complete with cigarette burns that might have been made by anyone from Charlie Rich to Johnny Cash. It was an eerie experience, because the studio, which is now managed by Sam's granddaughter Halley, looks just the same, and the ghosts seem all the more present.

It was a state-of-the-art facility when it was built, and in many ways it still is. The main room was built with foldout wall panels that had hard and absorbent surfaces on alternate sides, so the room could be made more or less reverberant by adjusting them. The large drum booth allowed the drummer to have eye contact with the other musicians while staying sonically isolated. The only substantial upgrade had been the replacement of the original Ampex three-track recorder and custom console with a twenty-four-track API console and a Studer two-inch tape machine.

Engineer David Farrell traveled to Memphis with me, where he was ably abetted by Phillips studio manager and ace engineer Roland Janes, whose good-natured personality made everyone feel at home, and who was a comforting presence for Charlie (although Roland's puns could be insufferable). Roland was a Memphis legend who had played guitar in Billy Lee Riley's band, the Little Green Men, as well as on Jerry Lee Lewis's early records, setting a much-emulated standard for rock and roll guitar. Roland ran his own Sonic Studio and several record labels for a number of years, finally settling in at Phillips in 1982, where he worked until his death in 2013.

Our strategy was to do two rounds of sessions: one week in late summer with an acoustic-leaning jazz band, and one week in the early fall with a rhythm and blues–leaning band, with electric bass. The nearly six-figure budget I received from Warner Bros./Sire Records was among the largest I had ever had to work with, but apparently not in the eyes of the record

company, because one of their attorneys called me to make sure I understood that I had to deliver the record on budget, and that I would get no
more money. I had to bite my cheeks to keep from laughing out loud.
We stayed at the Peabody Hotel in downtown Memphis, which was an
extravagance that my usual Rounder budgets could seldom have supported.

It might have seemed an odd choice to bring James Singleton and Johnny
Vidacovich up from New Orleans, because I could have found a musically compatible rhythm section in Memphis. However, if I believed that
Charlie Rich would not replicate the "capture the wind" experience that
James, Johnny, and I had been through with James Booker, I knew this would
not be a rote session, either. With the two of them onboard, I had musicians
who would play with their ears wide open, and who would roll with Charlie,
wherever he chose to go. They were, in a sense, my security blanket.

We generally made progress each day, whether we completed a track or
introduced a new song to the band, but it was slow going. After a number of
takes on different days, we got very good versions of the standards "Mood
Indigo" and "Am I Blue." These songs in particular were different for Charlie,
because even though he had been playing them for much of his life, they
revealed a side of him that very few had heard. The jazz chords were as
natural to him as playing the blues. Yet, on some days he did not feel like
recording, and I would get a call from Big Al, telling me that he would be
back at the studio the next day. Charlie was extremely sensitive to what
was going on around him, and the wrong word uttered in his presence
could send him to a withdrawn place. You could see it, like a cold wind
blowing across his face.

We tried a number of ideas that did not make it to the final record. In his
home studio, Charlie had improvised several long pieces ("Someday Baby
It Ain't Gonna Be That Way," "Dedicated," and "Back Home in Memphis"),
including a thirteen-minute piano performance that sounded almost classical. Peter and Joe both hoped we could capture something similar, but it
was difficult to direct Charlie to do so, because the only way it would have
worked was if it had been spontaneous. I asked Fred Ford if he would write
a big-band chart for "Am I Blue," but the session was a disaster, with the
horns playing out of tune, and with the part itself overwhelming the song.
We were better off with the small-band vibe. The impromptu "Every Time
You Touch Me (I Get High)" was when the group truly coalesced, perhaps
because it felt to Charlie like the jam sessions at his house.

We reconvened several weeks later with a new all-Memphis band. Guitarist Michael Toles was the key musician. I could see that Charlie appreciated his musical sensibility, which may have ranged as far as his own. On electric bass was Errol Thomas, who had recorded extensively with Isaac Hayes and Al Green. Rounding out the ensemble was drummer Doug Garrison, Charlie's friend who would later move to New Orleans to join the funky Latino band the Iguanas.

Right away, we captured tough, driving performances of the album's two blues tunes, Charlie's "Don't Put No Headstone on My Grave" and the standard "Juice Head Baby," which are about as raw as anything Charlie had ever recorded. Michael's guitar inspired him, and he fired back with strong piano solos of his own. Charlie had brought two previously unrecorded songs to the sessions, his own "Anywhere You Are" and Margaret Ann's "Go Ahead and Cry." Both are outstanding performances that pair Charlie's deeply felt vocals with laid-back grooves. We layered Michael's guitars on both songs, while Doug overdubbed percussion. In a way, both hinted at the lushness of Charlie's records with Billy Sherrill, but without the heavy orchestration. I imagined that back in the 1970s, both of these songs could have been hits. The Cindy Walker/Eddy Arnold standard "You Don't Know Me" was a continuation of the longing expressed in "Pictures and Paintings"—a heartbreaking performance that, to me, rivals the Ray Charles version.

There were two songs that Joe wanted to pursue. One was a new composition from Dan Penn called "Cry Like a Man." We all could imagine Charlie singing it, and we went after it time and again, but it was destined not to happen because Charlie did not connect with the lyrics, which he felt were coming from a woman's perspective. The other was Charlie's new song "Somebody Broke into My Heart," which Joe imagined with a Hi Records sound. We finally got a take, but it was not perfect. The tempo accelerated, and Errol's bass did not seem to lock in with the piano.

Finally, we recorded "Feel Like Going Home," with everyone in the pocket and with Charlie at his best. At first, it seemed that this song might not happen, because Charlie became frustrated as he strained vocally to hit several of the high notes. When I suggested that we lower the key, it all came together.

I brought him a rough mix on cassette at our evening get-together after the session, and he was satisfied with it. Then, he surprised me by quietly remarking, "You know, I could hear a gospel choir on this." I learned to listen closely to Charlie, because he might say something important in a such a muted tone that it was easy to miss. However, it did not take long for me to decide that we should give the choir a try. Knowing that Michael was the music director a church in West Memphis, and that he was well connected in the gospel world, I asked him if he could help to enlist the right singers.

Two days later, we double-tracked the little-known gospel vocal group Murphy and Company, who were thrilled to be recording on a Charlie Rich album. Their performance gave me chills when it went down, and when I played it for Charlie that evening, he teared up. It was one of the great moments of my career. Charlie's simple direction had transformed the song from one of desperation to one of surrender—maybe a fine line, but one that perhaps summed up the entire album. Regrettably, we were not able to properly credit the singers in the record's liner notes, as they were not members of the American Federation of Television and Radio Artists, the vocalists' union, to which Warner Bros. was signatory. Instead, they were paid directly, and I listed their names in the thank-you section of the liner notes.

We had our album. As Charlie's trust and comfort with the musicians, the studio environment, and me had grown, the sessions had become more productive. I took the tapes to New Orleans and did a few more overdubs, adding the brilliant gospel organist Sammy Berfect to "Feel Like Going Home." On "Somebody Broke into My Heart," I added Bill Samuel's horn section, and I asked my friend Lee Allen Zeno to think about a new bass part. The groove he came up with finally gave the track the propulsion it needed. We kept moving it closer to the dry, in-your-face Hi Records vibe that Joe was seeking, and I think we came close in the final mix session, with engineer Tina Hanson, although I was never happy with the way the track sped up.

I mixed the record with engineers Mark Wessel and Tina Hanson at Blue Jay Studio near Boston. The album hung together well in spite of the varied song styles, because you can feel the heart of each song in Charlie's vocals. It was a rare opportunity to be able work with such a pure artist, and perhaps the patience I had learned in sessions with James Booker and others helped to nurture the right moments for the songs to happen. *Pictures and Paintings* was Charlie's final record, and I think he may have revealed more of himself than ever before.

Charlie died of a pulmonary embolism in 1995 at the age of sixty-two, in a hotel room in Louisiana. He and Margaret Ann were on their way to Florida after having heard their son Allan perform at a casino in Natchez, Mississippi. I was lucky to be with him for the last chapter of his career, and to have been a part of the realization of Peter's vision of exploratory freedom for Charlie.

RECOMMENDED LISTENING:

"Pictures and Paintings" and "Feel Like Going Home" from *Pictures and Paintings*

Chapter 12

BEAU JOCQUE

MY CHEAP RENTAL CAR BEGAN TO SHUDDER AS IT REACHED EIGHTY-FIVE miles per hour. I was trying to keep up with Beau Jocque's van and trailer on the old two-lane concrete causeway that crosses the Atchafalaya Basin between Opelousas and Baton Rouge. We were bound for New Orleans to record his first album. As I was beginning to learn, nothing could be fast enough or big enough for Beau Jocque, neither his cars nor his sound system nor his dreams. He was embarking on a seven-year ride that would take him to the top of the Louisiana/Texas zydeco scene; to the pages of *Spin* and *Rolling Stone*; to the David Letterman and Conan O'Brien television shows; and finally, to an untimely death.

I had sought out Beau Jocque on the recommendation of Kermon Richard, who owned and managed the venerable Richard's Club, the wooden dance hall in Lawtell, Louisiana, that was a pivotal gig for every important zydeco musician. (In 2017, after Kermon's death, and after the club had been sold and renamed Miller's Zydeco Hall of Fame, it was burned down in an act of arson by a rival nightclub owner in Opelousas.) In 1987, I had produced the two-volume *Zydeco Live!* set at the club, with Boozoo Chavis and the Magic Sounds, Nathan and the Zydeco Cha Chas, John Delafose and the Eunice Playboys, and Willis Prudhomme and the Zydeco Express.

Kermon and I became friends, and each time I visited, I was proud to see Rick Olivier's photo of Kermon, Boozoo, and me on the wall behind the bar. In late 1992, he called to say, "Man, you've got to make a record with Beau Jocque, because he's hot as a firecracker." In Kermon's opinion, Beau Jocque would become the most popular zydeco entertainer yet. It was one of the best tips of my career.

On the phone, Beau Jocque was soft-spoken and polite, with a warm
Creole accent, but at the dark and run-down Quarterback Lounge in
Lafayette, there was something both exciting and ominous about the way he
goaded his band members to shout back at him. He pushed and pulled the
double bellows of his single-row button accordion harder and harder with
each repeated riff. At six foot six, with the build of a professional wrestler,
he made the accordion seem like a toy that he was about to tear to pieces.
He sang with the gruffness and intensity of the blues singer Howlin' Wolf,
while the band held down a groove that was more akin to James Brown
than Boozoo Chavis, the older musician who had been a major influence
on Beau Jocque's accordion style.

I immediately understood why Kermon had felt compelled to call me,
for it struck me that behind Beau Jocque's mighty nouveau zydeco dance
beat was a deep and complex soul. As the lyrics of old Cajun and Creole
two-steps and waltzes often tell of tragedy, death, and heartbreak, the air
of menace that hovered over his good-time Louisiana music made for a
potent combination. I had never heard anything like it.

Beau Jocque was the stage name of Andrus Espre, born on November
1, 1953, in French-speaking Duralde, Louisiana, in the heart of the Cajun
Prairie near Eunice. He was a true Louisiana Creole, with Native American
(Coushatta), German, and African American heritage. Among other musicians native to the area was the accordionist Amédé Ardoin, who made
the first Louisiana Creole recordings in 1929, and who helped to create a
recorded template for much of the French Creole and Cajun music to follow.

Beau Jocque's father, Sandrus Espre, played music in the style of Amédé.
Sandrus had performed house dances as a young man but had given up
music for a life of farming. Several times, I visited the tidy and comfortable
wooden home where Beau Jocque had grown up. Once, when I brought
a film crew to Duralde to document Beau Jocque's traditional roots for a
CD-ROM project I was producing, his father took his accordion down
from the shelf and played it beautifully, in an old-fashioned way, while
Beau Jocque accompanied him on the 'tit fer, or triangle. Creole music that
reached back to its earliest days was Beau Jocque's birthright.

Young Andrus enjoyed a boyhood of country pastimes, exploring on
his bicycle the fields, rivers, and small stands of forest near his home. He
also showed an early aptitude for music, playing trombone and guitar in
high school, and singing for his friends. It was then that he acquired the

nickname "Beau Jocque," which stood for, as he liked to recall with a grin, "big handsome guy."

Yet, there would be trying times before the emergence of the zydeco star called Beau Jocque. After high school, Andrus enlisted in the Air Force and became a member of the Elite Forces stationed in Germany and England. But something terrible happened to him there, something he would only talk about in vague terms. As I understood the story, in a secret operation, a man or men were killed, and only Andrus survived. He returned to the family home in Duralde after receiving a medical discharge.

Andrus's first post-military job was as a police officer in Eunice, but he found he could earn more money as a welder, first with the Miller Company and then with Tennessee Gas in Basile. But catastrophe struck again when a transformer exploded and knocked him from a twenty-five-foot tower. He landed on concrete and broke his back. The doctors removed three vertebrae and fused together several others, telling the paralyzed Andrus that it was unlikely that he would walk again. One year later, he got up. As his widow Michelle "Shelly" Espre recalls, "He just forced himself to get on his feet, using a walker. He endured great pain." The pain would stay with him for the remainder of his life.

It was during this time, in the mid-1980s, that Andrus began playing his father's single-row, button accordion. "That's a serious instrument," Sandrus told him, "and you'll never be able to figure it out." In fact, the elder Espre knew that his son would take these words as a challenge, and Andrus used his long convalescence to master his father's traditional style and songs. After he was released from his doctor's care, be bought a home and his first accordion with the settlement money he received from Tennessee Gas.

He put together a band, Andrus Espre and the Straights, and began playing at local dances, but he could not get the sound he was looking for. He and Shelly began following popular bands such as Boozoo Chavis and the Magic Sounds, and Zydeco Force, carefully noting the songs and the grooves that got people excited and onto the dance floor. He also considered the popular music he had listened to as a teenager. He assembled a new band and took tentative steps toward combining the deep Creole music learned from his father with the funk, rock, and blues sounds of ZZ Top, War, and Santana. Shelly suggested that he change his stage name to Beau Jocque. Andrus Espre was about to reemerge as the character and entertainer he and Shelly imagined, and he knew he would succeed. He was soon good enough to record an album, *My Name Is Beau Jocque*, for a small local label.

It was about that time, in 1992, that Kermon Richard introduced us. Beau Jocque was enthusiastic about recording for a label with national distribution, and, after we met in Lafayette, he signed a two-album contract. For someone who, as I would learn, was often suspicious of others, he was ready to give me his signature, document unread.

"Beau Jocque, it would be better if you read this before signing it," I advised him.

"Oh, I trust you," he said.

"No, really. I'm going to read it to you."

So, we sat at his kitchen table where I read aloud every word. When he asked about the royalty rate, I said I would ask the Rounder legal team if it could be increased by a percentage point or two. He also had questions about the artist price for CDs that he would buy to sell at gigs. Satisfied, he signed the revised contract a couple of days later, with a slightly higher royalty.

Beau Jocque had put together one of the best Louisiana bands of the 1990s, including the rhythm section that would remain with him for all six albums we made together. Bass player Chuck Bush, a veteran of funk and Top 40 bands, was the band's crucial musician, as he created thundering, fluid lines for each song that were unlike anything heard before in zydeco. Given the repetitive nature of the zydeco dance beat, it was Chuck's bass lines that gave each song its signature identity. Drummer Steve "Skeeta" Charlot was only eighteen years old when he joined the Zydeco Hi-Rollers. With Beau Jocque, he popularized the relentless "double kicked" beat that remains the foundation of much zydeco music to this day.

We rehearsed at Richard's Club. In his carefully considered way, Beau Jocque had not only made a list of the songs he wanted to record, but also the order in which he wanted to record them. But there was nothing careful or contrived when the tape started rolling at Ultrasonic Studio in New Orleans, for Beau Jocque gave himself completely to the moment and the music. When he launched into "Richard's Club," engineer David Farrell turned to me and said, "I've never heard zydeco that sounds like that before!"

With Ray Johnson, the first in a line of fine Hi-Rollers guitar players, and rubboard player Wilfred "Caveman" Pierre, the band laid down fourteen tracks in less than eight hours. I cannot remember a more exciting day in

Beau Jocque at Richard's Club. *Left to right:* Wilfred "Caveman" Pierre, Beau Jocque, Ray Johnson (photograph © Rick Olivier).

the recording studio. Skeeta punctuated Beau Jocque's deeply felt baritone vocals with his trademark yelping asides. Shelly danced in the control room, because she was her husband's biggest fan and the music moved her. In fact, on later sessions, I would notice if she was dancing or not, because if she was not, we did not yet have a take. I asked Chuck and Ray to overdub additional background vocals and shouts, as I had heard them do in performance, and I played a New Orleans street-beat cowbell, which I had learned from working with the Dirty Dozen Brass Band, on "Give Him Cornbread." Otherwise, the album was recorded live in the studio.

As we had done on previous zydeco records, we recorded the accordion acoustically, with a pair of microphones set up in Beau Jocque's isolation booth, in addition to the pickup (or small microphone) that was built into the accordion, which had a thin and wheezy sound. I have never understood why so many records feature only the sound from accordion pickups. David mixed the album with a huge low-end sound, which Beau Jocque later appreciated: when a car with a hopped-up sound system passed his house, playing the record, he boasted, "We made that pavement shake!"

The album, *Beau Jocque Boogie*, was released in the summer of 1993. It includes Beau's original zydeco dance songs, the slow blues "Brownskin Woman," and songs learned from his father and Creole tradition, but it was

"Give Him Cornbread," his reworking of the old "Shortnin' Bread" melody, that set the zydeco scene on fire. By the time of the Labor Day weekend Southwest Louisiana Zydeco Music Festival in Plaisance, the song was inescapable, blaring forth from every boom box and car radio in Creole Louisiana and Texas. During his set at the festival, women pelted the stage with cornbread they had baked for the occasion. We had a genuine local hit on our hands, so much so that bootleggers were selling burned copies of the CD from their car trunks in parking lots outside his shows.

Later that month, the film maker Robert Mugge was in Louisiana working on two films: *True Believers*, the story of Rounder Records, in preparation for the label's twenty-fifth anniversary, and *The Kingdom of Zydeco*, which documents the rivalry between Beau Jocque and his mentor Boozoo Chavis, as well as Boozoo's coronation as the new King of Zydeco (a title invented for zydeco pioneer Clifton Chenier, who had died in 1987). Their competition came to a head when musician and promoter Lawrence Ardoin (the nephew of Amédé) staged a battle of the bands at the Habibi Temple in Lake Charles, with fourteen hundred fans in attendance. If the contest was unofficially declared a draw, and if the musicians' sparring was more like that of two professional wrestlers, the film captures a remarkable event, with both bands (as well as young show-opener Chris Ardoin) performing at their best. In 2000, Beau Jocque's set from this show was released as *Give Him Cornbread, Live!*

It was a heady time because media opportunities kept growing, along with Beau Jocque's audience. He was opening large venue shows for Bobby Bland, Roger Troutman, and Tyrone Davis. At Richard's Club, parked cars lined Highway 190 for half a mile in each direction, and it was not uncommon for a thousand people to show up for a Beau Jocque dance. He was interviewed by Terry Gross on National Public Radio's *Fresh Air*. Things were moving so fast that we quickly returned to the studio, in October 1993, to record his second Rounder album, *Pick Up on This!*, which included a cover of War's "Low Rider Theme" and a ZZ Top–inspired version of John Lee Hooker's "Boogie Chillun." If the music borrowed heavily from funk and even rap (we hired a New Orleans DJ to add scratch sounds to "Give It to Me"), there was still no mistaking the deep and bluesy Creole roots of Beau Jocque's singing and accordion playing. Many of his compositions, such as the album's title track, start with little more than an accordion riff and a bass line, evolving into collective improvisation as Beau Jocque leads the band into variations that make his recordings more engaging than most dance records. Still, as his producer, I tried to balance his free-wheeling approach with a song-oriented awareness, often suggesting in preproduction that he add a bridge section to a song, or that he flesh out lyrics. We would occasionally write a song together, which he would suitably deconstruct in performance.

For Beau Jocque and Michelle, all their planning was paying off. They bought a sleek Ford Centurion truck to haul the band's equipment trailer, and a sound system that could knock down the walls of a small auditorium. Beau Jocque and the Zydeco Hi-Rollers were now the most popular band on the zydeco circuit. Yet, just as his performances could be terrifying in their single-minded intensity, he seldom seemed at rest with himself, and his humor could carry a malicious bite. If he could joke lightly with his band members as they traveled together to a dance, he could also taunt them when it came time to pay them at the end of the night. His eyes would take on a dark and suspicious cast that seemed to be straining to see something that was not there, as if he was trying to visualize his next move while worrying that someone would cheat him out of what he had achieved. He could also become irrationally jealous if he saw another man looking at Shelly, as I observed at a Christmas dance in Port Arthur when his silent rage seemed ready to explode as he loaded the equipment trailer. These dark moments seemed to pass quickly, but there was a threatening part of Beau Jocque's personality that I never was able to decipher.

Hoping to expand his audience beyond his home base, he signed with David Gaar's Sin Fronteras booking agency. He made his first trip to the West Coast, playing at the San Francisco Jazz Festival and the Ojai Blues Festival, followed by a July 1994 trip to England. The author Michael Tisserand, who would write about Beau Jocque extensively in his *Kingdom of Zydeco* book, signed on as his tour manager, and generally enjoyed the trip.

Between recording contracts, Beau Jocque decided to try his own hand at the record business, when he produced a four-song EP, *Beau Jocque's Nursery Rhyme* (which is not a children's record). With limited local distribution and sales, the release may have proven to be more work than it was worth. So, with a new appreciation for the art of selling records, he re-signed with Rounder that summer for three more albums. In September, we brought in the highly regarded Big Mo recording truck to make a live album at Slim's Y-Ki-Ki Lounge in Opelousas, and at Harry's Club in Breaux Bridge.

Beau Jocque, Michelle Espre, and Scott Billington at South by Southwest, Austin, Texas, 1996
(photograph © Scott Billington)

The media were still paying attention. In an exceptional acknowledge-
ment of a roots music act, *Spin* magazine gave him a full-page photo feature. In June, the band played "Give Him Cornbread" on the Conan O'Brien
show, a remarkable showcase that Beau Jocque was tempted to skip when
an offer of a big-paying gig in Texas came in. I was on the phone with him
at midnight, the day before his scheduled departure. All the air tickets and
travel logistics were in place.

"Scott, can we make the trip to New York some other time?" he asked.
"If we go tomorrow, I'm gonna miss a $10,000 show."

"Beau Jocque, I would not advise that you do that," I replied. "This is a
once-in-a-career opportunity that you can't afford to miss. It's a huge break."

Finally, he agreed, and the band made it to the New Orleans airport on
time the next morning. I met them in New York. Their performance was a
smashing success—probably the most visceral late-night television musical presentation that year, because they played with the energy of a night
at Richard's. Afterward, we had drinks at the Rainbow Room at the top of
Rockefeller Plaza, where Beau Jocque was courted by a disingenuous New
York publicist who read the ambition in his eyes and told him he could
have the world—that he could open for the Rolling Stones.

By 1996, the personnel of the Hi-Rollers included the talented Russell "Sly" Dorian, who specialized in talk-box guitar, and keyboard player Mike Lockett, whose brilliant Hammond organ work and synthesizer textures brought a more sophisticated musical sensibility to the band. In Austin, Texas, they played to an overflow crowd outside the Driskill Hotel for Rounder's block party at the South by Southwest festival, between sets by Johnny Adams and Irma Thomas.

A month later, we were back at Ultrasonic Studio to cut *Gonna Take You Downtown*. From my perspective, this is Beau Jocque's most satisfying album, with its varied songs, tempos, and grooves. In particular, the interplay between Mike's keyboards and Beau's accordions, including his new five-row Gabbanelli, made for an album that was as listenable from beginning to end as it was danceable. Engineer Steve Reynolds and I had also begun using recording studio technology as a bigger part of the creative process, especially as we realized that the new Pro Tools software could be used as a compositional tool, in addition to the flexibility it offered in editing, and in automating effects such as echo and distortion. Our experiments yielded "Make It Stank," with its drum samples, loops, and off-into-space sounds, again combining old and new. Beau Jocque loved it.

Yet the chemistry that made this album so special almost did not happen. When the band arrived at the studio, Steve "Skeeta" Charlot was nowhere to be seen. Instead, Beau Jocque had brought the excellent drummer Erick Minix. It turned out that Beau and Skeeta had argued, initially about the repossession of a living room suite that Skeeta had bought for his mother. Beau Jocque was not pleased and had fired Skeeta. We set up and began rolling tape, starting with the song "Just One Kiss." Beau Jocque liked to begin his songs by playing the song's signature accordion riff, and then to gradually accelerate the tempo as the band kicked in, like a jumbo jet careening down the runway before becoming airborne. But this time, the jet did not take off. Shelly was sitting behind me, and I could see her reflection in the studio control room glass. She was neither dancing nor smiling. It was not Erick's fault, because he was probably a better all-around drummer than Skeeta, but the energy and chemistry were missing. We tried a few more takes, but it did not get any better.

Beau, Shelly, and I conferred. At first, he was unwilling to budge. Skeeta's transgressions, whatever they had grown to be, were cause for a permanent separation. Yet, he knew even better than the rest of us that the music we were recording was not the sound he wanted, and he knew how important this album was. Eventually, Shelly and I prevailed, partly by advocating that he view his relationship with Skeeta as strictly professional. After three or four hours, Skeeta showed up, and, within minutes, he and Beau Jocque had resumed their good-natured verbal sparring and joking. The sessions resumed with full intensity, and Erick was still able to play on Beau's cover of Bob Dylan's "Knockin' on Heaven's Door." It was the variety that made this our most successful album, with dance hall numbers such as the title track, a sparkling version of War's "Cisco Kid," and a rocked-out version of the D. L. Menard Cajun standard "The Back Door" (sung in French).

Beau Jocque then signed with the large Monterrey Peninsula booking agency in Chicago and was performing on the road as often as at home, playing major festivals and traveling as far away as Guam. He pushed himself ever harder, with little regard for his once-broken body. At an employee Christmas party at a Texas chemical plant, I saw him lift a speaker cabinet that should have taken two men to carry. And he was putting on more weight. His older brother had died of cardiac arrest only a few years earlier, while still in his forties.

That fall, the Hi-Rollers embarked on the national Louisiana Red Hot Music Tour, sharing the bill with Marcia Ball, and Steve Riley and the Mamou Playboys, celebrating the twenty-fifth anniversary of Rounder Records. The itinerary would take them to most major US cities, and to audiences that sometimes expected something more traditional. In the *Chicago Tribune*, Brad Webber wrote that their set was "slightly off the evening's folk theme. Maybe that's because the group . . . is hard at work inventing its own hybrid of hard rock, blues and zydeco." Yet, "Beau Jocque worked his accordion's bellows like a steelworker raking molten metal."

Then, in Austin, Texas, after a long outdoor set in hundred-degree heat, Beau Jocque suffered a heart attack and was hospitalized. A stent was installed to open a blocked artery, and Geno Delafose was called to complete the tour.

I met Beau Jocque and Shelly at their home in Kinder when they returned from Texas. News that he was dead had been erroneously broadcast on several local radio stations, and word had spread quickly around town, so our trip to the supermarket to shop for dinner was a surreal experience. I had brought them a copy of Paul Prudhomme's cookbook *A Fork in the Road*, in which the great chef had modified many south

Louisiana dishes to be healthier. I had also volunteered to prepare dinner for them—greens and a brown rice jambalaya with shrimp and turkey tasso. The mayor rushed down the produce aisle to shake Beau Jocque's hand, while some shoppers just stared as if seeing a ghost.

"Beau Jocque!" he exclaimed. "We thought you was dead!"

Beau Jocque loved stories about superstition and magic. Once, when Michael Tisserand and I were visiting him at his parents' home in Duralde, he told of a haunted forest where old Creole men gathered and told stories, and he promised to take Michael there to gather stories for his book. When Skeeta and Chuck teased him with "Damballah," a chant from the *Child's Play* horror movie series and also the name of an actual Voodoo deity, he made it into a song to show that he was not afraid. Perhaps Beau Jocque enjoyed the idea of returning home as a ghost, even as he downplayed his heart attack. He had looked death in the eye enough times that he was not afraid, although I think he was acutely aware of his mortality. Perhaps this was the source of his driven personality, and his refusal to hold back in any way.

He began getting regular medical checkups, bought an exercise treadmill, and vowed to adhere to a better diet, but he did not slow down for a moment. He began playing regularly at the Rock 'n' Bowl in New Orleans, where Mick Jagger and his entourage showed up one night to see his show. When the ticket seller made them pay to get in, they had to scramble to find cash. He also traveled frequently to Houston, where the zydeco scene was rivaling that of southwest Louisiana, and he made an East Coast tour. His back was hurting him fiercely, and he now often played sitting down, but his music was uncompromised. At a Rock 'n' Bowl gig, he so impressed the producers of *The Late Show with David Letterman* that he was booked to perform on the program, when the producers brought an entire Louisiana audience to New York for a Louisiana-themed show.

Beau Jocque had the ability to create music on the spot. You can hear this on his first live album, where he makes a song out of an announcement telling a patron at Slim's that they needed to move their car. He would throw ideas back and forth with Chuck or Mike or Sly, always hitting each lick with clarity, always playing the spaces as well as the notes, always making it groove. Chuck, in particular, was his musical equal. Recording engineer Steve Reynolds comments, "Chuck Bush remains one of my favorite bass players, both in terms of sound and pocket. To my ears, he's right up there with Jaco Pastorius."

In 1998, we returned to the studio one more time for the album *Check It Out, Lock It In, Crank It Up!* Skeeta had been in and out of the band for the past year, and he almost did not make it to the sessions, but the diligent and now seasoned drummer Erick Minix was again on hand, and lent a contrasting touch to several songs, including the spacious groove on the slow blues "Going to the Country." Steve and I again experimented with sampling technology, creating two different versions of "Slide and Dip It," this time with Beau Jocque's full participation, as each musician created his own samples. The band continued to evolve, especially as Beau Jocque found jazzy chord voicings on his triple-row and five-row accordions, but songs such as "Come Go with Me" (with a riff borrowed from the young accordionist Chris Ardoin) and "Like a Pot of Neckbones" were as rollicking and down-home as anything he had ever recorded. For the album cover, I hired comics illustrator Don Simpson to depict Beau Jocque as a superhero, soaring through space at the controls of a massive spaceship/accordion.

With his Rounder contract fulfilled, Beau Jocque decided to try his luck with the New Orleans–based Mardi Gras Records, hoping that a change in label would result in new opportunities. His *Zydeco Giant* album featured the new two-guitar lineup that had become part of the Hi-Rollers sound, and the album was a local success, but in the summer of 1999, he re-signed with Rounder for two more albums.

Sadly, there would be no more recordings. On September 8, 1999, after driving home from a gig at the Rock 'n' Bowl and sleeping through the night, Beau Jocque had another heart attack and died while taking a shower the next morning. He was forty-six years old.

It is not a stretch to say that Beau Jocque invented the contemporary zydeco sound, just as he fearlessly reinvented himself, overcoming adversity with presence, courage, vision, and will. Like many other great figures in American music, he lifted his genre to a place where it had not been before, and his many imitators could not touch him. I'm glad I was along for the ride.

RECOMMENDED LISTENING:

"Give Him Cornbread" from *Beau Jocque Boogie*
"Gonna Take You Downtown" from *Gonna Take You Downtown*
"Going to the Country" from *Check It Out, Lock It In, Crank It Up!*

Chapter 13

RUTH BROWN

IT WAS A COOL FEBRUARY MORNING, AND WE WERE DRIVING THROUGH the last of the flat and fallow brown fields of the Mississippi Delta, heading up into hills near Yazoo City, where we could see the skeletons of the dormant kudzu vines that would again blanket the landscape once warmer weather arrived. In the van with me were singer Ruth Brown; her keyboard player and musical director, Bobby Forrester; and her two sons, Ron Jackson and Earl Swanson.

The evening before, at a casino along the Mississippi River in Greenville, Mississippi, Brown had performed before an audience of mostly older and elegantly dressed fans who remembered her as the biggest rhythm and blues star of the early 1950s. She put on a show that had everyone dancing in their seats, and if her voice was now grainier than on her early hit records, her timing, wit, and charismatic sass left no doubt that she remained a singer and entertainer of undiminished power.

We were on our way to New Orleans, where we would record her debut album for Rounder Records.

"You know," said Ms. Brown as we left the Delta, "We're about to leave spiritual territory and head into gospel country."

I thought for a few moments and asked, "What do you mean by that, Ms. B?"

"Well," she said, "When our people had no way out of this place, all we could sing about was the next life—crossing that River Jordan. Once we got out, we could celebrate life in the here and now. That's when we could sing gospel music."

She bore the scars of a segregated America with a keen sense of history and place. She had been one of the biggest stars on the Chitlin' Circuit,

Scott Billington and Ruth Brown at Ultrasonic Studio, 1997 (photograph © Barbara Roberds)

when her music, her style, and her ebullient personality were a beacon for her African American audiences, to whom she exemplified dignity and a measure of elegance in the face of indignities suffered each day. Yet, she bore this legacy with no bitterness.

It was that kind of perspective that Ruth Brown brought to her music: an occasionally world-weary acquaintance with the hardships and travails of life, coupled with the determination and resilience not only to get on with it, but to savor every moment of joy. On her later recordings on the Fantasy and Rounder/Bullseye Blues labels, on songs such as "Too Little, Too Late" or "A Good Day for the Blues," she brought grace to music about sadness and heartache, finding a universal truth that still resonated with her audiences. In songs such as the double-entendre "If I Can't Sell It, I'll Keep Sittin' On It," she carried forth a tradition of humor and stagecraft that endeared her to her fans as a complete entertainer.

In the early 1950s, Brown was the first recording star for Atlantic Records, which has sometimes been called "the house that Ruth built." In those days, the biggest challenge for an independent record label was getting paid by distributors, who were notorious for not paying bills until a label generated a new hit record that they needed. Brown's string of hits, including "Teardrops from My Eyes," "5-10-15 Hours," and "Mama He Treats Your Daughter Mean," meant the distributors had to keep paying Atlantic. She toured almost nonstop for nearly a decade, sidetracked once by a serious car accident. Her final minor pop hit was "Lucky Lips" in 1957.

The 1960s were lean years for Brown, as musical tastes veered toward a funkier sound, but she found her way back into show business, this time as an actress, in the 1970s, on television's *Sanford and Son*, and in the John Waters film *Hairspray*. She starred in Allen Toussaint's musical *Staggerlee*, and in Broadway's *Black and Blue*, for which she won a Tony award for Best Actress in a Musical as well as her first Grammy award, in 1989, for the related album, *Blues on Broadway*. She became the host of the National Public Radio program *Blues Stage*.

Concurrently, she and attorney Howell Begle began petitioning record companies to institute a standard royalty for legacy rhythm and blues artists, which led to the establishment of the Rhythm and Blues Foundation. Seed money from Ahmet Ertegun of Atlantic Records meant the foundation could provide financial support to artists from the golden era of R&B who had fallen on difficult times.

For much of the remainder of our trip from Mississippi to New Orleans, Ruth told us stories about the triumphs and challenges of touring in the South in the 1950s: about the camaraderie of the musicians; about the long drives after shows, when no hotel would take them; and about having to go to the back doors of restaurants to be served. When we stopped for lunch at a barbeque joint outside Jackson, Mississippi, she was initially hesitant to go inside, but then quickly relaxed when she realized that we were all welcome. She mused that perhaps some things had changed, at least on the surface.

It was a crazy time to make a record in New Orleans, because Mardi Gras was underway, and few hotel rooms were available. Through David Torkanowsky's acquaintance with the hotelier and fellow record producer Bubby Valentino, we found rooms for Ms. B and her crew at one of his comfortable French Quarter hotels, but that meant driving through crowds each day to get her to and from Ultrasonic Studio, located on the edge of the Gert Town neighborhood a few miles away.

On the day of our first recording sessions, we arrived to find the eleven-piece band I had assembled setting up in the studio, while engineer David Farrell was fine-tuning sounds and mic placements with drummer Herlin Riley. A great deal of preparation had gone into the sessions, and I had my fingers crossed that everything would click.

About two months beforehand, I had met with Ms. B and pianist Dave Keyes at a small rehearsal studio in New York, bringing with me cassette tapes of songs and song demos that I thought might be good for her. She brought Ketty Lester's "Love Letters" and the old Brenda Lee hit "Break It to Me Gently." She was excited about many of the songs I had found, including the Los Lobos song "That Train Don't Stop Here" and the new Dennis Walker/Alan Mirikitani composition "Too Little, Too Late." We worked on keys and tempos that suited her and made on-the-spot piano and voice recordings.

My next step was to get together with arrangers Wardell Quezergue and Victor Goines in New Orleans, bringing them our new demos. After discussion about the overall shape of each song, they went to work writing arrangements and hand copying charts for each musician in the band.

Early in the preproduction process, I decided that I wanted Herlin, one of the great drummers in New Orleans today, to be one of the key musicians on the session. At the time, he was playing with the Lincoln Center Jazz Orchestra, following an earlier stint with the pianist Ahmad Jamal. Herlin carries himself like a prince, and I knew that his elegance and class would set the right tone for the rest of the band. I had worked with him briefly on a few tracks for David Torkanowsky's solo record, *Steppin' Out*, but I did not know him well. So I called and told Herlin what I could pay him (which was exactly the same as every other person in the band, a practice that I have never deviated from). It was neither an insubstantial amount of money, nor was it extravagant.

"Well, that sounds interesting. Would you be willing to come out to my place to discuss the project?" was his reply.

I drove out to his airy, ranch-style home in New Orleans East, the newer neighborhood to which many New Orleanians had fled from the dereliction and crime of the inner part of the city in the 1970s and '80s.

He invited me in and offered me a drink of water.

"Do you play pool?" he asked.

"Well, I used to be pretty good at it when I was a kid. I played every afternoon at the YMCA, after school," I replied.

"Do you have time for a game?"

While we talked about the sessions—the other musicians, Ms. B, and the charts that Wardell and Victor would provide—we played two games, with each of us winning a round.

"OK, I'll play on your album," he said, and we shook hands.

Although I tried not to show it, I was nervous when Ruth stepped up to the microphone for the first song, "That Train Don't Stop Here." The band had just run through the chart, and I could see at least a small spark of excitement behind Ms. B's cool "let's see if these guys are really going to deliver" wariness. Then, as much like a professional athlete as a musician, she stepped up to the microphone and delivered the vocal that you hear on the record, with the band playing live behind her, complete with the ad-libbed "rap" at the end of the song (". . . soul train, Coltrane, night train . . ."). When she came back into the control room, she was glowing. "Baby, we're gonna have a good time," she said to me, and we were off and running. Her rapport with Herlin, who was in an adjoining recording booth to Ruth, separated only by a large glass window, was one of playful flirtation throughout the sessions, and I remember everyone laughing when we got each final take—always a sign that the music is happening. Hiring Herlin was the right call.

There are times when it makes sense to work by recording the rhythm section first, then adding other instruments, and finally overdubbing the singer at the end, but that was not what I wanted to do with Ruth Brown. Instead, we went for live-in-the-studio performances, always aiming for the moment when the spirit took over. We had the players to pull it off, in addition to Forrester and Riley: guitarist Duke Robillard, bassist James Singleton, and horn players Victor Goines, Barney Floyd, Charlie Miller, Delfeayo Marsalis, Wessell Anderson, and Ed Petersen. We did a few touchups after cutting each track—adding solos, fixing horn flubs—but what you hear on the record is music that, for the most part, happened in real time. The musicians were awed by Ms. B's improvisations and her ability to nail each song after only a take or two, and she responded with elan to their grooves. She stepped up to the microphone like a professional baseball player, ready to hit the ball out of the park. It is an attitude that I believe many younger singers would benefit from, because reliance on technology that allows the performance to be sung again (and again) can be more than a safety net, taking away the immediacy that a great singer can achieve.

We chose three wonderful guest artists to appear on the album. Clarence "Gatemouth" Brown, who had toured with Ruth in the 1950s, plays beautifully on Ivory Joe Hunter's "False Friend Blues." Ruth's duet with Johnny Adams on Willie Mabon's song "I Don't Know" (based on the boogie-woogie pianist Clarence Lofton's song of the same name) captures a wonderful chemistry, with Johnny playing straight man to Ruth's comedic come-ons.

Bonnie Raitt had become a great friend to Ms. B, taking her on the road as part of her show, along with pianist Charles Brown, for much of her 1995 touring. For their duet on "Outskirts of Town," we traveled to the Magic Shop in Manhattan to record, using Ruth's New York–based band: Forrester, drummer Akira Tana, guitarist Rodney Jones, and bassist Rufus Reid. There is a lot of love in the track, which features a beautiful slide guitar solo from Raitt. After the album's release, they would perform the song with the same band on the David Letterman show, where I was asked to help shorten the arrangement to three and a half minutes.

The resulting album, *R+B = Ruth Brown*, won a Grammy nomination the next year, and I was proud to be Ms. B's date for the ceremony. It is never easy to be with an artist when they do not win, but she took the loss in stride. She told me that she played the record over and over, enjoying it and reliving the sessions each time.

We made one more record together in New Orleans, in 1997, again for Rounder's Bullseye Blues imprint. Ms. B had a better idea of what to expect for *A Good Day for the Blues*, and she was enthusiastic as we began pre-production. This time, we would use more of her own band members, including tenor saxophonist Bill Easley (a soulful player from Memphis who would also write several arrangements for the album), drummer Akira Tana, keyboardist Bobby Forrester, and the talented twenty-five-year-old New Orleans–raised trumpet player Abram Wilson, with New Orleans players filling out the ensemble. Wardell Quezergue and Victor Goines were back as arrangers as well. For the first time, I worked exclusively with engineer Steve Reynolds, who had assisted on many other projects, and who had become David's partner at Ultrasonic.

I wanted to be more adventurous with the choice songs this time. If we were writing a new chapter in Ruth Brown's career, we both felt we should give her something new to say. My friend Joel Dorn, the producer who was responsible for many of the great jazz and R&B releases of the 1960s and '70s, especially at Atlantic Records (Les McCann and Eddie Harris's *Swiss Movement*, Roberta Flack's catalog, and the Allman Brothers), once told me that he most enjoyed working with artists either at the beginning or at the end of their careers, because that was when they had the most to say, and had something at stake. I believe that Ms. B had something new and important to communicate, a summation of a rich life that she could not have expressed at any other time.

I reached out my songwriting and publishing friends. Perhaps the track with the best story is the humorous Dan Penn/Bucky Lindsey/Carson Whitsett song, "I Can't Stand No Broke Man." The trio had made a trip to St. Francisville, Louisiana, a quiet and picturesque town that had become their songwriting retreat. When they stopped at a gas station, they spotted a woman with those words printed on her T-shirt, and they quickly wrote the song. It was perfect for Ms. B.

The album's title track, by Bucky Lindsey and Ricky Ray Rector, was written from a male perspective, but when we flipped genders, it worked even better. I received "H. B.'s Funky Fable" from Homer Brown, the tenor saxophonist I had met through Clarence "Gatemouth" Brown. This recitation gave Ms. B a quirky and clever vehicle for her theatrical skills. She had been performing R. Kelly's "I Believe I Can Fly" in her shows. I worried about it getting too sappy, but Victor Goines's chart and Davell Crawford's churchy Hammond organ kept it grounded, and she sang it with great power and conviction.

Her interpretation of the elegant Johnny Ace blues ballad "Never Let Me Go" recalls an earlier time, when blues and jazz came together after donning evening wear, with Wardell's gorgeous chart framing a perfectly delivered vocal. The sound is warm and enveloping, recorded to twenty-four-track analog tape.

In fact, this would be one of the last analog sessions I would conduct, as digital recording was both improving (when the twenty-four-bit sample rate was introduced) and becoming the more affordable standard. I am not an analog purist, especially because today's higher-resolution digital technology captures a broader range of frequencies, and because of the ease of editing and manipulating sounds and arrangements. However, I believe that the limitations of analog—especially the necessity of confining all the sounds to twenty-four tracks—can be a great asset, because it demands commitment. When a musician fills dozens of digital tracks with variations of the same vocal or instrumental solo, the editing process becomes a nightmare, and the oft-times Frankenstein construction project that ensues may result in a track so "perfect" that the spirit and life of the performance are lost.

And, yes, analog sound is warmer, I believe largely because of the gentle compression effect that occurs when the tape is slightly oversaturated with sound levels. The rough sonic edges are smoothed over, and the instruments seem to sit better in a common space. It is an effect. Even today, whenever I have the option, I will add a mix stage to half-inch analog tape, specifically to achieve that effect, before copying the mix back into the digital realm.

After the sessions, Abram Wilson's family invited Ruth, Steve, and me to dinner at their home in Marrero, Louisiana, outside of New Orleans. They were proud of their son, and clearly moved by the presence of Ms. B. It was as if Queen Elizabeth had entered their home, especially because Ms. B could not have been more regal or charming. I realized that afternoon, more than ever, what Ruth Brown meant to the older generation that knew her best, for whom she represented grace and pride, and we all recognized that there was royalty in the house. Tragically, Abram Wilson would die of cancer before reaching his fortieth birthday.

A Good Day for the Blues, the final album of Ruth Brown's career, won a Grammy nomination, and she added many of the songs to her live set. She continued performing for several more years, even as health problems were slowing her down, and she stayed at the top of her game until the end. In 2016, ten years after her death, she was awarded her second Grammy as the recipient of a Lifetime Achievement Award from the Recording Academy.

Ruth Brown was an artist and entertainer of the first rank, a singer who communicated joy and heartache in a way that allowed her audiences to celebrate their own lives through her music. She never second-guessed herself. She sang blues, jazz, R&B, and pop music with equal aplomb, but no matter what the song, the kind of in-the-moment emotion and engagement she consistently delivered is something that cannot be manufactured by tweaking and overdubbing in the recording studio, and it is a palpable presence on record. I learned from her that there is no substitute for that kind of talent, and, indeed, how rare that kind of talent is.

RECOMMENDED LISTENING:

"Too Little, Too Late" and "That Train Don't Stop Here" from *R+B = Ruth Brown*
"A Good Day for the Blues" from *A Good Day for the Blues*

Chapter 14

BOOZOO CHAVIS

WHEN WILSON ANTHONY "BOOZOO" CHAVIS DIED ON MAY 5, 2001, AT THE age of seventy, the world lost not only a wonderful and quirky musician, but a link to a way of life that today can only be imagined in Boozoo's Dog Hill neighborhood, on the rural outskirts of Lake Charles, Louisiana. Boozoo's reemergence as a musician in 1984, after twenty-five years spent training racehorses, reignited the Creole dance hall scene in Louisiana and east Texas, and his influence on contemporary zydeco, even thirty-five years later, remains pervasive.

Boozoo was a fireplug of a man who spoke in clipped, rapid-fire sentences. He was often outwardly stubborn and cantankerous, but once he made a friend (and he had many), he was unfailingly generous. With a can of Budweiser in one hand and a cigarette in the other, he would hold forth with his fans, conveying his pride in his Creole heritage, his family, and the deep roots of the songs he played. He was beloved by all.

When I first heard Boozoo's music, I did not understand it. His 1954 track "Paper in My Shoe" is generally regarded as the first modern zydeco recording, the result of Lake Charles record man Eddie Shuler's decision to pair Boozoo in the studio with a popular local rhythm and blues band led by guitarist Classie Ballou. Shuler claimed in several interviews that they spent days in the studio, waiting for the music to come together, and that on the final take of "Paper in My Shoe," Boozoo was drunk enough to fall off his stool, playing all the while. Boozoo told me that this was all nonsense. What is clear, however, is that Boozoo and the band are playing in different keys.

The bilingual "Paper in My Shoe" is one of the most unlikely hit records ever. The song itself, about folding paper inside your shoes to keep the dust

Boozoo Chavis at his stables at Dog Hill in Lake Charles, Louisiana (photograph © Rick Olivier)

and rain from entering through the holes in the soles, predated Boozoo, who told author Michael Tisserand that he learned it from Ambrose "Potato" Sam. Released originally on Shuler's Folk Star label, by Boozoo Chavis and His Orchestra, it was subsequently licensed and distributed by the national Imperial label. In spite of its strange tonality, Boozoo's signature dance groove is present, and the record reputedly sold over one hundred thousand copies. Many years later, its anarchic nature was compelling enough to draw the attention of Terry Adams, the leader of the rock group NRBQ, who would produce Boozoo for the Nonesuch, Antone's, and Rounder labels.

Clifton Chenier, widely acknowledged as the King of Zydeco, made his first record in Lake Charles the same year, but "Cliston's Blues" [*sic*] is a conventional if impassioned blues performance, sung in English, with his accordion accompaniment and a solid backing band. Boozoo's record was something else, with few references in popular music, hearkening back to the earlier and likewise otherworldly sound of accordionist Amédé Ardoin, the first Creole accordionist to record.

In fact, Boozoo and Clifton founded the two schools of zydeco that thrive to this day. Boozoo played the diatonic button accordion, with an emphasis on songs rooted in folk tradition, and with a rough, rural sensibility. In southwest Louisiana today, the pumping sound of this smaller accordion is favored by dancers who follow Chris Ardoin, J. Paul Jr., Keith Frank, and Rosie Ledet. Clifton played the larger and more versatile piano accordion, a sound carried forth by his son C. J., as well as Nathan Williams Sr., Nathan Williams Jr., and Buckwheat Zydeco. Clifton often characterized himself as a bluesman, while covering songs by artists as diverse as Ray Charles, Glenn Miller, and Professor Longhair, whose "Ay-Tete Fee" [*sic*] was the inspiration for Clifton's first hit, in French translation. Yet, it is clear that there was a degree of mutual influence between Boozoo and Clifton, the two founding fathers of zydeco.

Boozoo made a few more records for Shuler, but became disillusioned with the music business, believing that his records were selling many more copies than he was being paid for. He left music as a professional entertainer to train racehorses, maintaining his own stables at his Dog Hill home. He had been a jockey when he was younger, and he clearly loved working with horses. As his sons were born, he enlisted their help.

"Many was the time I got dusted breaking racehorses for my daddy," recalled Poncho Chavis. "If you got thrown from a horse, there would be a cloud of dust with a cowboy hat floating over the top, because no real cowboy would hit the ground before his hat." After being inspected for broken bones, young Poncho was expected to get back on the horse and try again.

"Dog Hill used to be a fun place," Boozoo's wife, Leona Chavis, told me. Named for the stray dogs in the area, set loose when a new litter of pups proved too many for nearby "city folks" to keep, Dog Hill was a weekend destination for Lake Charles residents from all walks of life. From the late 1940s through the early 1960s, Boozoo's mother, Marceline, ran two racetracks for quarter horses near the family home, as well as the Racetrack Club. With informal bets in place, two horses would run neck and neck down the straight dirt track.

"We hadn't heard of any big track in New Orleans or anything. She [Marceline Chavis] always did know how to make money," said Leona. "She was a good cook. She sold gumbo and barbeque sandwiches and beer. People would run from the city to the country on Sunday, because on Sunday you couldn't buy beer in Lake Charles. Sometimes, the law would come and close it down. And every fifteen days, Boozoo or Clif would play. They had benches along the wall, not like the tables and chairs you see in a club today." Clifton was accompanied by his cousin Morris on fiddle and his

brother Cleveland on rubboard. When Boozoo was not the featured musician, he tended bar, and sometimes he would play to give Chenier a break.

There were two other clubs in the area. Club 15 was operated by Leona's
father, Adam Predium. "He also had a baseball diamond. There would be
a game every Sunday, and if there wasn't a game they'd run motorcycle
races," recalled Leona. Club 16 was owned by Gilbert Martin, and nearby
was the Dog Hill Arena, where local cowboys could test their rodeo skills.
Taken as a whole, it was a scene. "When Boozoo sang, 'I'm goin' to Dog
Hill, where the pretty women at,' he wasn't fooling around!" she laughed.
In this environment, it's easy to understand how horses were as much a
part of Boozoo's life as music.

In 1984, Boozoo and Leona heard a radio advertisement, announcing
that a fake Boozoo Chavis was playing at an Opelousas club. Boozoo not
only became angry at this imposter (and, believe me, he could work up a
good head of steam), but figured there must be money to be made if after
all those years his name could still pull a crowd. With encouragement from
Leona and his family, Boozoo put together a band that featured his sons
Charles and Rellis, on rubboard and drums. With lead guitarist Carlton
Thomas Jr., rhythm guitarist Nathaniel Fontenot, and bassist Classie Ballou
Jr., the son of the guitarist with whom he first recorded, he soon had one
of the most formidable dance bands in southwest Louisiana. Ballou added
a virtuosic and colorful presence to the band, with bright scarves trailing
from the headstock of his bass as he danced and played, sometimes with
only his left hand hammering on the neck of his instrument. Boozoo's sense
of time could be quirky, and he often dropped or added half measures as
he played, but the Magic Sounds (sometimes spelled Majic Sounds on
posters) followed him without missing a beat.

When Boozoo came back on the scene, the excitement in the dance
halls was unmistakable. Only two years after visiting Richard's Club in
Lawtell for the first time, to hear Buckwheat Zydeco, I drove there from
New Orleans with the writer Jeff Hannusch to see Boozoo. I was surprised
that his audience was younger than Buckwheat's, and that the dancing was
even more athletic. If Buckwheat's music was polished and varied, with up-
to-the-minute Southern soul touches, Boozoo's sound was elemental, with
a hypnotic groove that seldom varied, and songs that could be a simple as
nursery rhymes. Some were utterly stripped-down versions of hits by other
artists, such as "Leona Had a Party" (Amos Milburn's "Bad Bad Whiskey")

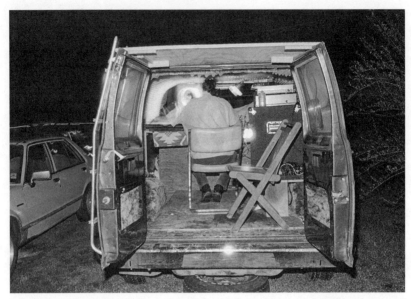

Engineer Mark Bingham in his "recording studio" at Richard's Club, 1987 (photograph © Rick Olivier)

or "Dance All Night" (Bob Wills's "Stay a Little Longer"), and others were his own compositions. "Paper in My Shoe," when performed by Boozoo's own band, had lost the atonal strangeness of the record, but it sounded just fine.

When Boozoo leaned over to pull the bellows of his accordion, dressed in his Stetson hat and plastic apron (which kept perspiration from damaging his accordion), he electrified the crowd. I wondered if it was his particular timing that made everyone want to move, or if it was the sound of the small accordion that spoke to people on the dance floor in a way that the larger piano accordion did not. The music seemed ancient and utterly contemporary at the same time.

He recorded a single, "Dog Hill," for fellow accordionist Rockin' Sidney's ZBC label, and soon signed with Floyd Soileau's Maison de Soul label in Ville Platte, where he made four albums that became staples on local zydeco radio programs. No other artist could come close to drawing the crowds that came to dance to Boozoo, and I was lucky to work with him for the first time during this period, when Floyd gave his permission to record his live set for the *Zydeco Live!* series that I would record at Richard's.

Working with club owner Kermon Richard, we had booked Boozoo Chavis and the Magic Sounds, along with Nathan and the Zydeco Cha

Chas, Willis Prudhomme and the Zydeco Express, and John Delafose and the Eunice Playboys. Engineer Mark Bingham brought his Sony F-1 digital recorder, which we set up in our "studio" inside the van belonging to the gifted blues guitarist and singer John Mooney, who served as second engineer. Rounder founder Bill Nowlin flew in for the weekend, which the photographer Rick Olivier would document. We all stayed at the nearby Cardinal Inn, a sprawling and frayed old motel with a good Cajun restaurant and an oyster bar.

Through Jeff Hannusch, we ordered hand-set, block-type posters from Gosserand Superior Printers on North Claiborne Avenue in New Orleans. We spent a good part of the week before the live recording sessions driving around southwest Louisiana putting them up; visiting radio stations, newspapers, and music stores; and telling people about our big show. I was slightly disappointed when I found out we were in the middle of Lent, to which I had never paid much attention, and that some people might have sworn off partying for the duration, but we nonetheless attracted good crowds, especially for Boozoo.

It was an exciting weekend, and we did a fairly good job of documenting the sound. We were recording direct to two-track, so there would be no after-the-fact mixing. However, with bass frequencies booming through the walls of the club, we were not able to accurately hear what was being recorded, so our mixes ended up with a deficient low end, but they were clear, and I think they gave a picture of how new and old Creole music styles were coming together in the venerable old dance hall. And the oldest musician was the star of the show.

It would be a few years before I would again work with Boozoo. In the interim, he made three albums with Terry Adams at the helm, the last of which was for Rounder. Boozoo had begun to tour widely, eventually overcoming his fear of flying. He was now booked by Jack Reich of Unmanageable Talent in Rhode Island, whose roster included Adams's band, NRBQ; Sun Ra and His Intergalactic Arkestra; and Boozoo himself. At venues such as the Rock 'n' Bowl in New Orleans, and at the Habibi Temple in Lake Charles, he often staged battles with Beau Jocque, his young rival who had taken the scene by storm. Their competition is documented in the Robert Mugge film *The Kingdom of Zydeco*, which includes pre-concert interviews with both musicians, each of whom describes the terrible defeat the other will suffer. In reality, they were friends.

Then, in 1998, Boozoo had a heart attack. He was released from the hospital and made a quick recovery, possibly taking his doctor's advice to cut down on cigarettes. He resumed performing with renewed vigor, playing exhausting hours-long dances. By the time we began talking about making a new album, he was back on top of his game.

Our first collaboration, *Who Stole My Monkey?*, was recorded at Dockside Studio. The band arrived early in the afternoon, and we were soon rolling tape. We planned a varied set of songs, including blues ("Baby Please Don't Go"), traditional Cajun/Creole tunes ("I Went to the Dance"), and new originals such as the title track, "Who Stole My Monkey," which exemplifies the current zydeco groove that was in demand by dancers. Boozoo did not like to spend a lot of time making records, and the session moved along quickly, with few multiple takes. He once bragged to a journalist that he had recorded a recent album in only half an hour. When the writer responded that he believed there were more than thirty minutes of music on the album, Boozoo replied, "Yeah, they couldn't believe it." *Who Stole My Monkey?* has that kind of immediacy.

The surprise of the session was that Boozoo agreed to rerecord the two "X-rated" songs that had been previously released on a 45-rpm single on the Kom-A-Day label (a Floyd Soileau imprint). Rounder Records, in its early years, had released an album of African American "toasts" called *Get Your Ass in the Water and Swim Like Me*, recorded by the ethnomusicologist Bruce Jackson in Louisiana and Mississippi prisons. That was my introduction to this folk tradition of recited poems that are filled with boasts, obscenity, and misogyny, and that are clearly the antecedent of gangsta rap. Characters such as Jody Grinder and the Signifyin' Monkey populate these narratives, which were a rich resource for comedians such as Rudy Ray "Dolemite" Moore.

Boozoo's characters, Uncle Bud and Deacon Jones, are no less formidable, embarking on sexual exploits that border on ridiculous ("Deacon Jones was a fuckin' fool, fucked his teacher on the first day of school"). If the songs might seem sophomoric, Boozoo delivered them with aplomb, and his audiences always had fun with them. In any event, we may have released the first traditional zydeco record with a parental advisory sticker. Boozoo thought that was a good idea.

In 2001, we made plans to go forward with a new record. Boozoo's health was steady, although he had lost the top two joints of two fingers on his left hand, which he used to play the rhythm side of his accordion, in an accident.

Undeterred, he adapted and kept playing. I asked him to think about songs he had heard as a young man, and we made plans to get together at Dog Hill to rehearse and go over repertoire.

Boozoo made a tape of many of the songs for the album at a gig at the Rock 'n' Bowl in New Orleans in late February 2001. His band was genuinely surprised as he introduced songs they had never before heard him play, among them Arthur Crudup's "Rock Me Mama," Hank Ballard's "The Twist," and Hop Wilson's "Broke and Hungry." It was clear that he had put some work into these songs, and he was itching to record. In late March, I headed to Lake Charles. For the recording sessions, Boozoo was open to my idea of augmenting his band with Lafayette slide guitarist Sonny Landreth and St. Martinville fiddler David Greely. His longtime guitarist, Carlton "Guitar" Thomas, was ill and unable to make the gig.

The evening before our rehearsal, on Saturday, March 31, Boozoo was billed as part of an R&B package show at the Lake Charles Civic Center, playing the middle set between local bluesman Big Ike and the main attraction of the evening, Mel Waiters. Many of Boozoo's fans were there, ready to dance. As always, Boozoo had arrived at the gig early, eager and ready to play, "high strung," as Leona would describe him. Whenever there was an opening act at a dance, he would pace back and forth, often in front of the stage, the barrel chest of his short frame thrust forward, listening with one ear cocked but impatient to take the stage and tear it up.

A local DJ/comedian was the master of ceremonies, and before Boozoo's set, he asked the audience for permission to get down, meaning that he was asking for license to pepper his monologue with explicit language, which he did.

Boozoo took the stage and played four or five songs, then asked if anyone wanted to hear "Deacon Jones."

"Ya'll want the X version?" he asked, as the audience screamed in the affirmative.

"I know some of you might want to know who Deacon Jones is," he exclaimed. "Well, I'm gonna tell you who he is. He's the short motherfucker with the cowboy hat and the accordion standing right here!"

Boozoo then proceeded to play his ribald song about his mythological character, who could make love to ninety-nine women in a row. It was right up to date with the latest rap boast. He was not about to be upstaged by a young DJ who knew a few off-color jokes!

The next day, we rehearsed in Boozoo's barn/carport at his home in Dog Hill. When I arrived at noon, the sound system was set up and ready to go, and the barbeque was smoking. In fact, it appeared that half the chickens in Lake Charles had given their lives for the occasion, augmented by several twenty-five-pound boxes of sausages. Boozoo's sons and nephew took charge of the barbeque while Leona made potato salad, dirty rice, and cornbread dressing, cooking up a down-home feast.

The Magic Sounds began to run through the new songs. Neighbors heard the music and soon an impromptu Sunday afternoon dance was under way. A small crowd gathered, and it became clear that our rehearsal was in jeopardy, because Boozoo was not comfortable working on the new material, with the requisite stops and starts, in front of so many people. When I reckoned folks had heard enough to leave happy, I asked Boozoo if we could move indoors with his sons Charles and Rellis, and he enthusiastically agreed. It took a while, because three teenage boys, including the talented Rellis Jr., took over on accordion, drums, and rubboard before the plug was finally pulled. The three followed us inside, and I wondered if we would again lose the necessary privacy to get any real rehearsing done.

For the next four hours, we worked on the new songs, including "I'm Still Blinkin'," the words for which Minneapolis musician Paul Cebar had written down for Boozoo a few weeks earlier. When Boozoo began to worry that he still lacked two or three songs for the album, at one point even suggesting that we wait another month or two to record, we searched his repertoire for bluesy songs that would give Sonny something to dig into. Boozoo recalled the "Henry Martin Two Step," the melody of which had been the source for his hit "Dog Hill," and we knew right away that this song would make a wonderful accordion/fiddle duet with David.

There was no need to worry about the teenagers, who sat quietly on a couch off to the side. When at last we finished, satisfied that we had a plan and all the songs we needed for our recording session, I asked Rellis Jr. if he had been bored. "No, sir," he replied, "I have a lot to learn from Mr. Boozoo." It was clear that the Dog Hill legacy was in good hands.

Listening to the album, there was no indication that Boozoo would be gone only a short time after the recording sessions, for there is, I think, an uncommon vitality and connectedness in his performances on this album. He was clearly delighted to have Sonny and David onboard. To begin the session, he called his familiar "Johnny Billygoat" to get everyone warmed

Scott Billington, Boozoo Chavis, and Kermon Richard at Richard's Club, 1987 (photograph © Rick Olivier)

up, and the chemistry was there from the start. If Boozoo was notorious for his impatience with the recording process, this time he did not want to go home. At the only lull during the session, when we were trying to get the right groove on "La poule pend p'us," Leona marched into the studio and told Boozoo to get it right, and he immediately did.

Boozoo's music does not adhere to normal musical rules, and that is a big part of the delight in listening. "Playing with Boozoo changed my life," said David Greely, "because this is music that follows the heart rather than form." Listen in particular to Classie Ballou Jr.'s bass lines, and you hear a musician who is not playing by rote, but by listening and responding with acute awareness. It was truly music played by feeling.

Early in his career, Sonny Landreth played with Clifton Chenier, and as he matured as one of the world's most distinctive and original slide guitar players (I would venture to say that he has reinvented his instrument), he maintained a deep connection to his native Louisiana roots. His playing on the album is fluid, dynamic, and ever soulful. It inspired Boozoo.

We did a few overdubs on the album, because Sonny wanted to work on a few of his guitar parts, and Boozoo had asked me to add harmonica to a couple of tracks. As a whole, I think *Down Home on Dog Hill* makes for a richer listening experience than most of his other sessions, and it remains one of my favorites.

Boozoo died in Austin, Texas on May 5, 2001, following a gig at Antone's Club. His funeral was well attended, not just by music fans, but by community members who held him in high regard. Posthumously, because it had already been announced, he was awarded a National Heritage Fellowship. Rounder Records released one more Boozoo record, because we had recorded his live show during his Habibi Temple battle of the bands with Beau Jocque. This time, the live sound, recorded by Ronnie Freeland in the Big Mo mobile recording studio, was superb.

Boozoo once immodestly told me, "After me, there ain't gonna be no more." You know, he was right.

RECOMMENDED LISTENING:

"Deacon Jones" from *Who Stole My Monkey?*
"Tell Me What You Want" from *Down Home on Dog Hill*

Chapter 15

BOBBY RUSH

ON THE EVENING BEFORE WE COMMENCED OUR RECORDING SESSIONS IN March 2016, I visited Bobby Rush at his room in the Old 77 Hotel, in the New Orleans Central Business District, for a final check-in before we began work. We had been preparing for a couple of months, with several songwriting sessions and rehearsals behind us, and we were both confident that we had a good album's worth of material ready to go.

That was when Bobby retrieved a plastic Piggly Wiggly bag full of old cassette tapes from a suitcase, along with a small portable player. The tapes were not well marked, but he knew what he was looking for, fast-forwarding and rewinding until he got there. Finally, he pushed the play button, and . . .

"Porcupine meat, too fat to eat, too lean to throw away," was the lyric to the chorus of the song demo he found, a line that was right up there with the best of his quirky, bawdy songwriting. He smiled with his boyish grin that made him look five decades younger than his eighty-something years.

"Do you like that one?" he asked.

"Bobby, I love it. That could be our title tune," I replied. "I mean, where did you come up with that song?"

"Well, I've had it for a few years. I was just wondering if you would like it."

Then, after more searching through his cache of cassettes, he found "Me, Myself and I" and "Nighttime Gardener." I knew then that he had taken an album that was already on track to be very good to one that might be great. I have learned that without songs and without adequate preproduction, booking a recording studio is usually a waste of time, and we had done our advance work well, but Bobby had just drawn three aces in a row from his old cassette deck.

Bobby Rush (photograph © Rick Olivier)

I first met Bobby Rush at a Recording Academy committee meeting, for which we both had been drafted as members, in the early 1990s, and we quickly became friends. Actually, just about everyone who meets Bobby Rush becomes his friend. Walking a few blocks with him in Jackson or Memphis or New Orleans always takes longer than it otherwise might, because shoppers, merchants, and even the UPS driver will stop to say hello. He acknowledges every one of them, taking time to listen with his full attention. It is safe to say that almost every African American in the South over the age of fifty knows about Bobby Rush. Like Sleepy LaBeef, he nurtures his fan base with genuine affection.

We stayed in touch over the years, seeing one another at Recording Academy functions, at the Blues Awards in Memphis, and at his gigs, which included the Memphis in May Festival and the North Mississippi juke joint where he taped his show for the Martin Scorsese PBS blues series. In the early 1990s, Rounder founder Marian Leighton-Levy approached him about making a record for the label's new Bullseye Blues imprint, but he decided to stay where he was, recording for companies that had access to the radio stations and programs that could reach his primary audience.

Emmett Ellis Jr. was born in Carquit, near Homer, Louisiana, in 1933 (or maybe 1937—he was delivered by a midwife, and it is possible that a birth certificate was not issued at the time), moving to Pine Bluff, Arkansas, at age eleven with his family. He began performing while still in his teens, when he met musicians such as the slide guitarist Elmore James and the pianist Pinetop Perkins. He called his first band Bobby Rush and the Four Jivers. Out of respect for his father, who was a preacher, he had changed his stage name to Bobby Rush.

In the 1950s, he moved to Chicago as part of the "second wave" of young blues musicians arriving from the South. He began recording in the late 1960s, scoring a major hit with the funky "Chicken Heads" in 1971, after former Vee-Jay Records executive Calvin Carter arranged to have the record released by the California-based label Galaxy Records. According to Bobby, the bass player on the session was not finding the groove he was looking for, so he picked up the bass and demonstrated the part, finally playing it himself on the recording. While in Chicago, Bobby told me that he became part owner of radio station WVON, as well as a station in Atlanta, revealing an entrepreneurial side that would enhance his business dealings in music in future years. In the mid-1980s, he relocated one more time, to Jackson, Mississippi, to be closer to the area where he most often worked.

Bobby's genius, though, was in creating a stage act that would keep him working on the Chitlin' Circuit of African American clubs and theaters long after many of his peers had lost their connection to that audience, and who now performed almost exclusively at festivals and mainstream clubs that catered to general audiences. First and foremost was his tight band, which played up-to-date grooves while never straying from a rich blues tonality. Bobby also has a knack for writing catchy songs, sometimes tapping a lode of common verses and verbal images that date back to the first blues recordings of the 1920s, but often with a humorous spin of his own. "Sue," "I Ain't Studdin' You," and "What's Good for the Goose Is Good for the Gander" are funky, Southern soul classics.

One of the most memorable features of Bobby's show is his dancers, who are often curvy and glamorous women in tight, sequined outfits, who undergo several costume changes each evening. It is a tradition that goes back many years in African American culture, manifested today in the bounce music of New Orleans and its attendant twerking. My own intro-duction to "shake dancing" was at Dorothy's Medallion Lounge in New Orleans in the early 1980s, when a lithe young woman performed with Walter "Wolfman" Washington, making her derriere move in ways I could never have imagined, much to the delight of the audience.

In many ways, it would appear that this aspect of Bobby's performance is archaic and even exploitative, but most people who experience the show become fans, and some come back expressly because of Bobby's comical take on sexuality ("Just look at it! It's speaking to me.").

"I have a secret," he told me. "If you listen to the words of my songs, the woman always has the power. If someone does wrong or acts a fool, it's me. I give the power to the women. I celebrate them." And somehow, it all works. One of his dancers, Mizz Lowe, has been with him for many years, and has cultivated a fan base of her own.

In the recent Eddie Murphy film *Dolemite Is My Name*, which depicts the colorful life of Rudy Ray Moore, the comedian, actor, and filmmaker who called himself Dolemite, Bobby plays himself in a nightclub scene, set in the early 1970s. There was no need to find actors to recreate Bobby's show, because he was still doing it, with an act that is both a reference to an earlier time, and strikingly timeless. In fact, Bobby describes the Chitlin' Circuit as a parallel universe.

He said, "In small cities around the South, there might be a major enter-tainment venue downtown, where people go on Saturday night. But across town, there's a club where I can draw two hundred people on a Monday or Tuesday night, and no one except the Black community will know about it."

In 2015, Bobby finally agreed to make a record with me for Rounder, and we began getting together whenever we could, to hone our strategy and to work on material. As we sat at a table on the mezzanine of the Peabody Hotel in Memphis, Bobby played a cassette tape demo of "Your Dress Is Too Short" and sang his concept for "Funkity Funk" to my wife, Johnette Downing, and me. Bobby and Johnette bonded right away, rein-forcing a tone of trust that carried through our sessions, and he soon visited us in New Orleans. At Bobby's spacious home in Jackson, I admired the

Bobby Rush and Scott Billington at their first preproduction meeting in Memphis, with Bobby's cassette player (photograph © Johnette Downing)

wrought-iron harmonica and music notes that decorated the façade. Finally, to make demos of the songs for the record, we traveled to the small studio owned by guitarist and producer Vasti Jackson in Hattiesburg, Mississippi.

Vasti is a remarkably talented musician who has been collaborating with Bobby for decades. A veteran of the Malaco Records house band in Jackson, he also was the musical director and guitarist for Southern soul and blues artists such as Z. Z. Hill and Johnny Taylor, with whom he toured for many years. Vasti grew up with the blues and gospel music that surrounded him in McComb, Mississippi, but his musical versatility and broad worldview have made him the go-to person for blues-related film, TV, and record making in Mississippi. He has toured the world with his own band for many years.

Bobby brought his stack of yellow legal pads on which he had written completed lyrics, lyrics in progress, and song ideas. When he found one he wanted to explore, he would sing his basic idea, and if we decided to go forward with it, we would work on the song structure. Then, Vasti would create a programmed beat, over which he would play a bass line and a guitar part.

Finally, we would add Bobby's vocal and harmonica parts. Johnette used her computer to type the final iterations of the lyrics (subject, of course, to further development and improvisation). For our second preproduction session at Vasti's, engineer Steve Reynolds joined us. Johnette and I had written a couple of songs with Bobby, and it was great fun to listen to them come alive, even in demo form.

We agreed on a recording date, and I began assembling the band. The rhythm section of bassist Cornell Williams and drummer Jeffery "Jellybean" Alexander had worked for many years with Jon Cleary's Absolute Monster Gentlemen, and I had done an album with them for New Orleans singer Theryl "Houseman" de'Clouet. Their gospel-rooted approach was as modern and funky as anything to ever come out of New Orleans, and they never overplayed. I had long harbored the dream of hearing Dirty Dozen Brass Band sousaphonist Kirk Joseph on a rhythm and blues session, because he is one of the funkiest and most versatile bass players I knew. This finally seemed like the perfect time, so I asked him to play on half the songs.

Keyboardist David Torkanowsky is one of my session mainstays, and for good reason, because his versatility and virtuosity never get in the way of his knack for finding the right part to play. He listens, with very big ears, to the artist and the musicians around him. The son of classical composer Werner Torkanowsky and the flamenco dancer Teresa Romero Torkanowsky, he studied with New Orleans jazz patriarch Ellis Marsalis. His playing expresses every one of these influences.

Shane Theriot, who played for years with the Neville Brothers and went on to become the musical director for Daryl Hall's *Live from Daryl's House*, would share guitar duties with Vasti, who would be our musical director. Taken as a whole, it was a dream band, and Bobby was excited.

We recorded the album at the Parlor, a newly built facility that is probably the best studio that New Orleans has ever had. With its vintage Neve 8078 console, live chamber, and isolation booths, each built on its own foundation to keep low frequencies from migrating, it gave us an environment that enabled us to record live with no bleed between the tracks (without instruments leaking into other microphones), and with sight lines that kept everyone connected. Owner Matt Grondin has created an inspirational space.

We began the sessions with Bobby's "I Don't Want Nobody Hanging Around," a song that builds on the theme of the blues classic "Outskirts of

Town." With Kirk's sousaphone driving the groove, the band settled into a pocket that went on for nine minutes. It felt so good that everyone danced while listening to the playback.

On the slow blues, "Got Me Accused," Bobby's live-with-the-track vocal and harmonica solo gave me chills. The interplay between Vasti and Shane seems telepathic, while Kirk's sousaphone adds a fatness that no electric bass could replicate. I recall David Torkanowsky saying something like "play this like it's your mama's funeral," which helped everyone attain the exquisitely slow tempo and sparseness that give the track its depth and soul. Bobby and I had worked together on the lyrics to this tradition-derived song, adding the line, "It seems like my life don't matter at all now, and this could be the last time you see me," in reference to the Black Lives Matter movement. All in all, it was one of those moments that I live for in the studio.

I could see that we were on track to accomplish what I had hoped for with Bobby—to make a "serious" blues record with a live band that would provide him with everything he needed to hear to be his best, without compromising his quirky and often double-entendre songs. Many of Bobby's most popular records had been made with sequenced and programmed tracks, a sound that was favored by the radio programmers who played them, mostly on small stations that catered to older African Americans. But that era and that format were fading. There were few of those radio programs left, especially as hip-hop has become the dominant force in contemporary music. Instead of aiming only for his traditional audience, I hoped we could make a record that would speak to the world at large.

The album's title track, "Porcupine Meat," came together quickly, with Vasti's beautiful chords and arrangement creating a "quiet storm" soul ballad feel, a groove that was perfectly executed by Cornell and Jellybean. Yet Bobby loses none of his grittiness, with Vasti's wah-wah guitar providing a counterpoint.

Bobby had played me a solo recording he had made of his song "I'm Tired," on which he had overdubbed an additional harmonica track. That gave Steve and me the idea to make a "Tangle Eye"–style track with Bobby, and he was excited about the prospect. We began by cutting two tracks of Bobby against a click track (or metronome), with his vocals and both diatonic and chromatic harmonicas. Then, we accumulated samples from the musicians, one at a time—different bass patterns, drum patterns, and guitar licks that could be edited into one- or two-measure blocks. Later, Steve loaded everything into Ableton software and made the mix, adding a few samples of his own. "I'm Tired" is the antithesis of everything else on the record, because it is a full-on studio construction, but several reviewers commented that it was the most traditional track on the record. Go figure.

A few weeks later, we reconvened at Jake Eckert's Rhythm Shack studio in New Orleans to add horns and backing vocals, and to complete work on Bobby's vocals. While most of his vocals were recorded at the Parlor, we had been tweaking a few of the lyrics, and now he had the final versions. When overdubbing vocals to a track, it is a rare artist who can summon the intensity and focus of a live-in-the-studio performance with the band, but Bobby may have been even more committed than he was in our tracking sessions, putting every fiber of his body into his singing. Trombonist Jeff Albert, with whom I had taught a music production class at Loyola University, and who had recently arranged the horns for a Meters reunion, wrote the horn charts.

That summer, after the mixes of the record were complete but before the album was released, Johnette and I traveled to meet Bobby at the Porretta Soul Festival in Italy, where Bobby was the headliner, and where Johnette and I performed her Louisiana Roots Music for Children show. Artistic director Graziano Uliani arranged a press conference for Bobby and me, and we played the record for the first time to a group of European music journalists. The feedback from them was encouraging.

Porcupine Meat received a Grammy nomination, so we made plans to attend the show. I had recently been elected a trustee of the Memphis Chapter of the Recording Academy, so Johnette and I had a busy week, attending all the official functions. When the album won, we joined Bobby onstage along with Vasti, Vasti's son Arsadia Harris, and Mizz Lowe. It was a triumphant moment. At eighty-something years of age, Bobby had won his first Grammy. Backstage, the champagne was freely poured, and I grabbed a glass for Bobby. He took one sip for a toast but declined to drink the rest. He later told me that he once drank two beers, in the 1950s. Until the Grammy win, he had not had another drink, not because it was a problem, but because it was a distraction from the business and joy of life.

Porcupine Meat went on to win the Blues Music Award for Best New Album in 2017, while a compilation, *Chicken Heads: A 50-Year History of Bobby Rush*, won the award for Best Historical Album. What is surprising is

Vasti Jackson, Bobby Rush, and Scott Billington backstage at the
Grammys, 2017 (courtesy of Scott Billington)

that any artist could win his first Grammy, along with an award for a fifty-
year retrospective, in the same year. In down-home fashion, we celebrated
the next day with lunch at Gus's Fried Chicken.

In the ensuing months, I interviewed Bobby twice onstage, at the
Grammy Museum in Cleveland, Mississippi, and at the Jazz and Heritage
Festival in New Orleans. These were two-part affairs, because we ended
each interview with a musical set, with Bobby on guitar and vocals, and me
on harmonica. For a kid from Massachusetts who had fallen in love with
the blues as a teenager, I could never have imagined a more meaningful
moment. And it was effortless.

To our disappointment, there would be no follow-up recording on
Rounder. As much as Bobby's record was acclaimed by his fans and by
the blues world at large, and even after our Grammy win, his contract was

dropped. There is no doubt that the record business had changed radically in the 2000s, and that blues fans were not yet generating enough streaming activity to compensate for lost CD sales, but it was a tough decision to accept. *Porcupine Meat* would be the final record I would make for Rounder as a staff producer, although I would continue on as a freelancer.

Of course, Bobby had been rolling with the ups and downs of record companies for fifty years, and he took the news in stride. He wasted little time in making plans for his next record, which he would release on his own Deep Rush label. This time, Vasti would be back in the producer's chair for most of the record, but Bobby asked the Mississippi-based producer Patrick "Guitar Boy" Hayes and me to each produce several songs for the album.

For the new sessions, I put together an all-star band from Lafayette, and for one day, on March 19, 2018, we convened at Dockside Studio in Maurice. Bassist Lee Allen Zeno was the cornerstone musician of the ensemble. Doug Belote, from nearby Carencro, was a former student of Lee Allen's who was now one of the first-call drummers in both New Orleans and Nashville. Rounding out the band would be Roddie Romero and Paul "Lil' Buck" Sinegal on guitars. Roddie's band, the Hub City All Stars, often features his accordion, but he is also a distinctive slide guitarist with a sound like no one else. It was exciting to finally have the opportunity to work with Lil' Buck, whose deep blues feel would be grounding for everyone. Sadly, it would be one of his last sessions, as Lil' Buck passed away at the age of seventy-five less than a year later.

We cut six songs that day, with Dockside's Justin Tockett engineering. Bobby, Lee Allen, and I would usually start by discussing overall groove ideas and a bass line for each song before we brought on the full band, when we would refine sounds and the overall arrangement. I was especially pleased with the harmonica instrumental, "Bobby's Shuffle," because it seemed to me that Bobby kept getting better at this instrument every year. He fired off one idea after another, never repeating himself. It was great fun, and I wish we could have continued for another few days.

I am often astonished at Bobby's vitality. He had worked very hard that day, recording for over eight hours, and he had the option of staying that night in the comfortable master suite at Dockside. Yet he chose to get in his car and drive home to Jackson, about four hours away. Maybe I was no better, because I headed to Lee Allen's Blue Monday Jam, where I sat in for most of a set, before heading back to New Orleans.

Bobby chose two songs from our session, "You Got the Goods on You" and "Bobby's Shuffle," for release on *Sitting on Top of the Blues*, telling me he wanted to save the wonderful "Boomerang Love" for a future release. Again, the album won a Grammy nomination. We all headed to Los Angeles for the ceremony in February 2020, except for Vasti, who was booked in Germany. Delbert McClinton won the traditional blues Grammy that year.

I have learned a great deal from Bobby Rush. Keeping his business solvent and his fans satisfied for almost sixty years is an accomplishment that cannot be denied, especially considering the hardship and challenges of being on the road most of the time, and holding together an organization that never seems to disappoint an audience. In 2001, he endured a bus accident, after his driver suffered a heart attack and drove off the road, in which one of his dancers was killed, and in which he and his band members were severely injured.

Yet, at least on the surface (and, I think, on a deeper level, too), he remains an eternally optimistic person who greets everyone with a smile. He approached our sessions with the enthusiasm of someone making his first record, and I have observed him as he approaches every new situation, gig, or even country with curiosity and gratitude. At the same time, he is directly connected to the deepest part of blues culture, inhabiting the same sensibility and shared traditions as the first Mississippi musicians to record in the 1920s. At an age when many people would be winding down, he lives in the present with an eye on the future. We should all be so blessed.

RECOMMENDED LISTENING:

"Got Me Accused" and "Catfish Stew" from *Porcupine Meat*

Chapter 16

ZYDECO MUSIC

THE PROPULSIVE, ACCORDION-DRIVEN DANCE MUSIC CALLED ZYDECO IS a quirky invention that could only have happened in southwest Louisiana, where descendants of French and Creole-speaking African Americans (who today call themselves Creoles) merged their traditional songs with a rhythm and blues beat. While zydeco shares partial and sometimes intertwining ancestry with Cajun music, it is its own distinctive modern form, even as it has incorporated influences from hip-hop and pop music. The essential instruments remain an amplified accordion and a rubboard or *frottoir*, a corrugated sheet-metal vest played with bottle openers that is surely one of the loudest percussion instruments ever invented. Electric bass, electric guitar, and a drum kit bring on the syncopation and funk.

No one could have predicted that such an idiosyncratic and regional style would flourish into the twenty-first century, or that southwest Louisiana's Creoles would hold so tightly to their music, even as English became their dominant language and as their rural lifestyle slipped mostly into the past. Yet, at trail rides, rodeos, dance halls, church dances, and almost any celebration, zydeco is a rallying point of the culture, and if many zydeco musicians have enjoyed the opportunity to tour the world, the music is sustained by the community at home. A zydeco dance or trail ride is a community ritual, with athletic young couples showing off their moves, and even the hippest young band must play an occasional waltz, as well as a "Harlem Shuffle"–type groove for the "electric slide" line dance.

The accordion itself is a relatively recent introduction. While there is evidence of accordions in Louisiana in the mid to late 1800s, possibly introduced by German-Jewish immigrants, they were not widely available until the late 1800s and early 1900s, either by mail order from a company

Left to right: Sid Williams, Scott Billington, Beau Jocque, Nathan Williams, and promoter Don "Apollo" Williams at El Sid O's Zydeco and Blues Club, 1990s (photograph © Philip Gould)

such as Sears, Roebuck and Company, or from a local merchant such as the Mervine Kahn store in Rayne. What is clear is that the loud, driving sound of the accordion was perfect for rising above the din of a house party or dance, and that the instrument was both durable and portable. The accordion was quickly adopted by Creoles, Cajuns, and Mexican Americans across Louisiana and Texas, and was already in use by the Czechs and Germans who brought the instrument with them. Today, many local craftsmen, including Marc Savoy in Eunice, Junior Martin in Scott, and Larry Miller in Iota, build most of the diatonic accordions that are favored by many musicians, while Italian-made Gabbanelli and German-made Hohner accordions, especially triple-row models, are cherished by others.

The specific origins of zydeco are likewise difficult to trace. In 1929, the Creole accordion player Amédé Ardoin and the Cajun fiddle player Dennis McGee made the first recordings of Louisiana Creole music. Their melodies and bluesy tonality remain a touchstone both for Cajun and zydeco players, as the shared legacy of their intermingling cultures. A closer antecedent might be the call-and-response music called *juré* (which means "to testify"), with its syncopated hand-clapping, The primary glimpse we have of this traditional style is on a few recordings made by the ethnomusicologist Alan Lomax in 1934, but Mrs. Florita Williams, the mother of Nathan and

Dennis Paul, was able to remember a *juré* song that she performed for my southwest Louisiana CD-ROM project, with her sons clapping along. There is also a possible Caribbean influence from the Creole-speaking Haitians who settled in the area in the 1800s, fleeing political turmoil at home. Yet, it was the post–World War II mingling of Creole music and rhythm and blues instrumentation that ultimately achieved the distinctive zydeco sound, as it moved further away from its Cajun cousin.

The word *zydeco* is a phonetic corruption of the French *les haricots*, or snap beans. The phrase, *les haricots sont pas salé*, signifying poverty so dire that there was no salt meat to add to the pot, appears in several of the Lomax recordings. Gradually, the term came to represent both the music and the event, as in "I'm going to the zydeco." Until the Houston folklorist Mack McCormack promoted the current spelling of the word in the 1960s, it was variously written as zorigo, zarico, or zodico on posters advertising weekend dances. Some older people recall that the music was once simply called "la la."

Clifton Chenier, widely recognized as the King of Zydeco, was a virtuoso of the piano accordion, an instrument with a full range of musical possibilities. He brought his own band, the Zodico Ramblers, to the recording sessions in Los Angeles that produced his 1955 Specialty Records hit, "Ay-Tete Fee," with its mangled French-Creole title. Chenier would often say, "I'm a blues man," for, in addition to Creole dance tunes, he played rhythm and blues hits, and down-home blues numbers. In doing so, he laid out the malleable parameters of zydeco that have always made room for the popular music of the day—rhythm and blues, soul, hip-hop, and pop—filtered through the perspective of an accordion-driven dance band.

In contrast, his contemporary Wilson "Boozoo" Chavis used the smaller diatonic accordion, a "bluesier" and louder instrument that can be played in only a few musical keys. By the time he was a teenager, he was entertaining patrons at his mother's racetrack and dance hall in the Dog Hill area on the outskirts Lake Charles, developing a repertoire of traditional songs and nursery rhyme–like originals.

In many ways, it is surprising that zydeco survived its early years. Chavis quit playing almost entirely, returning to his trade of training racehorses. Chenier kept working with his small band, but there was little awareness of his music outside the local Creole communities of southwest Louisiana and east Texas, and in the community of Louisiana Creole expatriates in

Clifton Chenier and band at Sid's One Stop in Lafayette, Louisiana, just before hitting the road. *Left to right:* Cleveland Chenier, James Benoit, unknown, unknown, unknown, C. J. Chenier, Clifton Chenier (courtesy of Sid Williams).

the San Francisco Bay Area. Both zydeco and Cajun music were often maligned as backward—it was the music of poor people, and, like speaking French or Creole, it was not socially progressive in an area that was just then assimilating into mainstream America. Yet, through the 1960s and '70s, zydeco and traditional Creole music maintained a steady if quiet presence. When Clifton Chenier signed with Arhoolie Records producer Chris Strachwitz, his star began to rise, and his records announced zydeco music to the world at large. He would eventually win a Grammy award.

It was a persistent tradition. Musicians such as John Delafose, Alton "Rockin' Dopsie" Ruben, Roy Carrier, Marcel Dugas, Delton Broussard, Ambrose Sam, and Hiram Sampy played weekend dances at churches and clubs. Dance halls such as Hamilton's Club and El Sid O's in Lafayette, Slim's Y-Ki-Ki Lounge in Opelousas, Papa Paul's in Mamou, the Offshore Lounge and Richard's in Lawtell, and the Double D Club in Parks were filled with dancers on Friday and Saturday nights. Yet, the full blossoming of zydeco was yet to come.

Music fans can look back to several junctures of time and place in American music when it was clear that something significant was happening. For Southern blues, it might have been Beale Street in Memphis in the early 1950s, when B. B. King and Bobby "Blue" Bland pioneered a modern blues sound that continues to resonate today. For bebop, it might have been 52nd Street in New York City in the 1940s, when Charlie Parker, Dizzy Gillespie, and Thelonious Monk deconstructed jazz. For zydeco, I would argue that it was southwest Louisiana in the late 1980s and early 1990s, when Boozoo Chavis came roaring back onto the scene at Richard's Club in Lawtell.

It was not long before Boozoo had his challengers, as a wave of younger musicians emulated his raw button-accordion sound. Bass player Robby Robinson enlisted Delton Broussard's son, accordion player Jeffery, to form the band Zydeco Force. Their sound emulated Boozoo's groove, but with modern touches such as harmony vocals and R&B-derived chord changes, and they quickly established a following that rivaled Boozoo's. Then, Beau Jocque arrived on the scene with a fusion of Creole music, funk, and rhythm and blues. The small and humble diatonic accordion had come to dominate the dance halls and clubs.

Like professional wrestlers, Boozoo Chavis and Beau Jocque carried on a rivalry—the zydeco forefather versus the young upstart. It was good for business. An even younger generation took note, and soon Keith Frank, Chris Ardoin, Step Rideau, and the tradition-leaning Geno Delafose joined the fray. The double-kicked bass drum beat inspired people from all over the country to begin dancing to zydeco, and a number of small booking agencies began sending zydeco bands around the country. John Blancher began booking a weekly zydeco dance at his Rock 'n' Bowl venue in New Orleans, while an enterprising travel agency booked a zydeco cruise.

Following the death of Clifton Chenier in 1987, his disciples carried his more sophisticated piano accordion sound forward, but usually not on their home turf. His former sideman Stanley "Buckwheat" Dural eclipsed his mentor's popularity, touring the world with a tightly disciplined show. Nathan Williams and the Zydeco Cha Chas soon followed. But the larger accordion never regained its popularity with local dancers.

Although live recordings are not often my first choice, given the greater creative possibilities of the recording studio, I undertook two live recording projects in southwest Louisiana clubs. Just as a traditional New Orleans brass band might play with more fire at a second-line parade than in a recording studio, I felt that a zydeco band might play with a more purposeful groove in front of dancers. The two-disc *Zydeco Live!* project was

Richard's Club poster advertising our 1987 live recording sessions (from the collection of Scott Billington)

recorded at Richard's Club in Lawtell in 1987 (for more details please see the Boozoo Chavis chapter), while *Zydeco Shootout at El Sid O's* was recorded a few years later in Lafayette. These projects offered a way to showcase lesser-known bands such as Willis Prudhomme and the Zydeco Express, and the irrepressible Pee Wee and the Zydeco Boll Weevils. "This is the song that brought me to the top," exclaims the Boll Weevil, as he sings "Don't Mess with My Ya Ya," which combines the titles of two of the most popular zydeco songs into a repeated refrain.

In 2020, most of the old zydeco dance halls have closed their doors, standing as decaying relics of what once were important community gathering spots. Yet, bands such as Lil' Nathan and the Zydeco Big Timers, Keith Frank and the Soileau Zydeco Band, Chris Ardoin and NuStep Zydeco, and

J. Paul Jr. and the Zydeco Nubreeds are more popular than ever, performing at a variety of mainstream venues, auditoriums, and festivals. Among the most popular zydeco-focused events are trail rides, in which members of Creole riding clubs load their horses into trailers and gather for a day or a weekend of horsemanship, dancing, and eating. Thousands of people, including many without horses, may attend a trail ride, and there is always a zydeco dance at the end of the trail.

Zydeco music is now as much a part of the American musical landscape as bluegrass or Chicago blues, and just as likely to show up in a fast food commercial. I am grateful that I was able to record so many of the most important zydeco artists during the breakout years of the 1980s and '90s. It is a sound that is here to stay. Here are stories about many of the musicians with whom I worked during those years.

THE ARDOIN FAMILY

The accordion-playing Ardoins could well be called the first family of Louisiana Creole music. In 2021, brothers Chris Ardoin and Sean Ardoin are at the vanguard of *nouveau* zydeco, fusing their mastery of traditional forms with hip-hop, rhythm and blues, and pop influences. Chris is one of the biggest draws in south Louisiana, while Sean often takes his Zydekool show on the road. Their father, Lawrence "Black" Ardoin, played traditional Creole through the lean times of the 1960s and '70s with his siblings Morris and Gustave in the Ardoin Brothers Band. His father, Alphonse "Bois Sec" Ardoin, played music that reached back to the early twentieth century. With fiddler Canray Fontenot, he performed at the 1966 Newport Folk Festival, bringing Louisiana Creole music to national attention for the first time. Bois Sec's cousin was Amédé Ardoin, the first musician to record Creole music, in 1929, accompanied by the Cajun fiddler Dennis McGee. When he was a boy, Bois Sec sometimes accompanied Amédé on triangle.

As fiddler Canray Fontenot told Michael Tisserand in *OffBeat*, Amédé was a carefree individual who lived for his music. "He never married, he didn't want to work. Amédé would put his accordion in that sack and every day would get to the gravel road with his accordion, hitchhike, and he didn't give a damn which direction it was—he'd go somewhere where he could pick up a few nickels." In spite of their scratchy sound, the early recordings

Chris Ardoin (photograph © Rick Olivier)

of Amédé Ardoin reveal an accomplished, fully formed accordion style that would not be out of place in a traditional band today, and many of his songs, such as "Midland Two Step" and "Les Blues de la Prison" are still played. His vocals are something else—bluesy and unearthly, with a sadness that can sound like crying. While Dennis McGee sometimes plays the melody of a song with him, the violin most often "seconds" the accordion by playing rhythmic figures. The records they made together are a crucial part of the foundation upon which much Cajun and Creole music was built.

However, whatever paragon of racial harmony might have been imagined in the musical partnership of Ardoin and McGee did not apply to Amédé's life in general. After accepting a handkerchief to wipe his face from the daughter of a Cajun employer, he was beaten by two men and left for dead in a ditch by the side of the road. He recovered enough to continue playing, but he was eventually confined to an asylum in distant Pineville, Louisiana, where he died in 1942 at the age of forty-four.

Duralde, Louisiana, an unincorporated and sparsely populated area northwest of Eunice, could be said to be the spiritual home of Creole and zydeco music. Amédé was born there, as was his nephew Alphonse "Bois Sec" Ardoin, future zydeco star John Delafose, and Canray Fontenot's father, the accordion player Adam Fontenot. Beau Jocque's parents, including his accordion-playing father Sandrus Espre, still lived there in the 1990s. One can imagine that the farmers and ranchers who lived there must have had a tradition of lively musical exchange.

Today, the Ardoins live in Lake Charles, where the now-retired Lawrence was employed by the electric company. I first heard Chris Ardoin there in 1993, when he opened for the epic battle between Boozoo Chavis and Beau Jocque at the Habibi Temple. Chris was a prodigy who could play the accordion well before he entered grade school. At nine years old, he joined the family band onstage at Carnegie Hall. Now, at the age of twelve, it was clear that Chris was an exceptional talent who was already pushing the limits of the diatonic accordion, playing impossibly fast lines.

By 1996, he had teamed up with Sean to form the band Double Clutchin' (with Sean playing drums), named for the double-kicked bass drum pattern that was favored by dancers. Lawrence would be their manager, for, in fact, they were taking over the family business. As such, he provided them with a sound system and a vehicle to haul it in. At sixteen, Chris possessed a burnished vocal style that made him sound like an old soul. He could initially be shy, but when he started playing, his authority was clear. Twenty-seven-year-old Sean had a lighter tenor voice that could deliver a sweet soul ballad, or that could recall the more plaintive sound of Amédé, especially when he sang an old family song like "Dimanche Apres Midi." He also had an ear for arranging vocal harmonies. With his voluble and outgoing personality, he worked for a time as a motivational speaker and, in 2021, became a candidate for mayor of Lake Charles. As of this writing, he serves as the president of the Memphis Chapter of the Recording Academy. Together, they were an unbeatable combination, especially when it came to writing zydeco songs with one foot in tradition and the other in the future.

We convened at Ultrasonic Studio in March 1997, along with bassist Derek Greenwood, rubboard player Tammy Ledet, and guitarist Gabriel "Pandy" Perrodin Jr., who was the son of southwest Louisiana legend Guitar

Gable. I appreciated the connection. Along with releasing a string of instrumental records, Guitar Gable was one of the defining figures of the swamp
pop style, especially with the ballad "This Should Go On Forever."

Chris and Sean arrived with a batch of newly written songs that included
the exuberant "We Are the Boys," based on a chant that Sean heard while
attending Louisiana State University, as a member of the Phi Mu Alpha
music fraternity. "I went to hang with the Southern University brothers, and
a song they sang gave me the inspiration," he said. Chris developed "When
I'm Dead and Gone" ("The way the world is going, I won't be here long"),
a somber assessment of the state of the world for someone so young, sung
over a 1950s rhythm and blues chord progression. Throughout the album,
the harmonies are as tight as only brothers could sing them. Steve Reynolds
contributed a sample-driven mix of "We Are the Boys," with Sean's double
kick turned into a triple kick, that Rounder released as a twelve-inch vinyl
single for the Houston dance club market. The album, Gon' Be Jus' Fine,
introduced the new generation of Ardoins with panache.

In the intensely competitive zydeco world, an accordion riff or motif
that made people dance could be a valuable property. When I recorded
Beau Jocque's song "Come Go with Me" in 1998, there was something familiar about it, but I could not identify exactly what it was. The next time I
saw Sean, he let me know, precisely, because the signature riff in the song
was the same as Chris and Sean's "Lake Charles Connection."

Taking a broader view, that is the way songwriting in traditional music
communities has often worked. However, we were not documenting folk-
lore, but making commercial recordings that would generate income for the
artists and composers. As part of my producer's job, I delivered songwriting
credits for every song on an album, which enabled the record company
and others to pay mechanical and performance royalties. This was relatively easy in the rhythm and blues world, where I would often obtain fully
formed and copyrighted original works from writers or song publishers.
However, when I asked an older musician such as Boozoo Chavis or John
Delafose if the song we had just recorded was their own composition, they
would inevitably say yes. It did not matter if it was an Amédé Ardoin or
Joe Falcón song, or if they had taken an older song or traditional melody
and added new lyrics. In a sense, the stylistic imprint that an artist can
bring to a traditional theme can be so strong that the song does indeed
become their own—a signature piece. Still, while Beau Jocque claimed to

have written "Come Go with Me," it is likely that he used Chris and Sean's original motif as its basis. It certainly sounds that way.

Folk tradition and the commercial songwriting world, with its attendant legal framework, do not coexist comfortably. The first person to record and publish a traditional song, and who takes the credit for writing it (as country music pioneer A. P. Carter did), receives the royalties from that point on, including those generated by subsequent recordings of the song by other artists. Then again, the exchange of ideas, verses, and motifs that might be a key part of a tradition could be stifled by a fixed copyright, which may simply be a snapshot of a particular time in a song's evolution. If the precedent of the recent successful lawsuit by the estate of Marvin Gaye against songwriters Pharrell Williams and Robin Thicke, for more or less copying the vibe of a Marvin Gaye recording in their "Blurred Lines," were applied to zydeco (or, say, to the blues), the lawyers would be kept busy for many years.

Another side to copyright law emerged after the release of *Gon' Be Jus' Fine*. Lawrence Ardoin received a call from a California fan who reported that she had heard Chris's song "When I'm Dead and Gone" in a Fourth of July commercial for a large supermarket chain. When Lawrence called me to ask if this was true, I verified that no one at Rounder had licensed the song for that purpose. The fan then went an extra mile (or two!) and taped the commercial from the radio. The supermarket chain's ad agency had edited the music from our record, removing the vocals, and had represented it as an original composition. At first, the agency responded with a strong denial, but when I made the same edits in our track to show that their advertising spot was identical, a settlement was soon reached. There is clearly a difference between the exchange of ideas in folk tradition and the theft of intellectual property.

We followed our success with 1998's *Turn the Page*, on which Chris and Sean began experiment with a broader range of material that included two non-zydeco songs: the Jackie Wilson sixties hit "Your Love Keeps Lifting Me (Higher and Higher)" and the reggae hit from Musical Youth, "Pass the Dutchie," which is melded onto their own "Stay In or Stay Out." The title cut is a classic soul ballad with a tender falsetto lead vocal from Sean and deftly stacked background vocals, with Chris's accordion romping over the chord changes. Pandy had been replaced by the double guitars of Bobby Broussard and Nathaniel Fontenot, which gave the music an extra push. There were also traditional songs such as Canray Fontenot's "Barres de la Prison" and "Double Clutchin' Old Style." We ended the record with another track made from samples, called "Fever for Your Flavor." Steve and I continued to explore the use of Pro Tools as a compositional aid, by making "building blocks" out of parts played by the musicians, and then arranging and rearranging them, often with other sampled sounds added.

As Double Clutchin' kept growing in popularity, Chris and Sean began growing apart musically. It was clear that each musician needed a creative space of his own. Sean, who is also an accomplished accordion player, decided to get out from behind the drums to front his own band, and to expand his travel sphere. Chris continued to build his local audience to become one of the top-drawing bands on the southwest Louisiana circuit. He also learned other instruments, to the point that he could play every sound on his records, which he eventually would sometimes do. With our next record, 2000's *Best Kept Secret,* he was on his way.

This time, we convened at Ultrasonic Studio with only four musicians: Chris, bassist Curley Chapman, guitarist Nathaniel Fontenot, and drummer Dexter Ardoin, Chris's cousin who would also go on to lead his own band, the Creole Ramblers. In addition to accordion, Chris played rhythm and lead guitar, bass, and rubboard. Chris and Curley sang the tight backing vocals, although I brought in New Orleans singer Charles Elam III to sing the high parts. The grooves were now even tougher, although Chris's sense of humor came through on songs such as his "What's in That Bayou?" We recorded covers of "Papa Was a Rolling Stone" and Sheryl Crow's "If It Makes You Happy."

With the changes in the record business that made selling zydeco to a national audience more difficult each year, this was our last record together, but Chris has continued to forge a vital contemporary embodiment of his family legacy. To my ears, especially because of his mastery of recording technology, he has achieved the most successful fusion of hip-hop, rhythm and blues, and zydeco to date. His NuStep Zydeco can be an arena-filling sound.

In addition to his Zydekool recordings, which won two Grammy nominations in 2019, Sean is also the force behind Creole United, an overall celebration of Creole music and language. Their 2014 recording, *Non Jamais Fait*, features Sean with his father, as well as with accordionists Andre Thierry and Jeffery Broussard, and fiddler Ed Poullard.

The Ardoin family legacy now includes almost a century of recording, and a level of musicianship that is still setting standards. It will be interesting to see how the next generation will carry it forward.

THE DELAFOSE FAMILY

I am often asked how long it takes to make a record. I have often spent months working on a project, from conception, to rehearsals, to tracking, to overdubbing, to editing, to mixing, to mastering. However, a record can sometimes materialize quite quickly.

After recording John Delafose as part of the *Zydeco Live!* project, I asked him if he would like to make a new record in the studio. He quickly agreed, saying he already had an album's worth of new material ready.

In December 1991, I booked two days at Ultrasonic Studio in New Orleans, along with rooms for the band at a nearby hotel. But when I called John to confirm, I was puzzled by his response. "Well," he said, "I don't know about all that, but we'll be there at eleven on Tuesday."

The following week, John Delafose and the Eunice Playboys rolled up in their van at exactly eleven on Tuesday. By this time, engineers David Farrell and Steve Reynolds had developed a zydeco studio setup that we used each time. The drummer occupied the big, main room; the rubboard player went into his or her own small isolation booth; and the accordion player occupied the larger piano room, with a matched pair of B&K 4011 microphones set up to record the accordion, and a Neumann U-87 microphone for the vocal. We also took a direct signal from the accordion pickup, which sometimes would make the sound thicker if we added just a small bit in the mix. I believe the zydeco records we made at Ultrasonic are distinguished by exceptional, acoustic accordion sounds, which seemed to sit better in the track than the inevitably wheezy pickup sound that is often heard on other records.

As we were setting up headphone mixes, fine-tuning the placement of the microphones, and adjusting the sound of Charles Prudhomme's guitar amplifier, John was tapping his foot, clearly impatient. "What's taking so long?" he asked.

Finally, we started rolling tape. John breezed through a set, just as if he were playing a dance. The music was bright and full of energy, and the

Geno Delafose and John Delafose (photograph © Rick Olivier)

band, which featured his sons Tony on bass and Geno on drums, followed John's every move. The only time we stopped was to change reels of tape, and once when the band was stymied by a chord change that they were not expecting. I asked John is he would do the song again.

"Well, we could," he replied, "but it'll be just like the one before."

They played the song again, and this time no one missed the chord. We also recorded five songs that featured young Geno on accordion and vocals, with Germaine Jack switching from rubboard to drums, and John taking over on the rubboard.

In two and a half hours, we recorded twenty-two songs, and I figured we were done. I called the hotel to cancel the reservation (which, somehow, I got away with). We had captured a set of traditional Creole music played as well as it could be played, as if John had conjured a packed house of dancers. I went out into the studio to shake his hand and to pay him.

"I don't know if you realize what you just did. You made a fantastic record in way less time than it usually takes most musicians to record just one song," I said.

"Well, that's the way we do it," he replied with a slightly boastful tone.

I told him, "If you can stick around for about two hours—maybe we can order lunch—I can give you rough mixes to listen to on the way home."

He looked at his watch. "No, why don't you mail them to me. We have to go home to feed the horses."

And there it was—*Pere et Garçon Zydeco* (in Louisiana, "pere et garçon" translates as father and son, not father and boy)—a perfect record made in two and a half hours. Even my friend Chris Strachwitz, the producer and owner of Arhoolie Records who had also recorded John Delafose, complimented me on the record. One of the previous criticisms I had received from him was of the overprocessed "whipshit" drum sounds on Walter "Wolfman" Washington's first record for Rounder. He was right on both counts.

But my lasting impression of the record was the beauty of John's unself-conscious attitude toward recording. Many musicians and singers, especially younger ones, will fret over every note and line, asking to punch in (or to record snippets of new parts, one line or phrase at a time) over and again until a part is "perfect." I have at times been guilty of that myself. The result can be a disjointed final track that loses its spark and groove in the service of flawlessness. In post-tracking overdub sessions, if a singer such as Irma Thomas or Johnny Adams had made a mistake or flubbed a line, I would ask them to sing the entire song again, while making a note of the part we needed. That way, the continuity of the performance could be maintained, even if we pieced together a final vocal performance from multiple takes.

John Delafose would have none of that. The session was also a credit to David, who created headphone mixes that reinforced that confidence. John knew that music felt right, and he did not let the recording process get in the way.

Born in 1939 in Duralde, Louisiana, John Delafose was a farmer, which is how he supported himself for the first half of his life, especially after his marriage to JoAnn Ceaser. As a boy, he learned the harmonica well enough to play at dances, and he had fooled around with both the fiddle and the accordion, but it was not until later in life that he picked them both up again. He was a folk musician in the best sense of the term, working with the floating verses and melodies that were the heritage of his native area, where Amédé Ardoin had once hitchhiked with his accordion on his back in a flour sack. John also had a knack for quirky original compositions, but no song was a set piece. Rather, the songs flowed with the dancers as he elaborated on their themes. French was his first language. Unlike the Creolized language that was spoken around St. Martinville, a dialect of standard French was native to both Cajuns and Creoles in the Eunice-Duralde area.

At the time I met John, in 1987, he was one of the most popular artists on the southwest Louisiana and east Texas circuit, playing church dances and clubs such as Richard's. Once he had made up his mind to pursue music, he did so with passion and focus, creating an energetic style that made even the most traditional song sound like his own. He loved entertaining people, and he was proud of the success he had achieved, especially the national touring he had done. He now made his living almost exclusively from playing music, although his home in Eunice remained a small farm, with horses and chickens. The kitchen in the Delafose home was a hub of activity, with people coming and going all day long, but John was often outside, tending his animals.

Geno had been playing rubboard and then drums with his father since he was eight years old, developing a muscular, rolling style that gave the music an edge. His father then tutored him on the accordion, and he was all ears, augmenting his lessons by learning traditional Cajun and Creole tunes from compact disc reissues. Geno had gone to Eunice High School as a classmate of the Cajun bandleader Steve Riley, where they played in the same band. Both John and Geno blurred the lines between Cajun and Creole music, perhaps finding that two forms were sometimes not all that different. For instance, the melody his "Down in Texas Way" is based on fellow Eunice resident and Cajun fiddler Dewey Balfa's "Quand J-étais Pauvre," but in a different key, with different lyrics.

When we started planning a follow-up record, in 1993, John told me that he wanted to record a few tunes on violin, which he had taken up again. With Geno consistently gaining more confidence in his accordion play-ing, it was thrilling to hear John return to an instrument that once had a

John Delafose and the Eunice Playboys. *Left to right:* Tony Delafose, Germaine Jack, Geno Delafose, unknown spectator, John Delafose (photograph © Rick Olivier).

prominent place in Creole music, playing traditional melodies such as "Joe Simien Special" and "Co Fe" with his son. On accordion, John presented a stripped-down and thoroughly zydeco-ized arrangement of the Delmore Brothers' country classic "Blues Stay Away from Me," which became our title track, while Geno boldly covered Walter Mouton's Cajun song "Scott Playboy Special."

We also decided that it was time for Geno to make the first album of his own. John had cut back on his touring schedule, and had partially handed the reins of the family business over to Geno. Booking agent David Gaar and his Sin Fronteras agency now represented the Eunice Playboys, with or without John.

By February 1994, Geno had his repertoire together, with seven of his own new songs, including several written in French, and adaptations of music by Canray Fontenot and Cajun accordion player Iry LeJeune. David Gaar suggested the Shirley Bergeron song "French Rockin' Boogie," which became both the album's title and the new name for the Eunice Playboys. I thought it would be fun to add a rhythm and blues song, so I brought Charles Wright's "One Lie (Leads to Another)."

For me, the highlight of the sessions at Ultrasonic was Geno's "C'est Pas la Peine Brailler (There's No Need to Cry)." I had asked the two saxophone players from the New Orleans band the Iguanas, Joe Cabral and Derek Huston, to join the sessions for a few tunes, and the simple, harmonized tenor saxophone part they added to this track gave it just the right push, making the song seem to float in the air. On "One Lie," I added trumpet player Steve Howard and tenor saxophonist Jon Smith, who perhaps unfortunately called themselves the White Trash Horns (because they had played in Edgar Winter's band of that name). Altogether, I felt the variety of the album made it a great success, even as Geno never lost his footing in the Duralde tradition.

Then, in September 1994, John suffered a heart attack onstage at Richard's Club, and died that night. He was a popular and respected figure in the community, not only for his music, and it seemed that half the town attended his funeral at the St. Mathilda Catholic Church in Eunice, where he was buried in the church cemetery.

The band had a full itinerary of gigs, and Geno bravely became their full-time leader, with his grief expressed through performing his father's songs. At the age of twenty-three, he was a handsome figure on and offstage, in his cowboy hat, pressed jeans, and colorful western shirts. He quickly became one of the most popular artists with zydeco dancers across the country, where zydeco had become as popular as swing or ballroom dancing.

We followed up with *That's What I'm Talkin' About!* in 1996. Geno continued to dig deeper into the traditional music around him—Creole, Cajun, and swamp pop—consolidating his reputation as a young keeper of the flame, delivering his music with the energy of the most groove-oriented zydeco bands. He had also mastered the larger piano accordion, giving him the facility to play almost any style of Louisiana Creole or Cajun music. In the album's liner notes, he told Todd Mouton, "I'm not saying, 'Well, I'm just trying to preserve zydeco or the Creole culture.'"

At the same time, Geno was creating a life at home that was a refuge from the rigors of the road. At his Double D Ranch in Duralde, he raised cattle and indulged his love of horses by erecting a new barn. While he was away, he enlisted family members to do the daily chores. It was a timeless place. When I visited Geno during Mardi Gras in 1997, I watched the dust rise and move ever closer, as the Courir de Mardi Gras—the masked horse riders and revelers on wagons—slowly made its way down the gravel road toward Geno's house. It was a scenario that might not have changed in a hundred years.

Geno's synthesis of tradition was no better exemplified than on the final record we made together in 1998, *La Chanson Perdue* (the Lost Song). He now had a band, French Rockin' Boogie, that could go wherever he wanted, with Germaine Jack on drums, Steve Nash on rubboard, Joseph "Cookie" Chavis (a Beau Jocque alumnus) on guitar, and John "Popp" Esprite on bass. More importantly, we brought in several like-minded neo-traditionalists from the Cajun world: guitarist and *'tit fer* player Christine Balfa, fiddler and acoustic bassist Dirk Powell, and fiddler Steve Riley. Several songs, including the title track and "'Tite Monde," were played with only acoustic instruments, with the musicians gathered around one stereo pair of microphones. Amédé Ardoin's "Valse de Opelousas" had the raw immediacy of his old records with Dennis McGee. It was a thrilling sound.

With Geno's road-seasoned rhythm section, we cut high-energy versions of John Delafose's "Bernadette," Iry LeJeune's "Bayou Pon Pon," and Geno's own "Je Va's Jamais La Voir Encore (I'll Never See Her Again)." On the pop-leaning side, we recorded Billy Swan's "I Want It All," with Geno tracking the song on accordion and then overdubbing drums. While this song might have suggested a swamp pop treatment, we settled on a ska beat.

Geno had staked out his own territory, approaching his craft with discipline, and with the curiosity of a music scholar. His advantage was in the musical lessons absorbed from his father. He was writing new songs in French, playing the left-hand rhythms on the diatonic accordion that many musicians had left behind, and generally insuring that the Duralde sound remained an exciting and vibrant American roots music niche.

LIL' BRIAN AND THE ZYDECO TRAVELERS

Zydeco music is almost exclusively identified with Louisiana, but Gulf Coast Creole culture extends beyond the Louisiana-Texas border, into Port Arthur, Beaumont, and Houston (as well as to the community of Creoles in the San Francisco Bay Area). The Continental Zydeco Club in Houston's Third Ward was a regular stop for artists such as John Delafose and Clifton Chenier, who also regularly played church dances in the area. And the family connections between Texas and Louisiana Creoles remain strong. For instance, the wife of the renowned Houston bluesman Sam "Lightning" Hopkins, Annette, was Clifton's second cousin.

Brian Terry, from the Houston suburb of Bartlett, began playing accordion at the age of thirteen. His learning curve accelerated quickly after spending two months in Eunice with the Delafose family, who are distantly related to the Terrys. Geno, who is only a few years older, taught him three songs on the diatonic button accordion. Brian sent me his first demo tape when he was fourteen years old, at the recommendation of Stanley "Buckwheat" Dural Jr., and we stayed in touch. He responded to each suggestion or criticism with a new tape, and he worked hard, developing a formidable accordion technique. With the help of his guitar-playing brother Patrick, he began writing his own songs and playing with him in a band that evolved into Lil' Brian and the Zydeco Travelers.

Brian also listened intently to records by Clifton Chenier and Buckwheat. He told me, "Piano accordion I just picked up from watching Buck and listening to Clif." His father, Felmon Terry, saw that his sons were serious about what they were doing, and they found in him an unwavering sponsor. Said Brian, "From day one, he pretty much fronted us the money for guitars, accordions, speakers—he was our backbone, and he gave us support whenever we needed it. He encouraged us to keep going."

Brian jokes about the band's first gig at a Mexican bazaar. Their regular drummer failed to show up, but they went on anyway with a drummer borrowed from a conjunto band that was also on the bill. They were subsequently booked at the Continental Club and at the Juneteenth Festival. In 1990, they won an award for Youngest Zydeco Band at the Southwest Louisiana Zydeco Music Festival in Plaisance.

A critical turning point for the band came when my friend Lee Allen Zeno, the bass player for Buckwheat Zydeco, began rehearsing with them, teaching them instrumental parts, and helping with arrangements. Even though most of the players were just out of high school, they proved to be adept musicians, and the band soon developed a funky, edgy sound, anchored by the tight rhythm section of bassist Emerson "EJ" Jackson, rubboard player Kenneth "Skin" Terry, and drummer Charles "Red" LaMark, III. Red was also an accomplished singer with an ear for vocal harmonies. When Brian sent me his next demo tape, it was clear that he was ready. We decided that Lee Allen and I would coproduce, and that we would record with engineer Tony Daigle at Dockside Studio.

The two albums we made together, *Fresh* and *Z-Funk*, pushed into new territory for all of us. "When Buckwheat came out with *Waitin' For My Ya*

Ya," it changed the whole scenery of zydeco," Brian told Michael Tisserand in the liner notes for *Z-Funk*. "It showed people that zydeco didn't have to be played in one direction." If Buckwheat looked to Southern soul music and classic rock as a way of expanding his musical reach, Lil' Brian was similarly influenced by Tupac, Snoop Dogg, and the Fugees. He continued, "Just because I got an accordion and a scrub board, it doesn't mean I can't play hip-hop and rap." Even his double-kicked dance hall songs such as "H-Town Zydeco" and "Bad Time Woman" are subtly different, with repeated instrumental motifs that are as clearly defined as if they were samples (snippets of music that have been digitally copied and "sequenced" to play over and over).

On *Z-Funk*, we covered James Brown's "Back Up and Try It Again," which Steve Reynolds remixed by creating actual samples of what the musicians played and recomposing them in a new form, while adding or manipulating the sounds. Of course, James Brown's records of the late 1960s and early 1970s were a harbinger of what was to come in popular music production, not only for their beats (which are among the most sampled in hip-hop), but because of their focus on repeated, interlocking parts. In a way, every instrument was playing a "looped" percussive part, with few chord changes to distract from the groove. Now, it was no longer necessary for a musician to perform a repeated part like this in a recording session, as long as he or she played it the right way just once. When digital sampling and recording tools such as Pro Tools and Logic became widely available in the mid-1990s, the idea of creating a record from samples nearly superseded earlier technologies and devices such as MIDI and drum machines.

This method of record production was a world apart from John Delafose's two-and-a-half hour session, but it was enlightening to consider how sampling technology was affecting the way that many musicians conceptualized recording, and how Brian and his bandmates could hear how these two worlds could relate to one another. It could also be great fun, because recording technology had become its own fully creative medium. A collection of samples could serve like the colors of paint on an artist's palette.

The challenge of putting together the right songs and the right people to make a record, and the elation of capturing a one-time magical performance, are the experiences I cherish and value most when it comes to making records. However, Steve and I were both drawn to the world of the more abstract process of sample-based composition and sound design, especially if we could use this technology without losing the essence of the roots music we valued.

That said, for the album's one pure hip-hop performance, "Z-Funk," we cut an old-fashioned live track, although we did add a low-frequency sample to the bass drum sound. Darius "Third Leg" Barnett's rap declares, "Believe it, you know that I'm here, grew up on that blues and that Clifton Chenier." On Lee Allen Zeno's composition "Sunday Walk," Red and I found that our voices blended well, so we stacked them to build the song's harmonized refrain. Lee Allen's arrangement of the King Floyd rhythm and blues song "Baby Let Me Kiss You" would do any New Orleans funk band proud. A modern touch comes from Brian's overdubbed accordion stabs on the one and three beats throughout the song.

The two albums by Lil' Brian and the Zydeco Travelers fared decently in the marketplace, but, by 1997, zydeco had just about run its course as a national phenomenon. I could see how waves of world and regional music, from Cuban to Cajun to South African choral singing, would suddenly reach public consciousness and then just as quickly fade back into their communities, especially when the driving medium was a movie such as *O Brother, Where Art Thou?* or the *Buena Vista Social Club*. With zydeco, it may have been the film *The Big Easy*, and Brian may have caught its last wave. He signed on with North Carolina–based Intrepid Artists, and the band toured steadily, including several trips to Europe. His records remain among the most creative in the last golden age of zydeco.

RECOMMENDED LISTENING:

Geno Delafose and French Rockin' Boogie, "C'est Pas la Peine Brailler (There's No Need to Cry)" from *French Rockin' Boogie*
Chris Ardoin and Double Clutchin', "We Are the Boys" from *Gon' Be Jus' Fine*
Lil' Brian and the Zydeco Travelers, "Z-Funk" from *Z-Funk*

Chapter 17

RHYTHM AND BLUES

BY THE TIME I BEGAN MAKING RECORDS IN LOUISIANA IN 1981, THE TWO golden eras of New Orleans rhythm and blues had faded into the past. From the late 1940s through the early 1960s, the recording scene had been so hot that national record companies were sending artists such as Roy Brown, Little Richard, and Big Joe Turner to New Orleans to catch the hit-making vibe of the city's musicians. As the New Orleans sound got funkier in the 1960s and '70s, a plethora of local labels emerged. Arranger and producer Wardell Quezergue (Nola Records), engineer Cosimo Matassa (White Cliffs Records), record distributor Joe Banashak (Instant Records), "Seafood King" Al Scramuzza (Scram Records), and the team of Marshall Sehorn and Allen Toussaint (Sansu Records) vied for local hits that might earn them a modest return on their investment in studio time and session fees. A few major labels achieved national hits with Toussaint-produced records by artists such as the Meters, Dr. John, and LaBelle.

Each era had its key songwriter and producer. Dave Bartholomew, working especially with Fats Domino, wrote, cowrote, or produced at least a few of the greatest songs of the rock and roll era of the 1950s, including "I Hear You Knocking," "One Night," and "I'm Walkin." Allen Toussaint wrote elegant songs for a handful of singers such as Irma Thomas, Lee Dorsey, and Ernie K-Doe, establishing an urbane and funky sound in the 1960s that resonated around the world. His major hits included Dorsey's "Workin' In a Coal Mine" and K-Doe's "Mother in Law."

Much of the action took place at the succession of recording studios operated by Cosimo Matassa—J&M Recording Studio on North Rampart Street, Cosimo Recording Studio on Governor Nichols, and Jazz City on Camp Street. Later, after having been one of Matassa's regular clients, Allen

Toussaint opened his SeaSaint Studio (a combination of his name and the name of his business partner, Marshall Sehorn) in the Gentilly neighborhood. Matassa—Cos to everyone who knew him—was a modest man with big smile and a corny sense of humor. He is often credited as one of the architects of the rock and roll sound, because of the driving beat of his records, but he told me it was a simple thing. "I just went out into the studio and listened to the sound the instrument was making, then I would go into the control room and record it to see how close it was. I kept moving the microphone or the instrument until I got it right." His method remains good advice for anyone interested in recording today.

In 1981, the New Orleans recording scene was in a lull. The New Orleans Jazz and Heritage Festival was just beginning to prod interest in the city's music, while the pop music of the 1980s had become increasingly reliant on programmed tracks—the antithesis of the loose and syncopated New Orleans sensibility, in which successive measures of a drummer's groove are seldom played exactly the same way. Cos had closed up shop. Yet, all the musical resources that gave New Orleans rhythm and blues its character were still as vibrant as ever—the gospel music, the second-line street parades, the brass bands, the Afro-Caribbean rhythms, and the chants of the Mardi Gras Indians. It had been the genius of both Bartholomew and Toussaint to channel these resources as the foundation of their own productions. The beauty of New Orleans roots music is its connectedness to the lives of the people who play it, sing it, and dance to it, often in neighborhood and noncommercial settings. It is a living tradition, or a related group of traditions, that do not necessarily require a formal stage. I understood how precious this deep musical culture was, as it revealed itself to me in layers over the years. Even New Orleans rappers such as Juvenile and Mystikal tap deeply into these roots, with a sound that embraces New Orleans street beats and funk, even in the context of programmed or beat-centered tracks.

My challenge, as I understood it, was not to look backward for a model of record making, but to try to create situations that allowed the musicality of New Orleans to come forward again in new ways. I relied on a core group of musicians who could help to accomplish this objective, usually working with engineers David Farrell and Steve Reynolds at Ultrasonic Studio on Washington Avenue. The studio was often booked months in advance, because Black Top Records owners Hammond and Nauman Scott were recording artists such as Earl King and Snooks Eaglin there at the same time.

Choosing the right cast for each record was critical, especially when it came to drummers. Herman Ernest III was funky and precise at the same time. Once he learned the arrangement of a song and made his cryptic-looking chart, he would nail the track every time, with every accent perfectly in place. Johnny Vidacovich had a lighter but no less funky approach. He listened to the other musicians and could flow with the moment, giving a different performance with each take (although he could perfectly execute a big-band chart, too). Shannon Powell could pack a deep groove into an often minimalist approach, leaving plenty of space around him. It was like choosing colors for a painting.

For many years, perhaps until Ultrasonic was destroyed by Hurricane Katrina, I felt that I could imagine almost any sound, and know the right person in New Orleans to call to make it. The studio became a hub that, if it never rivaled Cosimo's studio in its busiest years, constituted a third era of recording in New Orleans. Here are stories of many of the musicians I produced during those fruitful years.

WALTER "WOLFMAN" WASHINGTON

It was 2:30 a.m. on Saturday night when Walter Washington and I arrived at Ultrasonic Studio. We had come straight from his gig at the Maple Leaf Bar, where he had played two long sets that left him drenched in perspiration, and still a little bit high. I had become perhaps unreasonably obsessed with getting his vocal right on his recording of a new song written by Doc Pomus and Mac Rebennack called "Hello Stranger," and we had decided this might be the right time.

It was a perfect song for Walter, with a lyric about staring at a stranger in the mirror, an unrecognizable specter who warns that the good times may be over. He had sung it with such exquisite focus and resignation in one of our rehearsals that the musicians and I got goosebumps. A week later, at our initial recording sessions, we had recorded a very good basic track, but it took a while—too long for Walter to be able to summon the feeling he had channeled at the rehearsal, especially as we recorded take after take. David Ellington's MIDI-connected keyboards gave the track a spooky bed,

Walter "Wolfman" Washington (photograph © Rick Olivier)

while Jack Cruz's floating bass line harmonized with Walter's guitar on the chorus. I figured it would not be difficult to add the final vocal later.

We tried to record his vocal and guitar (for they spoke with one voice) on several more occasions, but the spirit still eluded us. Walter knew what I wanted, and he wanted it too. He could always deliver a good performance, but Walter at his best pushed himself past rote performance, seeking a spiritual transcendence that danced into the territory of art.

Now, in the middle of the night, David Farrell set up Walter's amp and vocal mic. Walter was ready. He gave it his best effort for two or three takes, but then he was trying too hard, and the fatigue of the evening overtook him completely. His performance got close, but it still was not all there, except for a magical unison vocal and guitar section toward the end of our second pass.

We did not give up. Finally, one afternoon, Walter plugged in and effortlessly delivered the vocal heard on the record in one take, although we used the section from our 3 a.m. session at the end of the song. I cringed when I thought about how much of our recording budget I had spent chasing this one performance, but it was worth it.

I was introduced to Walter Washington at Dorothy's Medallion Lounge on Orleans Avenue, where his band, the Solar System, backed Johnny

Adams every Friday and Saturday night. Walter would play most of the first set before bringing Johnny on, usually at around 2 a.m., and they would play until the sun came up. He was an integral part of Johnny's first Rounder album, *From the Heart*, which accurately reflects the live vibe of the band, especially the songs they played on the set, such as "Feel Like Breaking Up Somebody's Home."

Born in New Orleans in 1943, Walter became a professional musician while in his teens, backing Irma Thomas in her band the Toronados, and recording with Lee Dorsey on "Ride Your Pony" and "Workin' in a Coal Mine." He traveled to New York to play with Dorsey at the age of nineteen. Walter's recording debut under his own name was the funky Eddie Bo production "Pony Express" for Scram Records in 1969. In the 1980s, he made an album for the producer Senator Jones, on the local Hep' Me label.

On both of these early sessions, his guitar sound and concept are nearly fully formed. While he is often regarded as a blues artist, his playing is more akin to that of a blues-informed jazz guitarist like George Benson, although the choked, machine gun-fast runs he extracts from his guitar are funkier than that. His sound is immediately recognizable, in the same way that B. B. King's or Jimi Hendrix's is. With his command of harmony and the deep spirituality of his singing, he remains one of the last of the New Orleans rhythm and blues iconoclasts, because no one sounds like Walter.

When I approached him about making a record for Rounder's new Modern New Orleans Masters series in 1985, his long-term gig with Johnny Adams at Dorothy's Medallion Lounge had ended, and he was working for a time on Bourbon Street. It was not a prosperous time for Walter, who was living in a small, unheated apartment in the back of a friend's house in Mid-City. It was cold in January 1986 as we went over songs for the record, even with all four burners of the gas stove turned on high. He was in the process of putting together a new band, which included the talented bass player Harold Scott Jr., rhythm guitarist Elijah Rodgers, drummer Van Odom, and his longtime percussionist, George Jackson Jr. I added David Torkanowsky on keyboards and commissioned arranger Bill "Foots" Samuel to write horn arrangements.

Walter's guitar, a Hohner Les Paul copy, was an important part of his signature sound, but the frets were so worn that they were almost level with the furrowed wood of the neck, and the intonation of the instrument was badly off. When soloing, Walter could force the notes into tune, but it was hard work. I asked him, then, if I could take the guitar away for three days, to have new frets installed and to have the neck set up by New Orleans guitar-repair wizard Jimmy Foster. He agreed, and when I returned it to him he seemed happy enough, although it was not the transformative playing experience for him that I thought it would be. Nonetheless, I had learned to check intonation on stringed instruments before heading to the studio, and I am glad I did with Walter.

The sessions with engineer David Farrell at Studio Solo in Slidell went well. We were joined by singer Timothea Beckerman, with whom Walter had been writing songs such as the clever "Thinking for Yourself" and the slow blues "One Way or Another." I mixed the record with engineer Gragg Lunsford at Blue Jay Studio in Massachusetts, and I am afraid we went all out with mid-1980s mixing tricks. The gated snare drum sound, with the reverb seeming to fall off a cliff, and excessive processing of the vocals gave the record a modern sound, in a way. But it also sounded immediately dated, at least when listening in retrospect, even if Walter loved it. The record, *Wolf Tracks*, was well received in blues and soul circles around the world.

Looking back, I can see that it is easy to identify records by the studio effects of their day: the gated snare in the 1980s; the Yamaha DX-7 electric-piano-with-bells sound that seemed to appear on every ballad in the 1980s and '90s; the overly compressed and very loud recordings, with sound files that look like two-by-fours, of the early 2000s; and the auto-tune effect on contemporary records that somehow refuses to go away today. And then there's the Roland TR-808 bass drum sound from the early 1980s, which went away and then came back when it was reintroduced as a common sampling sound. If, when I started out, I was entranced by the *au courant* sounds of novelty technologies used in pop music, I soon endeavored to mostly avoid them.

By the time of Walter's next album, *Out of the Dark*, he had put together his great band, the Roadmasters. Walter and bassist Jack Cruz had made a pact to stick together as musical partners for life, and so far they have, even as almost every other imaginable relationship around them has changed. Saxophonist Tom Fitzpatrick also signed on for the long haul, save for a spell when his own sobriety took precedence over the band's inclination, at the time, to party. Wilbert "Junkyard Dog" Arnold had been performing with Walter since he was a boy. Walter had directed him to play tambourine behind his drummer for two years, until he was ready for the actual drum chair. Lately, Wilbert had taken to securing his drums with a hefty plastic orange chain to keep his cymbal stands grounded. The synchronicity of his playing with Walter's is remarkable.

We also enlisted the young pianist Jon Cleary, who had recently relocated to New Orleans from England, organist Kermit "Champ" Young, and the horn section led by arranger and saxophonist Bill Samuel (with trumpeter Terry Tullos and trombonist Ernie Gautreau).

The band was disciplined and ready to play. The Johnny "Guitar" Watson song "You Can Stay but the Noise Must Go" became an immediate funk favorite on New Orleans radio station WWOZ, while Walter's reading of the Buddy Johnson ballad "Save Your Love for Me" builds to one soulful crescendo after another. In the liner notes to the record, Johnny Adams told writer Tom Smith, "I imagine there are a lot of guys who can play as good as Walter, but they don't have the soul that Walter has." We now had the record to prove it. This time, I was pleased that the mix that I did at Blue Jay Studio with engineer Rob Jaczko was clear and gimmick free, but Walter expressed disappointment that we had not kept the trendier edge that he had appreciated on *Wolf Tracks*.

His next record, *Wolf at the Door*, should have continued our upward trend. In addition to "Hello Stranger," it includes the pop-soul balled "It Doesn't Really Matter," written by Denise Rich, Allan Rich, and Michael O'Hara, who between them had penned hits for Barbra Streisand, Natalie Cole, and Luther Vandross. I was proud of Walter's Teddy Pendergrass–inspired vocal, the horn-driven arrangement, and the backing vocals by ELS. We might have taken a step too far away from the New Orleans funk that was Walter's signature, because the sound veered toward contemporary rhythm and blues without really getting all the way there, but it was satisfying to hear him stretch into new territory. His own composition "Don't Say Goodbye" is a classic jazz-blues ballad with a beautiful solo from Tom.

However, any problems with the record had more to do with overall focus than with songs. One morning, Wilbert's brother arrived at the studio, and the two went around to the back of the building. I had never before heard of click-ems, which are joints soaked in formaldehyde, but I learned that morning that they could rob even the funkiest drummer of his groove, on the day we were scheduled to record live with the horn section. There were also issues with the liquor left over from the Ultrasonic

Studio Christmas party. I have never minded a little bit of stimulation in recording sessions, but if a musician comes to party, he or she can go home.

The record was nonetheless well received, but Walter decided to make a change for his next record, and to sign with the new Virgin Records blues imprint, Point Blank, which had been formed in the wake of the modest success of independent labels such as Rounder, Alligator, and Black Top. Label head John Wooler was a genuine fan who was astute in his signings, which included Albert Collins, Pop Staples, Solomon Burke, Duke Robillard, Johnny Winter, and John Lee Hooker, in addition to Walter. The band stepped up its international touring, and the record they made for Point Blank, *Sada* (named for Walter's young daughter) gained him new fans around the world.

I had assumed I was at the end of my professional relationship with Walter, but when Point Blank folded, as perhaps most major label roots music endeavors eventually do, Walter was again available. He first made a record for a Swiss label, featuring the JB horns (also saxophonist Maceo Parker, tenor saxophonist Pee Wee Ellis, and trombonist Fred Wesley, from James Brown's band, in addition to Tom), but by 1997 the time seemed right to talk about working together again. The band was tighter and funkier than ever—and operating on a higher plane on several levels. Walter now carried his own horn section, which included the formidable arranging chops of trumpet player Larry Carter, and many of the band members had been writing.

Most New Orleans music fans would agree that *Funk Is in the House* stands with Walter's best recordings. If he excels on ballads such as Jerry Butler's "I Stand Accused," the many years the Roadmasters had spent playing together made them one of the sharpest funk bands in New Orleans. In fact, New Orleans was enjoying an all-around funk revival, with younger bands such as Galactic making the sound as relevant and compelling as it had been the first time around. Of course, Walter had been there all along. His playing on the record is alternately ferocious and sweet, always executed with authority and feeling, especially on funk songs such as "Funkyard" and "Wolf Funk."

At the age of seventy-eight, Walter is still at the top of his game. In 2018, he made a wonderful, stripped-down record with Galactic saxophonist and producer Ben Ellman, on which he sang three songs that he had first recorded with Johnny Adams on Rounder, as a sideman. With supporting musicians who include vocalist Irma Thomas, bassist James Singleton, drummer Stanton Moore, and keyboardists Ivan Neville, Jon Cleary, and David Torkanowsky, he was accorded a new round of respect both by his peers and a new generation of fans.

I learned about dedication from Walter, who, in spite of setbacks and the grind of the life of a working musician, never lost the spiritual center that kept him and his band members making music. If the precarious infrastructure of the New Orleans music business left many musicians who came of age in the 1960s by the wayside, Walter's talent and belief in his life mission carried him through. And no one sounds like Walter.

DAVELL CRAWFORD

Perhaps more than any musician working in 2020, Davell Crawford maintains a direct connection to earlier eras of New Orleans rhythm and blues. His grandfather James "Sugar Boy" Crawford recorded the first version of the Mardi Gras anthem "Jock-A-Mo," which he had put together from the Mardi Gras Indian gang songs that he heard in his Central City neighborhood while growing up. Recorded at Cosimo Matassa's J&M Studio and credited to Sugar Boy and His Cane Cutters, it was released nationally by Checker Records in 1954, achieving moderate success. When the song was recorded as "Iko Iko" by the Dixie Cups a decade later, it became a national hit. Sugar Boy's career came to a tragic end when, in 1963, he was brutally beaten by Louisiana State Police officers after a traffic stop. Following years of convalescence, he recovered, but he sang thereafter only in church.

Davell Crawford was a child prodigy who, according to his grandmother Catherine Celestine, was playing competent boogie-woogie piano at the age of five. James Crawford told Jeff Hannusch in *OffBeat*, "He could play better than I ever could [when he was] twelve." I first heard him at the Crescent City Brewhouse on Decatur Street, where he was playing a duo with bassist James Singleton, when he was fourteen.

If much of post–World War II, pre-hip-hop American popular music was emblazoned with the sound of the electric guitar or the tenor saxophone, the best-known stars of New Orleans music have played either trumpet (Louis Armstrong, Louis Prima, Nicholas Payton, Terence Blanchard, Al Hirt, Trombone Shorty) or piano. In fact, it is the long line of New Orleans pianists that most clearly set the city's sound apart. Jelly Roll Morton, Tuts Washington, Professor Longhair, Fats Domino, Eddie Bo, Dr. John, James Booker, Sweet Emma Barrett, Allen Toussaint, Jon Cleary, Henry Butler, Tom McDermott, David Torkanowsky, Harry Connick Jr., and Jon Batiste trace the full history of New Orleans music.

Davell Crawford is one of the latest musicians in this elite lineage. His impeccable gospel-rooted technique gives him the ability to play anything he chooses, from jazz ballads, to modern funk on the Hammond B-3 organ, to the rhythm and blues piano styles of the 1950s. In fact, it has sometimes been difficult for Davell to focus his vision on one musical objective at a time, and his performances can be impulsive. Yet the sublime artistry he achieves when it all comes together dances across genres with glee. He often brings his audiences to their feet. At times, Davell has been compared to James Booker, but Davell's gregariousness is the opposite of Booker's self-medicated isolation. Even when Davell and I were not seeing eye to eye, I appreciated his kind and outgoing nature.

At the time we began working together, he was living with his grand-mother in the apartment behind her beauty parlor on North Broad Street. Ms. Celestine, a vivacious woman who is originally from Lafayette, raised Davell during his adolescent years. She was one of his biggest fans, and he respected her immensely. Once, I said something to her about how her precocious grandchild must have been a handful. She smiled and said, "Child, you don't know the half of it."

When he signed with Rounder Records, he may have been the first art-ist I produced who had been modestly influenced by some of the records I had made. For new recordings of three of his grandfather's songs, he wanted a big rhythm and blues band conducted by Wardell Quezergue, with trumpet player Charlie Miller, guitarist Renard Poché, saxophonists Alvin "Red Tyler and Fred Kemp, and drummer Herman Ernest III among the musicians. We also recorded three solo pieces, and several classic blues ballads, including the album's title track, "Let Them Talk," which Davell had learned from James Booker's recording.

On "Can't Nobody Do Me Like Jesus," Davell enlisted the sixty-voice teenage choir from John F. Kennedy Senior High School. We could not afford to pay each singer, so we made a donation to the school's music program and bought everyone lunch from McDonald's. At his young age, Davell was already in demand as a choir director and arranger, and I was impressed with his efficiency as he masterfully taught parts to the singers. For a second gospel song, we recorded the standard "Walk Around Heaven" as a duet with Davell and his grandfather, James "Sugar Boy" Crawford.

We discovered that Mr. Crawford owned a locksmith business, and that he often serviced cars at the body shop behind Ultrasonic Studio. We would often see his van parked there, and every now and then, he would stop in to say hello to David and Steve.

Through Davell, I gained a deeper understanding of the depth of the New Orleans gospel world, as he brought in backing singers and the tambourine player Charles Cockerham, who had raised his instrument to a virtuosic level. Later, Davell introduced me to one of his mentors (both as a musician and as a gay man who was prominent in New Orleans gospel music), Raymond Myles, who was one of New Orleans most beloved gospel artists before he was murdered at the age of forty, by an acquaintance while carjacking his new SUV. I came to appreciate the space made in the church, however discretely, for talented gay artists.

Davell was understandably new to the recording process, and it could be difficult at times for me to temper his desire to keep adding more layers of sounds to our tracks, even if each idea he had sounded good on its own. But I also learned to be flexible. When resinging several of his vocals, he was uncomfortable with standing still in front of the studio's wonderful Neumann U-87 microphone. After engineer David Farrell set up a handheld Shure Beta 58 microphone, Davell could roam the studio as he sang. If the sound might not have measured up to the Neumann, the performances Davell delivered were worth it. And, sometimes, the least expensive microphone can be best suited to a singer's voice, so a blind comparison of microphones with each artist can often be worth the effort.

Upon the album's release in 1995, Davell was heralded, especially in Europe, as the new savior of New Orleans rhythm and blues. At the age of seventeen, he had an assured presence, whether interpreting older songs or improvising as a solo pianist. Yet he was no retro act, and his versions of the Sugar Boy Crawford songs "I Bowed on My Knees," "She's Got a Wobble When She Walks," and "No More Heartaches" managed to avoid a revivalist tone, because of the unforced tone of his delivery, Wardell's charts, and Herman's drumming. His virtuosity was clear.

On the strength of the album and on my recommendation, my friend Graziano Uliani booked Davell at the 1996 Porretta Soul Festival in Italy, with a five-piece, all-star New Orleans ensemble that included the keyboardist and saxophonist Thaddeus Richard, an alumnus of Paul McCartney's band. But when Davell arrived at the rehearsals in Porretta, along with his attorney and new manager, Ellis Pailet, three young Italian musicians were in tow. Graziano was livid, especially because this was his first all–New Orleans band in what had generally been a Memphis-oriented festival.

"I am paying for an all-star New Orleans band, not Italian boys!" he exclaimed.

The solution was obvious to me. Davell would perform solo, as the festival's opening act. I knew he could do it, and that he would likely put on a show so exciting that he would be a tough act to follow. He agreed. I let Graziano know. He suggested that the fee be reduced by half, which seemed like a fair proposal. I then asked Ellis if this arrangement would be amenable to him.

"It doesn't say anywhere in his contract who the musicians have to be," was his response, in spite of having provided biographies of the musicians that were printed in the Porretta program. "Davell gets his full fee, or he doesn't go on."

It came down to a suspenseful moment, just before Davell was scheduled to perform. Ellis insisted that unless he was paid the full fee, there would be no show. I told Davell, "I think you know the right thing to do." And then he did, over his manager's objection, playing Hammond B-3 organ and piano in an unforgettable show. The audience and Graziano were happy. The incident reminded me of why I did not want to be an artist manager, because I found the episode very stressful.

Back in New Orleans, we started thinking about what direction to take with Davell's next recordings, and where he wanted his career to go. He could be the next Little Richard or Fats Domino if he wanted to, but that did not feel right, nor did any other purely retro course. Ultimately, we decided to make two very different albums that would both continue to attract the attention of the European jazz festivals and promoters. The first would be an all-instrumental jazz/funk album with Davell playing the Hammond B-3 organ, while the second would be an album of romantic jazz ballads and instrumentals, played on piano.

He told me he wanted a change of environment from Ultrasonic Studio, so we decided to record with engineer Jim Albert at the American Sector, a new studio that had opened in the old Masonic Temple, downtown at 333 St. Charles Avenue (the number was significant to Masons). The Egyptian-themed décor of hieroglyphics, human figures in profile, and intricately painted columns had been left in place, giving the studio an *Indiana Jones* vibe that was indeed a contrast to Ultrasonic.

On *The B-3 and Me*, Davell plays the complete instrument, using the bass pedals to accompany the chords and melodic lines he plays with his hands, so there was no bass player—just a core group of Shannon Powell on drums and Clarence Johnson III on tenor saxophone. Davell found his perfect foil in the twenty-three-year-old Johnson, whose rough rhythm and blues tone is coupled with a harmonic sensibility that verges on the avant-garde. Shannon always makes the music feel good. I am almost sure there is no other musician on the planet who expresses so much joy when he plays, and he is a great asset on any session. In the tradition of the great organ combo records by Jimmy Smith, Brother Jack McDuff, and Dr. Lonnie Smith, the record would be funky, occupying a zone between jazz and rhythm and blues.

The sessions were fun, especially when the trio caught a groove on an up-tempo song such as Davell's arrangement of the Aretha Franklin song "House That Jack Built," which features the wah-wah guitar of June Yamagishi, or Sugar Boy Crawford's "Ooh Wee Sugar." Davell's compositions "The Cat" and "Uptown" manage to be hot and cool at the same time, with his sure-footed walking bass, and very much within the organ combo tradition. Perhaps the album was not the great artistic statement of Davell's career, but it was clear that he was among the upper echelon of New Orleans musicians.

The following album, 1998's *Love Like Yours and Mine*, reveals a more mature and gentler—but no less soulful—side of Davell, with bassist Mark Brooks and drummer Shannon Powell in support. His wistful, slowed-down take on the standard "Fly Me to the Moon" sets the tone, with a vocal that reminds me of Sarah Vaughan. He told liner note writer Geraldine Wyckoff that he composed the instrumental "Adenika" (which means "affectionate" in Swahili) when he was fourteen years old, after betting his grandmother that he could write a song in twenty-two minutes. Thaddeus Richard added a wonderful flute part to the track. The underappreciated pianist Henry Butler, who could play everything from avant-garde jazz to Professor Longhair–style rhumbas with great authority, and who was one of Davell's mentors, accompanies Davell's vocal on "Detour Ahead." The songs "Sunday Morning" and the masterful solo version of "Let It Be," with its churchy chord substitutions, have Davell's gospel chops on full display.

In an era when artists such as Diana Krall were selling out concert halls, I was excited about the album and this artistic path for Davell, who was still not twenty years old. He could sing a ballad such as "Detour Ahead" with unerring clarity and class, but he could also get funky.

The sessions were not without conflict. As we progressed, Davell began gravitating toward a sound that had more in common with contemporary artists such as Maxwell or D'Angelo than with the classic-sounding jazz direction we had chosen. At times, it was neither easy to keep the session focused nor for Davell to keep his attention on one direction long enough to get something constructive done. He could be so impetuous that he would not finish the idea at hand before moving on to the next one. As with many of the most gifted artists I have recorded, the sessions were far more productive when a spirit of in-the-moment connectedness visited us. With Davell, the spirit was worth waiting for, but we spent way too much time between productive moments, often waiting for Davell to arrive at the studio. We went so far over budget that he did not get the full advance he had been planning on. Ms. Celestine let me know she was not pleased, but when I explained, she countered with a look of resignation that let me know she had been there before with Davell. He once told me that the name of his music publishing company, Crawpita, was not an homage to some Cajun-Middle Eastern fusion dish, but that it stood for "Crawford Pain in the Ass."

I never produced another full album with Davell, but we continued to work together on sessions by Ruth Brown, Chuck Carbo, and Irma Thomas, and on the Tangle Eye record of remixes of Alan Lomax recordings that Steve Reynolds and I made. After Hurricane Katrina, Davell moved to New York City, where he still spends much of his time, but he visits home often. At a recent concert at Snug Harbor in New Orleans, Davell introduced me as his uncle, saying that I had taught him some things he did not necessarily want to hear at the time.

I still puzzle over Davell. What does a musician who might well be the preeminent embodiment of a deep and magnificent tradition do to stay relevant to him or herself as an artist? How does an artist or producer bring that tradition forward without repeating the past, or repeating something that has already been said? I love listening to old New Orleans rhythm and blues records, but I generally dislike recordings that seek to recreate the sounds, songs, and attitude of those eras. I mean, what is the point? Then again, losing a musical tradition that is performed as part of a living social environment seems akin to losing a language—a valuable resource that future generations will be poorer in not knowing.

Davell Crawford remains one of the most immensely talented musicians with whom I have worked, and I cannot wait to hear what he does next.

THERYL "HOUSEMAN" DE'CLOUET

If New Orleans rhythm and blues has remained relevant in 2021, it is largely through its variant known as funk. Pioneered in the 1960s by groups such as the Meters and producer/pianist Eddie Bo (who employed the wildly gifted drummer James Black), New Orleans funk may be the most rhythmically sophisticated and syncopated sound in American popular music.

New Orleans funk may be a part of the legacy of Congo Square (located today in Armstrong Park), where, beginning in the early 1800s, enslaved people of African descent were permitted to gather on Sundays to dance, play music, and engage in trade. Unlike most areas in the United States, where African cultures were often violently suppressed, the French and Creole hegemony in Louisiana sometimes allowed a small shred of humanity and shared culture to endure, even if the participants were from many different countries. The gatherings even became a sort of tourist attraction.

New Orleans is often called the northernmost port of the Caribbean. The interchange with countries such as Cuba and Haiti provided an influx of influences and immigrants with different variants of African- and Spanish-derived rhythms, such as the habanera, rhumba, tango, and mambo. The pianist and composer Jelly Roll Morton considered Latin and Caribbean rhythms to be an essential part of New Orleans music. As he told Alan Lomax in his Library of Congress interviews, ". . . if you can't manage to put tinges of Spanish in your tunes, you will never be able to get the right seasoning, I call it, for jazz." The rhythms of the bamboula and the clavé permeate New Orleans rhythm and blues, traditional jazz, and the street beats of second-line brass bands and the Mardi Gras Indian gangs.

Yet there is no exact parallel to New Orleans funk in Africa or in the Caribbean. With its blues influences, it remains a uniquely American invention that perseveres especially in the city's drummers. In 2021, it remains easy to hear the inimitable funk sound in New Orleans in the drumming of musicians such as Terence Higgins, Herlin Riley, Russell Batiste, Shannon Powell, Stanton Moore, Joe Dyson, Johnny Vidacovich, and Raymond Weber. They could be from nowhere else.

After the original Meters broke up and splintered into different groups (the Neville Brothers, George Porter's Runnin' Pardners, the Funky Meters, and others), the funk sound never went away. Then, in the mid-1990s, a young group of college-aged musicians calling themselves Galactic Prophylactic (quickly shortened to Galactic) began playing Meters-inspired music and appearing in clubs around town. While their sound grew to embrace other influences, they became fixtures on the jam band circuit, inspiring many other musicians to follow in their path, and generally spreading the funk message. Their New Orleans–born drummer, Stanton Moore, had the funk feel in his bones.

For most of their first decade, Galactic's vocalist was Theryl "Houseman" de'Clouet, an experienced singer who was a decade or two older than his bandmates. His rough-edged voice had been hewn not only by decades of experience with vocal groups such as the Lyrics and Hollygrove (named for the New Orleans neighborhood where he was born in 1951), but, by his own admission, years of hard living. Of his experiences on the road with the Lyrics, he told Jonathan Tabak in the liner notes of *The Houseman Cometh*, the album we made together, " . . . we were too drug-laden and strung out, so we eventually had to come home after a year. We had a chance, man, but we didn't have all the right ingredients behind our talent." He had acquired his nickname when a fight broke out at a craps game at his house. When he slammed a pistol down on the table, it mistakenly fired, putting an end to the fight. He declared, "I'm the house man," and the name stuck.

With Galactic, he was now clean in more ways than one, appearing onstage in brilliantly colored custom-tailored suits and achieving the kind of success that had eluded him when he was younger. He was an easygoing person with a big smile for everyone, and a hard-won perspective on the ups and downs of life. When we met, he seemed to be enjoying every moment, often projecting the aura of a stoned Zen master. He was living with his aunt Meriel in her neat Hollygrove home, and I could not help but notice his immaculately made bed and the general lack of clutter when we went to his room to listen to songs for the record we would make.

Theryl's deal in 2000 with Rounder Records was facilitated by Edgar "Dino" Gankendorff, an attorney who (some would say, "at long last") was providing New Orleans musicians with fair and expert legal advice. If New Orleans has never had the music business infrastructure of other Southern music cities such as Nashville or Austin, it had grown to the point that musicians who needed help could get it. Perhaps a New Orleans music industry has not developed further because the music itself is not an easy-to-package commercial commodity, and because a culture of songwriting has never been as strong as its grooves.

I loved the idea of working with Theryl, because, like his idol Johnny Adams, he was a singer who valued a good song, and who had the kind of big ears that enabled him to approach each song as its own story. There is nothing I love more than putting together a team behind a singer—the writers, musicians, arrangers, and engineers who will give them everything he or she needs to put each song across. It is an old-school approach, since many artists and groups today are more self-contained, or rely on a producer for a programmed track or beat. But the idea of a group of specialists coming together to create something greater than any of us could accomplish as individuals has never lost its appeal to me.

Now, with Johnny gone, here was an opportunity to bring everything I had learned in working with him into play again. As Theryl and I made our plans, it was clear that we would embrace the funk of Galactic, who would appear on two tracks, but that we could also reach into the realm of orchestrated rhythm and blues that we both loved. This would be his debut recording as a solo artist, and he was ready to show the world what he could do.

Theryl brought several excellent songs to the table that he had written with his friend and former musical partner, the percussionist Michael Ward. Prior to joining Galactic, Theryl had fronted Michael Ward and Reward, one of the funkiest and perhaps least-appreciated bands in the city, that would surely have ridden the new wave of funk to greater success had Ward not died in 1998. I also reached out to my regular songwriting friends, including Dan Penn, Bucky Lindsey, and David Egan, who each sent material that Theryl loved.

The core of our recording band would be bassist Cornell Williams and guitarist June Yamagishi, with whom Theryl had worked in Michael Ward and Reward, abetted by drummer Jeffery "Jellybean" Alexander and multi-instrumentalist Thaddeus Richard, the New Orleans musician who had been a member of Paul McCartney and Wings. Horns would be arranged by Ed Petersen and, on the recommendation of Thaddeus, Don Vappie, who is best known as a purveyor of traditional Creole music, and for his substantial chops as a traditional jazz player. He is one of the city's most versatile musicians. We would bring in guests who included rappers Derrick Freeman and Menace, and pianist Henry Butler.

Two of the songs that I am most proud of in my career as a record producer appear on *The Houseman Cometh*, both written by Theryl and Michael Ward. "Ain't No Yachts in the Ghetto" could be played to an initiate as the definition of funk, with a locked-in groove that left me on the edge of my seat as it went down. It is not a big production—only the four musicians in the rhythm section, playing interlocking, syncopated lines, without wasting a note. Each musician is essentially playing a percussion part, like a multilayered expansion of a New Orleans street beat. Perhaps the track's alchemy was inspired by the loop of a conga sample played by Michael Ward, which we had obtained from producer Mark Bingham. June added an extra guitar part, and Menace added a rap where a solo might have gone. The song talks about the complicity of government agencies in ferrying drugs to inner-city neighborhoods.

The second song is "Two Wrongs." With its steady, Steely Dan–like groove, the song builds to a swinging close, with a big horn section riffing behind tightly harmonized background vocals by Cornell, Charles Elam III, and Earl J. Smith. It reminds me of Thom Bell's records by the Spinners, which were a marvel of grit and gloss in the same moment. I played the solo on harmonica.

The album closes on a yearning, gentle note with the David Egan and Buddy Flett song "If That's What It Takes." Theryl's vocal is supported only by June's acoustic guitar and Stanton Moore's pandeiro (the Brazilian hand drum).

The two tracks with Galactic, "I Get Lifted" and "Ready Willin' and Able," were as natural as breathing, but a legal issue emerged. The band's label at the time, Capricorn Records, refused our request for the band to appear on the record, so we had to replace bassist Robert Mercurio's parts with new ones played by Cornell Williams. It seemed like such a stupid technicality, especially after the label was soon sold to another company, and the band's involvement with the label ended.

The album was not the major success that Theryl and I had hoped for, but it has achieved a kind of cult status among New Orleans rhythm and blues fans. Perhaps if we had stuck with only funk, we would have struck a better chord with the jam band audience that knew Theryl through Galactic, but we were both proud of the depth of the record. He passed away in New Orleans in 2018, following a period of declining health.

CHUCK CARBO

It was not often that I had the opportunity to work with the New Orleans rhythm and blues pioneers from the first golden era of the 1950s. With Chuck Carbo's 1996 album, *The Barber's Blues*, I had the good fortune to work with two of them. Carbo himself was the lead singer of the preeminent New Orleans vocal group of the 1950s, the Spiders, who scored two Dave Bartholomew–produced national hits on the Imperial label in 1954. The other was pianist Edward Frank, who was an integral part of the band at Cosimo Matassa's studio, where he supported local artists such as Lloyd Price, Bobby Charles, and Shirley and Lee, as well as national figures like Big Joe Turner and Elmore James.

Born in Houma, Louisiana, in 1926, Hayward "Chuck" Carbo was one of the great voices of New Orleans rhythm and blues, and if he did not have the range of slightly younger singers such as Johnny Adams or Aaron Neville, his smooth tenor had earned him the nickname "the Voice of New Orleans." But, by the mid-1960s, he had more or less retired from the music business to raise a family, although his 1970 Eddie Bo–produced single, "Can I Be Your Squeeze," is a quirky only-in-New Orleans recording. With backing by Eddie Bo's band, the Soul Finders, and likely featuring James Black on drums, the track is a classic example of sputtering period funk, with Chuck, Eddie, and other singers sharing the vocals.

In 1989, he and Edward Frank got back in the game with *Life's Ups and Downs*, for the local 504 record label. The album yielded two local hits: the jaunty "Second Line on Monday" and a version of the Jimmy and Jeannie Cheatham blues "Meet Me with Your Black Drawers On." The feel of the

Mac "Dr. John" Rebennack, Chuck Carbo, Dave Bartholomew, and Edward Frank at Ultrasonic Studio, 1990s (photograph © Rick Olivier)

record was timeless and relaxed, more informed by traditional jazz than by funk or any other more recent developments. It was a stylish and elegant musical approach that once prevailed in nightclubs such as the Mardi Gras Lounge at Mason's Las Vegas Strip on South Claiborne Avenue, where Edward Frank often performed. (In 1996, when we made our record, all that remained of Mason's was a run-down hotel with a bulletproof reception desk window, and optional hourly rates.) It also had an inimitable New Orleans feel that was brought to the session by drummer Shannon Powell. In spite of Shannon's relatively young age, he has always impressed me as an old soul who can summon the spirit of the earliest jazz.

Chuck was signed to Rounder by Marian Leighton-Levy, and his first Rounder album, *Drawers Trouble*, was produced by Ron Levy. I was asked to take the reins for his second Rounder release, *The Barber's Blues*, named for the ribald Doc Pomus/Dr. John song that Dr. John had given Chuck. Dr. John had been a longtime Chuck Carbo supporter, going back to sessions he produced for Chuck in the 1960s for Jackson, Mississippi–based Ace Records.

Edward Frank is one of the unheralded heroes of New Orleans music. I had gotten to know him on the sessions for the *Jelly* album by the Dirty Dozen Brass Band, on which he arranged the compositions "Sidewalk

Blues" and "Milenberg Joys." Edward had a keen ear, knowing how to build a song and to voice a small horn section to make it sound huge. Arrangers often get short shrift when it comes to credit for making records, because the right arrangement can make a good song sound magnificent. While record production inherently involves arranging—choosing, coaching, and balancing the different parts the musicians play—the ability to hear harmony and moving chords in the abstract, and then to write them down, is a specialized talent. A downside of the skill is that, unlike for the artist, songwriters, and musicians, there are no mechanisms in place for arrangers to share royalties. Because Edward had put so much work into the Chuck Carbo record, I thought it was appropriate to give him a coproducer credit.

Edward Frank was also a wonderful pianist who had overcome a major obstacle. While in his twenties, he had suffered an aneurysm that left him partially paralyzed on his left side. As a result, he became a one-handed piano player. Because of his ability to voice chords and to play bass notes with a stride-like technique, he remained one of the first-call pianists in the city, especially for traditional jazz gigs. His recordings with his own modern jazz quartet appear on the Kalamu ya Salaam–produced *New New Orleans Music* series on Rounder.

When I arrived at Ultrasonic Studio, the band was ready to go. For the first time, I met and worked with the old-school rhythm section of Fats Domino bass player Erving Charles and the talented drummer Bernard "Bunchy" Johnson. Guitarist Eugene Ross, an alumnus of the Ray Charles Orchestra who lived in Baton Rouge, played on most of the album. Perhaps more out of habit than comfort, he wanted to stay at the dilapidated Mason's Hotel (which is how I was able to view the lobby, when I paid the bill). Edward played piano on most of the tracks. Steve Reynolds, who was now the solo engineer on many of my projects, joined me at the console.

Edward had already arranged most of the songs, including a few that I might not have chosen, such as the Ray Noble composition "The Very Thought of You" and the blues standard "Every Day I Have the Blues," both of which had been recorded so often that they deserved a respectful retirement. Yet, the classic feel of the arrangements and Chuck's vocals seemed to reflect a place and a time that was slipping away, and I could not bring myself to jettison them. I brought a new Dan Penn/Charlie Taylor soul ballad, "I'd Rather Beg," which is an answer to Dan's "Dark End of the Street." To add additional depth to some of the songs, I augmented the band with Davell Crawford on Hammond B-3 organ and piano, as well as with guitarist Cranston Clements and keyboardist David Torkanowsky on one cut each.

The highlight of the album may be "Hey, Mardi Gras (Here I Am)," a new composition by Chuck, Edward, and their songwriting partner Ruth Durand. In New Orleans at Carnival time, the songs of the season are as pervasive as Christmas music in December. Adding a new song to the canon is never a bad thing, and this one captures the spirit from the first note. Davell's soaring organ and percolating piano lead the way.

The Barber's Blues, I think, offers a window into the music of an earlier time, when, as Irma Thomas told me, a parallel world existed for African Americans in New Orleans (and for many, it still does). Commercial strips along North Claiborne Avenue, Dryades Street (now Oretha Castle Haley Boulevard) and other areas offered not only entertainment, but clothing stores, legal services, and groceries. These were the Black Main Streets of New Orleans. Irma observed that the civil rights movement of the 1960s, for all the hard-won progress it achieved, also sounded the death knell for these centers of community life, even if no one would choose today to go back in time. The nightclub scene of that era had provided both work and an incubator for the talent that fueled the New Orleans rhythm and blues years. I was fortunate to get a glimpse.

DALTON REED

One day in 1991, I was sitting at the bar in El Sid O's Zydeco and Blues Club in Lafayette, Louisiana, talking with owner Sid Williams, when the employee who was mopping the floor began playing the jukebox. The song was Otis Redding's "Chained and Bound," but it was not Otis's recording. The voice was impassioned and tender, and it demanded my full attention.

"Sid, do you know who that is?" I asked. "What a great voice."

"Oh yeah," he replied. "That's Reed. He lives up the street."

And that was my introduction to Dalton Reed, whom I met later that day.

Born in Cade, Louisiana, in 1952, Dalton was a gentle, big-hearted man who made his living as a welder, and who cherished his role as a father. We were just about the same age, and we immediately bonded over our shared musical interests. He performed around town every now and then, including at El Sid O's, and had released the 45-rpm record of "Chained and

Dalton Reed and Scott Billington (photograph © Scott Billington)

Bound" a few years earlier on the Reed Brothers label, which he founded
with his brother. My friend Lee Allen Zeno, who also knew Dalton, told
me how much he appreciated him.

Back at the Rounder Records offices in Massachusetts, I played Dalton's
record for the three founders, who agreed almost immediately to give me a
modest budget to make a record with him. Dalton had not been expecting
anything from our meeting, so when I called him with the good news, he
did not know what to say, although I could envision him smiling in disbelief. I proposed that Lee Allen and I coproduce the record, and asked Dalton
to think of musicians in the area with whom he might be able to rehearse.

We began working on finding and writing songs, which came to include
the new Delbert McClinton/Johnny Neel "Read Me My Rights," the Gary
Nicholson/Dan Penn/Carson Whitsett "Blues of the Month Club" (which
later became the title track of a Joe Louis Walker album), and the Doc
Pomus/Mac Rebennack "Full Moon." When we convened for rehearsals with our primarily Lafayette-based band in late 1991, it was clear that
Dalton had put a great amount of work into learning the songs and plotting
his approach. He knew exactly what he wanted to do with them, so no lyric
sheets were needed. Dalton's voice could be rougher than the prevailing
style of the 1990s, but he also had a sweetness in his delivery that gave him
his range as a song interpreter.

The album, *Louisiana Soul Man*, announced to the world that a new and compelling soul music voice had arrived, even surprising local music critics. Dalton stepped up his performance schedule, which included a New Orleans Jazz and Heritage Festival debut that unfortunately coincided with a major thunderstorm and ensuing deep mud in front of the stage. When Rounder sent him a stack of black-and-white publicity photos, I asked him if he was able to use them. "Well, I put one of them on the wall, and all the rats and roaches disappeared," was his tongue-in-cheek response. He began to imagine the crazy idea that he might have a career in music.

Everyone at Rounder loved the album, and we made plans for a follow-up. Of all the records I have made, I think Dalton's *Willing and Able* may have come closest to the my ideal of a rhythm and blues record that lives within the tradition while succeeding as contemporary music, something along the lines of what a song-driven Bonnie Raitt album might accomplish. I had reached out to every songwriter and publisher that I thought might have the right songs, and they came through. The musicians would constitute a pan-Southern dream band that included bassist Lee Allen Zeno, Memphis guitarist Michael Toles, Lafayette keyboardist Chet Blakistone, Baton Rouge drummer David Peters, and New Orleans musicians and singers David Torkanowsky, Sammy Berfect, Charles Elam III, and Earl J. Smith. Bill Samuel would provide horn arrangements.

Then, over Thanksgiving weekend in 1993, we worked almost around the clock, with David, Steve, and Jay Gallagher tag teaming engineering duties. I asked a great deal of everyone, because I had committed the bulk of the budget to the musicians, travel, and hotels, and we had had no choice but to get the recording done in a relatively short period of time. Part of my job as a producer was to bring each record in on budget, but this one was tight. I had little time to sleep, and even when I managed to get to bed, the music in my ears kept me awake.

Yet neither the energy of the record nor the crew ever flagged. In the time that had passed since the first record, Dalton's confidence had grown, and he was not afraid to push himself to his limits. While cutting the title track, composed by Tower of Power's Ellis Hall, Dalton reached for a note at the modulation that made us all gasp. "You better keep that, because I don't know if I could ever hit that again," he said with a smile. We completed the track with an orchestration by Bill, and smooth backing vocals from Chuck and Earl.

Michael Toles was the album's instrumental star. On the tough Bonnie Hayes–composed "The One Thing," he played two interlocking rhythm parts that set up Chet's clavichord, while on the Zeno/Reed song "Back on Track" he harmonized with himself on the solo. He worked at blinding speed, dialing in sounds from his SansAmp, a new device that emulated classic tube amplifiers. While David, Steve, and I were at first skeptical, Michael knew what he was doing, and we saved the substantial time it would have taken us to set up an amp and microphone for each new part.

Jonnie Barnett's "Never Never Land" lands on a deep funk groove, while the Dan Penn/Bucky Lindsey song "I Guess You Didn't Love Me Enough" takes a lazy, Jimmy Reed–type blues groove to new territory on the bridge. On each of the ten songs, Dalton sings with power and grace, and with an unerring sense of storytelling. We were all proud of what we had done. I was sure that Dalton was on his way to becoming a successful international music festival attraction, and a bright star in the Lafayette music world.

Then, Dalton died at the age of forty-two. He had traveled to Minneapolis for a gig at the Blues Saloon, where he would be backed by a local band who would subsequently back him on a short tour. After a rehearsal with them, he returned to his hotel room, where he suffered a heart attack. He was being treated at the time for high blood pressure, but otherwise was a healthy man in the prime of life. I do not think the death of any other musician with whom I had worked had a more profound effect on me.

At the funeral, his two compact discs were placed in the coffin with him. His dream had come true, but the world had lost one of the most promising roots music talents of the 1990s.

RECOMMENDED LISTENING:

Walter "Wolfman" Washington, "You Can Stay but the Noise Must Go" from *Out of the Dark*
Walter "Wolfman" Washington, "Hello Stranger" from *Wolf at the Door*
Davell Crawford, "I Bowed on My Knees" from *Let Them Talk*
Davell Crawford, "Fly Me to the Moon" from *Love Like Yours and Mine*
Theryl "Houseman" de'Clouet, "Two Wrongs" from *The Houseman Cometh*
Theryl "Houseman" de'Clouet, "Ain't No Yachts in the Ghetto" from *The Houseman Cometh*
Chuck Carbo, "Hey Mardi Gras (Here I Am)" from *The Barber's Blues*
Dalton Reed, "Willing and Able" from *Willing and Able*

Chapter 18

TANGLE EYE

AFTER A DECADE OF EXPERIMENTATION WITH CREATING SAMPLE-DRIVEN remixes of tracks we had recorded with Beau Jocque, Chris Ardoin, Corey Harris, and many others, Steve Reynolds and I began imagining a bigger project. We had heard Moby's remix of the Vera Hall's "Trouble No More" (released as "Natural Blues"), and I had been intrigued with Beck's *Odelay* record from the moment I heard it. But we wondered. What if we could use sampling and editing technology to extend the feeling conveyed by the artists we might sample, rather than making remixes strictly for their danceability and sonic novelty? Could we bring an authentic roots sensibility to the craft of the remix, rather than using samples simply as atmospheric ornaments on an otherwise unrelated dance track or musical collage?

The source of the recordings that we might remix became obvious. Throughout the 1990s and into the early 2000s, Rounder Records had embarked on an ambitious program of compact disc reissues of the field recordings of Alan Lomax, who was perhaps the most prolific ethnomusicologist of the twentieth century. His thousands of recordings, generally made on location—on front porches, in churches, and at work—are a unique overview of locally based, noncommercial American roots music. In all, Rounder released over one hundred albums, not only of Lomax's work in the United States, but of recordings he made in Great Britain, the Caribbean, Italy, and Spain.

The son of the pioneering American folk music researcher John Lomax, his work was not without controversy. Like others before him, such as country music founding father A. P. Carter, Alan Lomax listed himself as the cowriter (and, therefore, songwriter royalty recipient) on many of the songs he discovered and recorded. Currently, 979 works are registered in his name at the performing rights agency BMI, including "Tom Dooley," which was a number-one hit for the Kingston Trio, and folk standards such as "Red River Valley." This was not an uncommon practice. For instance, record impresario Morris Levy is listed as the cowriter of hits such as Lee Dorsey's "Ya Ya," which became the most popular song I produced by Buckwheat Zydeco. In the 1950s, it was even common to give cowriting credit to a powerful disc jockey, such as Alan Freed received on Chuck Berry's "Maybellene." Contemporary standards might dictate that someone like Alan Lomax make publishing agreements with his artists, rather than taking a cut of the songwriters' royalties.

Nonetheless, in a quirky manifestation of song publishing practice, Alan Lomax is listed as a cowriter on Jay-Z's song "Takeover," which uses a sample with an underlying composition derived from his recording of "Rosie" in a Mississippi prison in the late 1940s. He is also listed as a coauthor of Beyoncé's "Freedom" because samples of his recordings are used in the track.

What is more important, though, is that over and again Alan Lomax recorded music that otherwise might have been lost to time. He sought out songs that had been passed on from person to person and that represented the character and struggles of a community or a culture, although it has been argued that he led his musicians toward his own vision of authenticity. He knew what he was after, and if one of his subjects began performing a song that he or she had learned from a recording or from the radio, he would stop them. The acceleration of the folk process began with radio and with the first records of the 1920s, spreading repertoire and songs faster than oral tradition ever could, especially when a song became popular. Today, it could be argued that this acceleration has become complete. With almost all music available on streaming services all the time, regional music traditions survive by choice and by the nature of their functionality in their communities, and not because of their isolation.

Steve and I were drawn to Rounder's fourteen-disc overview of Alan Lomax's Southern Journey recordings, because they tapped the heritage of the exact musical territory in which we lived—blues, work songs, hymns, and old ballads. Lomax had made these recordings between the late 1940s and early 1960s, and there were many a cappella vocals in the collection, perfect for sampling and rearranging.

The salient quality of these performances, and of most of the music that Lomax recorded, is that they were made by singers and musicians who were not seeking a professional advantage of any kind. For someone like me who has made a career in the music business, it is all too easy to forget that, for most of human history, folk music was made for the pure joy of singing and performing, whether in a communal setting, singing to pass the tedium of work, or perhaps for spiritual solace. Listening in this context, it is breathtaking to hear Mrs. Sidney Carter sing the old hymn "Pharaoh," or to hear the crying tone in the voice of a prisoner called Jimpson, at Mississippi's Parchman Farm penitentiary, as he sings "No More My Lord."

I contacted Anna Lomax Cheratakis Wood, Alan's daughter, to ask if we could make an agreement to work with her father's legacy; to let Steve and me "recompose" twelve tracks that used samples from the Southern Journey recordings. I explained that our objective was to honor the voices he had recorded and to integrate them into new contexts that might expand their original intent, however subjective that judgment might be. Almost immediately, she agreed. We decided to call ourselves Tangle Eye, from the nickname of one of Mississippi singers recorded by Alan Lomax. After we presented a few samples of our work to Rounder, we were signed to the label as artists.

If I had spent most of my career attempting to bring out the best in my artists and to create situations for them that would inspire them to perform at their least self-conscious and most emotive peak, we were now presented with a wealth of performances that had already achieved that high mark. Our goal was not to create an environment that would inspire the best from a singer or musician, but rather to create new music that might amplify the voices we would sample, like making new settings for precious gemstones.

Our remixing process began with building a time-based grid and a basic beat for each track. Because the tempos of the a cappella singers that Alan Lomax recorded often sped up or slowed down, the process of editing the vocals to fit a consistent time pattern without losing their groove was often laborious—it could take the better part of a day to make the vocal in just one song feel right. Sometimes, we would create a verse-chorus structure, or a refrain, where there had not been one before. Steve comments, "It took intense concentration and tedium to make the hundreds of micro-edits to organize and structure each song, but it was well worth it for the creativity, fun, and excitement we all had reimagining music around the vocal."

Next, we would refine our percussion elements, adding samples from Steve's library and building different textures for different sections of our song. Finally, we added new parts played by our musician collaborators, who came from the full spectrum of American roots music. It was great fun to build our "toolbox" of samples, which were usually two- or four-bar segments that could be looped and stacked. Using Pro Tools made the process slow. Today, newer software such as Ableton would have made the time-stretching, tuning, and syncing of elements much easier.

Of all the musicians I asked to participate, both famous and little known, only one turned us down. Because we were footing the bill for the project, we could not offer them big paychecks, but they were as intrigued with the idea as we were. It started one day when Steve and I were working on the track we would call "Parchman Blues," based on that performance by Jimpson of "No More My Lord." "Wouldn't it be cool if George Porter could play bass on this track," I said to Steve. "Let's call him up and see if he's around." Within half an hour, the bass player for the defining funk group the Meters was at Ultrasonic, laying down the fat, funky part on the record (which we then edited and sampled).

The first track we worked on was based on the performance of a field holler called "Whoa Buck," by a convict called C. B. It was the kind of work song that might be sung while working, with humorous, self-deprecating verses alternating with an eerie yodel, which gave us contrasting sections. We added samples of hand percussion, and a Delta-style blues guitar that we sped up, distorted, and retuned. The song had achieved the feel of a Mississippi juke joint stomp, which made me think of Howlin' Wolf's early records. The final touch, added a few months later, was James Singleton's percussive acoustic bass.

Sometimes, Steve and I played parts ourselves. He is an accomplished guitarist and bassist, while I added harmonica on "Heaven," which is based on Mississippi Fred McDowell's recording of "Wish I Was in Heaven." A few times, Steve and I would sketch out reharmonizations—adding chords to the melodies—but these parts were almost inevitably replaced by our master reharmonizers: keyboardists Henry Butler, Davell Crawford, and David Torkanowsky.

My favorite track is called "Chantey," which is based on "Menhadden Chanteys" by the Bright Light Quartet, a group of fishermen from Lancaster County, Virginia. Steve immediately heard a rock-steady reggae groove in their voices, so he added a "one drop" drum loop. Next, I took the track to Chris Wilson, the Jamaican-born musician who managed Rounder's reggae label, Heartbeat. Chris overdubbed guitar, bass, and Nyabinghi-style bongos, while his keyboardist friend Dow Brain added Hammond organ. Back in New Orleans, we enlisted fourteen-year-old bandmates Troy "Trombone Shorty" Andrews and James Martin to play solos, and a horn ensemble part I had written, after listening to Skatalites records for inspiration.

Another improbable mashup was the juxtaposition of Arkansas ballad singer Almeda Riddle's "Gallows Tree" with a Mississippi fife and drum loop played by Ed Young and group. I cannot remember exactly how we discovered how compatible these performances were, but they fit together organically, in the same key and tempo, with very little tweaking. I could hear the chord changes to Charles Mingus's "Goodbye Pork Pie Hat" behind the melody, so I played a variation of them on Wurlizter piano, before George Porter Jr. and Johnny Vidacovich added bass and drums. Finally, I sent the track to the bluesy bluegrass fiddler Ron Stewart, who sent us several takes of alternately rhythmic and crying fiddle. Everyone was then sampled, and Steve assembled the final mix.

For our reimagination of the Georgia Sea Islands singer Bessie Jones's "O Death," Steve assembled a percussion loop inspired by Dr. John's "Walk on Gilded Splinters." When we added Dirk Powell's acoustic bass and tuned-down fiddle parts, the haunting vocal was made even more spooky and ominous. The track was ultimately licensed for the soundtrack of the HBO series *Deadwood*.

In all instances, I hope we created music that the original singers would have enjoyed—and that they might have been surprised that their encounters with Alan Lomax had transcended time and become part of a new medium. But, of course, we will never know.

After almost two years, we finished. Then, a problem emerged. At the South by Southwest festival in Austin, Texas, Anna Lomax Cheratakis Wood and I were on a panel together, to talk about Alan Lomax, his legacy, and the Rounder series of recordings. At the end of the hour, I played one of the completed Tangle Eye tracks. Almost immediately everyone in the audience applauded enthusiastically, except for one curmudgeonly (in my opinion) man who raised his hand to comment that he hated hearing the freedom of the singers locked to the steady time of a grid. He planted a seed that grew in Anna's head until, perhaps amplified by a member of her staff, she began to worry that our project would be seen as a desecration of her father's work. She called to tell me so, asking why we could not simply bring the musicians together to play along with the original tracks. She did not want to proceed.

I was distraught, because I did not feel that she understood what we had done. I was sympathetic to her mandate of honoring her father's work, but I felt that we had done exactly that. I had made a big mistake in not obtaining a written agreement ahead of time. I wrote to her to plead my case, and finally made a trip to New York to meet with her and her attorney Jeffrey Greenberg.

I am not sure exactly what changed, but the face-to-face meeting solved the impasse. I believe that Jeff's perspective was instrumental in Anna's decision to let the project go forward. If anyone were to be blamed for the sacrilege of distorting folk tradition, and for exploiting these deceased voices, it would be Steve and me. On the positive side, we might bring a few more people into the world of Alan Lomax, and Anna had little to lose. We made a formal agreement and were on our way, but I learned never again to use a sample without clearing it first. Two years of our work might never have been heard.

Today, the Association for Cultural Equity has made a great number of Alan Lomax's recordings accessible online, rendering the old CD reissues obsolete. In exploring their website, I made a revelatory discovery. The song "No More My Lord," with the heartrending lead vocal by Jimpson, had first been recorded with a full work-gang vocal ensemble. Alan Lomax must have had the presence of mind to hear how special Jimpson's vocal was, and asked him to perform the song a cappella, with his percussive axe the only other sound. So, maybe the great documentarian had the ear of a record producer, as he influenced the music he recorded.

The Tangle Eye album was released to considerable acclaim, by media as diverse as the British folk music magazine *Froots* and *Billboard*. I was interviewed by Liane Hansen for National Public Radio's *Weekend Edition* program, after which I traveled to Europe for two radio interviews at the BBC, and several more with journalists in Holland. For someone who was accustomed to staying in the background, this was a new experience. Steve elected to truly stay in the background and to let me be the Tangle Eye mouthpiece, but the experience of making the record cemented a creative relationship and deep friendship that has persevered. None of the fears of tarnishing the Lomax legacy materialized. We had entered a new world in which sampling has become an accepted part of the creation of a new recording, perhaps in a similar way to musicians a hundred years ago who were inspired the music they heard around them, reshaping it to suit their own purposes.

Will there be another Tangle Eye record? It is possible, but the hurdles of licensing samples and paying the required advances have not made the prospect easy. As recently as 2019, we made a Tangle Eye mix of the song "Bulletproof," the opening track on Samantha Fish's *Kill or Be Kind* album. So, just maybe . . .

RECOMMENDED LISTENING:

"Chantey" from *Alan Lomax's Southern Journey Remixed*
"O Death" from *Alan Lomax's Southern Journey Remixed*

Chapter 19

ROUNDER RECORDS

WHEN I JOINED THE ROUNDER RECORDS STAFF IN 1976, IT WAS NOT WITH the express objective of becoming a record producer. Going to work for Rounder simply felt right, because I knew that the three founders, Ken Irwin, Marian Leighton-Levy, and Bill Nowlin, were in it for the music, and that they were fans of much of the music I loved.

In the mid-1970s, the record business was exploding. I often think, perhaps idealistically, that the late 1960s and early 1970s were a golden era for recorded music. The cutting edge of contemporary popular music was played on Top 40 radio, with records by artists like James Brown, the Doors, Joni Mitchell, and Jimi Hendrix permeating mass consciousness. Even B. B. King scored a 1969 Top 40 hit with "The Thrill Is Gone." For a few years, it seemed that music was again driving the business, as it had briefly during the original rock and roll revolution in the mid-1950s.

By 1975, FM radio had become the relevant medium, with formats that evolved into AAA (Adult Album Alternative), AC (Adult Contemporary Music), AOR (Album Oriented Rock), and others, as record companies and radio stations sought to compartmentalize and consolidate the new culture into a business model. The record companies were also seeking to have influence over a more controlled airplay structure, after the free-form model that had been embraced by many of the early and influential FM stations and disc jockeys. On a smaller scale, the same thing was happening in the record store where I worked, when in-store airplay and prominent display space were bought by the major labels (usually with free goods). Instead of choosing the music we wanted to play in the store, as we had a few years earlier, we were directed to play certain albums several times each day, all the way through, so much that customers would ask why we were playing such crap.

As the manager of New England Music City, the largest record store in Boston, I was a prime candidate for recruitment to be a major label promotion person or sales representative. Quite a few of my friends had gone that route, quickly climbing the record company corporate ladder and making real money. I had been approached a few times, by labels such as Arista Records and ABC Records, but it was not the kind of career I wanted. It felt too much like the corporate job that I believed had been complicit in robbing my father of his life.

One experience in particular soured me. Each Tuesday, I received calls from the trade magazines—*Billboard*, *Cash Box*, and the somewhat hipper tip sheet *Walrus*—asking for my list of best-selling records. This data was used as part of the information that determined chart positions, which were an influence on what chain stores and big retailers would buy.

At the time, every major label had its own branch distribution office in Boston (as in other regions throughout the country). If a store wanted to buy records on the Capitol label, for instance, at the best price, it bought them from the Capitol branch. Sales representatives from each of these distributors visited me each week to tell me about their new releases, and I generally enjoyed their visits. Before leaving, some of them might suggest records that I could do them the favor of reporting to the trades, whether they were selling or not.

Columbia Records took this concept a step further. Each Monday, I would receive a call from a Columbia employee, giving me a list of four or five singles and two or three albums that were the answers to that week's "contest." She would call back on Thursday, and if I was able to read back the same list, my salesman would show up the next week with a bottle of booze. It was not difficult to imagine a connection. For a while, I accumulated an office closet full of bottles of brown liquor that I usually gave to my employees.

I was also editing the music magazine called *Pop Top* and contributing an editorial each month, usually about an uncontroversial but interesting topic such as the distribution of "cut-outs" (discontinued albums, often with the corners cut off) that were sold inexpensively, or that, in some instances, were illegally manufactured (the Beatles' Vee-Jay album may have sold millions of copies as a cut-out). I decided to write about how record companies tried to influence the sales reports that stores provided to the trades, much as I have done here. Of course, books such as Fredric Dannen's *Hit Men* documented far more serious instances of radio and airplay manipulation, but this was my own experience.

I turned in the editorial to the publisher of *PopTop*, who quickly sent it to Columbia for "fact-checking." Within hours, I received a call from my boss and one of the owners of my store, Howie Ring.

"Scotty, you can't publish this. I mean, this is our business," was his direction. I believe he may have secretly admired my stab at corruption, but it was difficult to argue with him. If *PopTop* published the editorial, as I came to understand it, there would be curtailed Columbia advertising dollars for both the magazine and the store, and I would be fired. The piece was never published.

When the idea of working for Rounder Records was first proposed, it seemed like the most natural and logical step I could take, because it would not only sidestep the hustle and chicanery of the mainstream record business, but also meant that I would be representing the music that I most cared about. Simultaneously, I began touring around New England with the swing band Roseland, making it difficult to be at the store every day. I needed more flexibility. I had gotten to know Ken Irwin better, because he was my Rounder sales representative at the store. Until the 1990s, Rounder not only produced and released its own records but also distributed records on hundreds of other labels, so he had a lot to sell. Once, we went together to the press party for the Pointer Sisters' first album at the club Paul's Mall, just down the street from the store, and we became friends.

I initially approached Rounder as half of a team. An ex–major label promotion person was starting his own company that would cater to independent labels, and I agreed to be his partner and sales rep. He would promote the records to radio stations, and I would sell them to stores. Yet, that scenario did not work out, because, after only a few weeks on the job, my partner was caught selling promotional copies of Rounder records intended for radio stations to a used-record store. So, I settled in on my own as Rounder's first hired salesperson. It still did not seem like a career, though, because I was focused on being a harmonica player.

The Rounder founders had not set out to create a major independent label. They were fans of old-time American folk music and bluegrass, along with other roots music styles, and they had a left-leaning political bent.

When Ken was hitchhiking in West Virginia, after attending a fiddlers' convention in Galax, he was picked up by Ken Davidson, the owner of a tiny bluegrass and old-time music label called Kanawha. When Ken returned home, he suggested to his friend and roommate Bill Nowlin that they might start a label. With third partner Marian Leighton-Levy, they subsequently visited Davidson and licensed the master recordings of an album by the banjo player George Pegram, for $125. It became one of Rounder's first two releases.

They were a well-balanced trio. As I saw it, Bill's organizational skills, business instincts, and attention to detail kept the company running. He worked on artist contracts, and on such tasks as developing systems for paying royalties. Marian was the perfect spokesperson for the company, projecting confidence and poise. She was very good at talking to both artists and the press. Ken remained the heart of the company's mission, with a steadfast commitment to genuine soulfulness in the all the music the label released. If at times I had difficulties with each of them (I could be strong headed and inflexible), we always continued forward together. In fact, we eventually reached an understanding that if I could get two of the three of them to agree on a recording project I wanted to do, I was good to go.

There was a degree of anarchy at Rounder in its early days, with all tasks open to whoever felt best suited to do them, and I thrived in that environment. I loved traveling around New England and selling records, mostly to small stores. Every Monday and Tuesday, when the band was not working, I made my rounds in Boston and Cambridge, where I would sell our new releases and sometimes do inventories of our labels. The Harvard Coop, Discount Records, Briggs and Briggs, and New England Music City, all in Harvard Square, were especially good accounts, often ordering hundreds or occasionally thousands of records each week. It was the golden era of the vinyl LP, with some customers buying several every week.

Since I needed tools to sell records, I began designing and writing marketing materials for Rounder Distribution, creating a new release sheet to mail to accounts. I also began a co-op advertising program for the labels that Rounder distributed, tagging retailers who would buy the records in quantity. All of this awakened my interest in graphic design, especially after observing the "mechanicals" of album cover art delivered by the designer Susan Marsh. In addition to studying her work and asking her questions, I enrolled in the Art Institute of Boston, taking classes in mechanical preparation and typography. I eventually designed hundreds of album and compact disc covers for Rounder, serving as the label's art director in the late 1980s and early 1990s, and again in the early 2010s. When desktop publishing was in its beginning stages, staff designer Nancy Given and I were quick to jump onboard, giving a presentation of our new cost-saving skills at the National Association of Independent Record Distributors. For much of my time at Rounder, I enjoyed graphic design as a respite from the intensity of the recording studio.

When the first Rounder album by George Thorogood and the Destroyers began to pick up airplay on rock stations, I started making a fair amount of money, selling LPs by the box. But one of my biggest "hits" was the catalog of a group called the Mom and Dads, on GNP Crescendo Records, a label that Rounder distributed. This group of mostly senior citizens played pol-kas, hymns, waltzes, and sentimental music from the 1930s and '40s. When a campaign for their music hit late-night television in New England, the distributor in Maine ordered thousands of their albums. I loved it that people responded to something so basic and conventionally unhip.

Ironically, the first Destroyers album put the company under consider-able financial stress. The general practice within the network of indepen-dent distributors that handled Rounder was not to pay bills within thirty days. In fact, outstanding invoices might not be paid for three or four months. In the meantime, the album jacket printers and pressing plants demanded to be paid promptly. No bank would give a loan to a such a scruffy bunch, and we all had to economize.

The practices of not wasting anything, of eschewing the glitz of the major label record business (secondhand clothes stores outfitted many on the staff), and of furnishing the offices with found or used fixtures, along with a musical philosophy that disdained pretense, became known as "the Rounder way." Ken soaked uncanceled stamps from envelopes that had arrived, and we all endeavored not to make long-distance phone calls or use any kind of expedited delivery service. The company pulled through.

By the time of the release of George Thorogood's second album, *Move It on Over*, Rounder was enjoying a level of success that the founders could never have imagined. George's music was clearly part of the roots music world, and an extension of the Rounder aesthetic, but a hit record was not what anyone had expected. It was a game changer for my career as a record producer, both because of the blues-oriented artists who began approaching Rounder and the infusion of cash that George's success brought. (Ultimately, George became too big for Rounder to market properly, and he was signed to EMI Records, with Rounder's participation.)

We hired a second local salesperson, my friend Richard Seidel, who would eventually go on to pursue his passion for jazz at Contemporary Records and Verve Records, but not before the founders offered us positions as joint general managers of Rounder Distribution. As was becoming my pattern when confronting a business-oriented opportunity, I declined (as did Richard), but we were given the opportunity to help interview candidates for the job. Duncan Browne, who had owned and managed an independent record store in Boston, was chosen. He was an asset for many years, with a fair-minded management style.

But there was another side of Rounder's new success. When it came to compensating a staff that had grown to over thirty people, "the Rounder way" was not sufficient. The employees could see the number of records going out the door, and they wanted better benefits and compensation, especially those who had hung in through recent lean times. The founders were now the owners of a thriving business, with employees who wanted more than to work in a hip and relevant place, for many of the Rounder staff were as committed to the company's mission as the owners. It seemed a contradiction, because of the owners' sustained vision of their solidarity with working-class rights. After all, the company had released records that drew attention to the plight of coal miners, and their struggles to unionize.

Nonetheless, a group of employees began organizing to petition for a union, to be affiliated with Service Employees International Union, Local 925, AFL-CIO. The founders resisted the idea, and there were bitter feelings on both sides, but when the ballot was cast, the vote was nearly unanimous. My ballot was blank, because I felt that I was better off negotiating on my own. Yet the union ultimately proved to be a good thing for everyone, including the founders, because it gave them a defined platform for fairness. The contractual definitions of Rounder's benefits and ideals, including a clause in that prohibited discrimination because of sexual preference, were in many ways ahead of their time. Health insurance, parental leave, and other benefits were near the top of what any company offered at the time.

The record business of that era was perfectly aligned with Rounder's aesthetic. We knew that if we made a good roots record that did not stray from our instincts, it would likely sell enough to pay for itself, while putting

The Rounder Records staff in the Rounder warehouse, ca. 1981 (photograph © Scott Billington)

some money in the artist's pocket. An album such as *Masters of Turkish Folk Music*, a reissue of rare 78-rpm recordings, could sell ten thousand copies or more. A working artist such as Beau Jocque could sell thirty-five thousand or forty thousand compact discs. With every record I made, the side musicians as well as the lead artist were paid decently for the sessions, and we used the best studios, engineers, and mastering facilities. Photographers, liner note writers, and graphic designers were also employed.

If Rounder had initially been inspired by labels such as Kanawha, Folkways, or Arhoolie, which also released high-quality roots music, it now differed from those labels by offering increasingly effective radio promotion, publicity, and marketing services for the artists it signed, when appropriate. We now had, on staff, a publicity director, a radio promotion director, and a marketing director.

The company kept growing, eventually releasing over one hundred records each year. There was a series for children's music; an expanding international series, fueled by Bill Nowlin's travels and the records he licensed, especially from Africa; the purchase of the Philo label, which became a singer-songwriter imprint; the founding of the Heartbeat reggae label, in partnership with Duncan Browne; a series of recordings by contemporary artists such as Jonathan Richman and Barrence Whitfield; a series for Cape Breton fiddle music; and much more. Of course, when Ken Irwin signed fourteen-year-old Alison Krauss, not knowing that the young, award-winning fiddler would become the most popular bluegrass-based star and singer ever, Rounder was set on an even bigger trajectory.

My contribution to this web of activity was the Modern New Orleans Masters series, which grew to include almost fifty titles. As I began making records by James Booker, Tuts Washington, and Johnny Adams, I envisioned a larger-scale project that would better focus attention on our releases. Initially, I was inspired by Sam Charters's *Chicago: The Blues, Today!* 1960s series on Vanguard, a three LP set with two or three artists on each album. I still have my original proposal, which included an all-star rhythm and blues album, with backing by Dave Bartholomew's orchestra.

Yet, the project grew bigger than that. I produced new records by Johnny Adams, Irma Thomas, Walter "Wolfman" Washington, and Alvin "Red" Tyler. Marian's new husband, the keyboardist and producer Ron Levy, came onboard by producing records by jazz saxophonist Earl Turbinton Jr. and the Mardi Gras Indian gang the Golden Eagles. Marian had befriended the New Orleans Jazz and Heritage Festival producer Quint Davis, who facilitated Rounder's acquisition of records by the Dirty Dozen Brass Band and Professor Longhair. I designed a logo and wrote the promotional copy. The objective of attracting attention worked, because the series was featured in a full-page *Newsweek* article, with a photo of Marian, Ron, and me.

Along the way, I signed several artists that I did not produce, including Ted Hawkins, who was discovered by my friend Bruce Bromberg. It was an improbable signing, because Ted was incarcerated at the time. With the warden's permission, our photographer brought Ted a shirt and a guitar for the cover photo. The album, with notes by Peter Guralnick, nonetheless received a four-star *Rolling Stone* review. Bruce was ready to sign Robert Cray to Rounder, but I could not convince the founders that Robert was destined to be the blues star I believed him to be. As a result, Bruce and his new partner Larry Sloven went on to found the HighTone label, and to sell enough copies of Robert Cray's *Strong Persuader* album, through a license with Mercury Records, to earn a gold record.

In the early 1990s, Marian and Ron were the architects of the Bullseye Blues label, with initial releases that included Charles Brown and Champion Jack Dupree. Many people today think of Rounder primarily as a bluegrass and Americana label, but in the 1990s, the label released more blues and R&B records than those in any other genre. For Bullseye, I made records by rhythm and blues songwriter Paul Kelly, Dalton Reed, Ruth Brown, and, with coproducer Andy Breslau, New York's Little Buster and the Soul Brothers.

As the label grew even larger, Duncan Browne left and was replaced by two former major label executives: general manager Paul Foley and sales manager Sheri Sands. One of Paul's initiatives was to arrange for the most commercial part of Rounder's catalog to be distributed by Universal Music. When Alison Krauss's 1995 *Now That I've Found You: A Collection* was released, the company now had enough muscle to do a first-class marketing and promotion job, and it did, selling over two million copies.

In 1998, the founders appointed John Virant to be the label's first president, as they sought to implement a better structure for operations. John had been Rounder's counsel for a few years, having joined the company as an intern after graduating from Harvard Law School, and his integrity kept the company solidly on track. As part of his custom-tailored job, he was given the opportunity to found his own label, Zoë (named for his daughter), as an outlet for alternative rock and folk music, with signings such as Juliana Hatfield and Kathleen Edwards.

Under John, I became vice president of A&R. I did my best to be a productive "artists and repertoire" person (responsible for signing new artists and acting as their liaison at the label), but I had always seen A&R as the necessary but unpleasant work that had to be done before making music in the studio—it seemed to entail all the work and none of the creative satisfaction I got from making a record. For the most part, I continued on as I had, signing artists that I would produce. But I was also proud of my signing of the British soul singer James Hunter, and of an agreement to release Laura Nyro's final album, on which I completed production. Rounder hired a second A&R person, Troy Hansbrough, who had none of my misgivings about the role, and he performed brilliantly, signing Madeleine Peyroux, whose 2004 *Careless Love* album garnered Rounder another gold record.

An even bigger record was 2007's *Raising Sand*, by Robert Plant and Alison Krauss, which won five Grammy awards and which truly put the Americana music genre on the map. I had met Robert several years earlier at El Sid O's Zydeco and Blues Club in Lafayette, which he had found while looking for music, especially the style known as swamp pop, on a day off from touring. I had stopped by the club on a whim. When club owner Sid Williams saw me enter, he ran up to say, "Scott, there's someone here you have to meet. He's from England and I know he's a big shot." Robert and I talked about Excello Records, swamp pop, and southwest Louisiana music in general.

To be clear, I had nothing to do with *Raising Sand*, but when Robert visited the Rounder offices a year or two before its release, to talk about a possible partnership for his previous album, he and Paul Foley walked past my office, and he spotted me. "Is that Scott—from that club in Lafayette?"

Paul motioned for me to join the meeting with Robert, where we spent the first fifteen minutes talking about Warren Storm and Slim Harpo in front of the entire marketing and promotion teams, much to their bewilderment. Robert is a true roots music fan.

After *Raising Sand*'s Grammy triumph, Rounder hosted a celebration party on the roof of the art deco Oviatt Building in downtown Los Angeles. With Robert's friends Priscilla Presley and Knox Phillips, the son of Sun Records founder Sam Phillips, in attendance, it was a triumphal moment. Rounder's commitment to old-time American music, blues, and roots had, however improbably, manifested itself in a record that had just been honored as the best of the year in any and all genres. And we were partying in high style.

Rounder now had over one hundred employees, and the company would move in a few years from its funky headquarters in North Cambridge to a swanky, two-story building in an office park in the Boston suburbs. Marian worked with a decorator to choose the lime green and dark orange color scheme. All the furniture was new, including massive wooden tables in two conference rooms, which were shaped roughly like a banjo and a guitar. We had a climate-controlled vault for Rounder's tape library, and I was able to oversee the construction of a small recording studio. It was a thoroughly impressive facility, although it was isolated from the Boston-area music clubs that were so easily accessed from the old Cambridge office. As comfortable as it was, it never quite felt like "the Rounder way."

It was not a surprise when, in 2012, the founders called the staff together to announce that the company would be sold to Concord Music. With CD sales falling and with significant streaming revenue nearly a decade away, the record business had been contracting. In spite of new releases by Willie Nelson, Mary Chapin Carpenter, John Mellencamp, Gregg Allman, and others, all signed in the wake of *Raising Sand*, the size of Rounder's business was not sustainable, and we had already downsized considerably. For a time, I had resumed duties as Rounder's art director.

Nothing much changed until 2014, when Concord revealed that it would move Rounder to Nashville. Many employees were given the option to relocate, and I initially decided it would be a good move, to be Rounder's head of A&R in Nashville. Johnette thought it could be an opportunity for both of us. Then, a few weeks after the announcement, I was invited to dinner at the Pacific Palisades home of Norman Lear, the influential television producer who was then a part owner of Concord. Also present were John Burk (Concord's head of A&R), another Concord staff member, and a veteran Nashville record executive whom Norman thought might make a good addition to the Rounder staff.

The idea was put forth that Rounder could become a home for legacy country stars who no longer had a place on the major Nashville labels, but who still had large fan bases. I was asked what I thought of the concept.

Really, I had no idea. I had been to Nashville three times in my life: once as a teenager, once for Sleepy LaBeef's sixtieth birthday party, and once to go to the Americana Music Association awards ceremony. Apart from traditional country music of the nature that Sleepy played, and records by artists such as Hank Williams and Lefty Frizzell, I had no connection to Nashville. If that was the agenda for Rounder A&R, it was clear to me that I was being asked to do something I was unqualified to do. After talking to acquaintances in Nashville, I also concluded that I would be perceived as an outsider. It seemed to me that the executives at Concord did not know what my role at Rounder had been. It also seemed that no legacy country artist, no matter how long it had been since his or her last hit record, was going to sign with a label that could not generate country airplay, which was out of Rounder's reach.

Instead, I joined the majority of Rounder employees who asked for the severance package that was being offered, opting not to go to Nashville. By this time, Johnette and I were living for most of the year in New Orleans. The response from Concord was that they did not want to lose me, and that I could live where I wanted. I could not get the severance package, because I was no longer being asked to leave. John Virant opted for the same arrangement, working out of his hometown of St. Louis. In the end, only three Rounder employees moved from Boston to Nashville.

I have wondered if the Concord Music executives thought they were buying a company with its finger on the pulse of what was happening in the roots music world, with an eye for winnowing out the most commercial artists, or whether they simply saw the value in the catalog. In the wake of *Raising Sand*, Rounder had enjoyed a run of records that sold well, and the label had attracted a number of prominent artists. Yet, the Rounder A&R team (the founders, John Virant, and official A&R people like me) rarely arrived at a decision based on whether we thought something would sell. There were certainly commercial expectations and carefully considered marketing plans when, in later years, we signed Mary Chapin Carpenter or Gregg Allman. But decisions were always based on an aesthetic—it was either soulful music that was connected to the roots sensibility that we cherished, no matter how traditional it was or how many boundaries it pushed, or it was not. If it moved enough of us in that way, it was a candidate for signing. Rounder's hits, from George Thorogood to Alison Krauss, grew organically out of that philosophy, but so did many of the records we were most proud of that never sold much at all, from bluegrass singer James King to soul singer Dalton Reed. "The Rounder way" had been successful for many years.

A few years later, when I sat down with Tom Whalley, the former Warner Bros. CEO who was now responsible for running all the active Concord labels, he told me that he valued that sensibility, but that he wanted only records and artists that had major cultural and commercial potential. I agreed that it was not usually possible to stream or sell enough of, say, a zydeco record for a fully staffed record company to break even. So, I fully understood his point, even if it ran contrary to many decisions that I had made in the past. Today, would Rounder have signed James Booker, a frail, addicted genius who could not leave New Orleans? Would we have signed Ted Hawkins while he was in jail? Those recordings are now regarded as highlights of the Rounder catalog. I think we might even have missed at least a few of our major artists. But it was a different time.

Today, there is no place in the mainstream record business for many roots, jazz, classical, children's, and other artists, who are left to record and distribute music on their own, and who are often not able to afford to record in a top-tier studio. To the credit of the investors that now owned Rounder, they did not shut down the ongoing recording operation, because marketing the existing catalog and other assets might have been an easier route.

Not long after Nashville attorney John Strohm replaced John Virant as president in 2017, I retired from Rounder, after forty-two years. I became a consultant for Craft Recordings—Concord's catalog division—working primarily with the Rounder catalog. I have enjoyed working with the Craft team on reissue projects by Béla Fleck, Jimmy Reed, George Thorogood, Madeleine Peyroux, Doc Watson, and many others. I have also continued as a freelance producer with Rounder proper, producing new records by Samantha Fish, and The McCrary Sisters. Under John Strohm's direction, Rounder continues as a major creative force in the Americana music world (but without those legacy country artists—an idea that never came to pass).

Looking back, I can see several pivotal moments in my life when I made my best decisions, based on feeling rather than any sort of calculation. One of them was when I went to work for Rounder, for three nonbusiness-oriented music fans who ultimately afforded me the opportunity to pursue my passion in a way I never could have envisioned. Yes, I was at the right place at the right time. I will forever be grateful.

Chapter 20

AFTERWORD

IN AN ERA OF INSTANT ACCESS, IN WHICH A SONG CAN MOVE DIRECTLY from the recording studio to worldwide distribution in a matter of hours, and in which a developing musician or style of music may be revealed online at the very earliest stages of growth, the idea of roots-based music evolving within a community over time is an archaic concept.

In the Production of Recorded Music class that I teach at Loyola University in New Orleans, I marvel at many of my students as they sample music from every possible source, creating fully realized beats and tracks while sitting at their laptops, listening on headphones. Only at the end of the process might they go into a live recording space to add a performance by a musician, vocalist, or rapper. While many of them have a specific target audience in mind, the boundaries between genres have become vague. The possibilities for an artist to create his or her own sonic world, and to create a piece of art that will have cultural significance, are endless, at least if they have the ideas and conceptual skills to do so. If they have something to say, the entire history of recorded music can be fodder for getting their point across (although, of course, there are the legal issues attendant with using samples).

Sometimes, it can seem that my stories about my adventures with musicians are little more than amusing anecdotes for them. But I also feel that my students may be missing something. There can be joy in solitary creation—the "aha moment" when everything comes together. But the emotional journey of a recording session can be deeper than that, both in frustrating instances and in the exhilaration of capturing a moment that suddenly materializes, seemingly out of the air. The collective energy of a group of talented people makes for a socially dynamic experience that can result in music greater than any of the individuals involved could imagine creating on their own. When a recording can harness that kind of feeling, listeners can feel it, too, and they will come back to it time and again.

In many ways, sampling is nothing new. Most American roots music styles, from bluegrass to zydeco, are the result of the musical cultures of different immigrant groups butting up against each other, and of musicians who adopted and adapted the new musical ideas they heard. Thus, Boozoo Chavis could play a German instrument, sing in Creole French, and cover a song by Bob Wills and the Texas Playboys. Traditional New Orleans jazz and brass band music used the format of German and Italian brass bands, added the syncopation of ragtime, rhythms from Cuba, and finally the blues tonality of African Americans. Cajun music, with its blues influence, sounds nothing like the French music of Canada or France. The Mardi Gras Indian gangs of New Orleans adopted their suits and jargon from Native Americans, while their chants and rhythms may represent a direct survival of African traditions that persevered through two centuries of slavery. These music styles could not have coalesced anywhere else but in America, and specifically in Louisiana. The constant interplay of cultures gave us our wealth of American roots music.

Of course, this happened throughout the Americas, wherever European, African, Indigenous, and other cultures met; Brazil and Cuba have histories of musical fusion that are no less exciting than those in the United States. Musical evolution was perhaps quieter when people stayed in one place, although, for example, itinerant Roma and Klezmer musicians spread their influence as they traveled throughout Europe, and there is substantial Arab influence in the flamenco music of Southern Spain.

Nonetheless, the music played by artists such as Boozoo Chavis or John Delafose was their cultural imperative. Even when they borrowed a song from, say, Bob Wills or the Delmore Brothers, it came out as Louisiana Creole music. For a younger artist such as Chris Ardoin or Nathan Williams Jr., Creole Zydeco music is a choice, even as each of them built on the foundation of his family legacy. Both of these musicians could just as well have chosen to play contemporary rhythm and blues, or hip-hop, or country music, had that been their inclination. The sustenance of musical tradition is now a conscious decision.

And that is what has happened in New Orleans as well. If one of the great concerns that followed the flooding of New Orleans after Hurricane

David Farrell and Scott Billington at Studio in the Country, 1983 (photograph © Rick Olivier)

Katrina was that the culture would also be decimated, there are now more brass bands and Mardi Gras Indian gangs than ever. The conservation of musical culture became a badge of survival. The Mardi Gras Indians were once strictly an inner-city phenomenon, more or less shielded from citywide view because they did not leave their neighborhoods, but now the Mardi Gras Indian Super Sunday event in March is now celebrated by everyone, with families and people from all walks of life lining the streets to admire the "pretty" Indians, as they parade by and chant their boastful songs. And if traditional New Orleans rhythm and blues is no longer an especially relevant style, most of the elements that gave it birth are still present: the high school marching bands, gospel music, and a way of speaking, dancing, and moving that conveys the inherent musicality of the city.

That is the reason it made sense to bring someone such as Ruth Brown to New Orleans to record—the resource of the city's musicians could not be found elsewhere. It was the same with other artists I brought there, such as the talented New England singer Michelle Willson and the New Hampshire singer-songwriter Bill Morrissey. Dan Penn once told me that he believed Memphis was the most soulful place to record, but that the low frequencies present on a record made in New Orleans had a resonance that could not be replicated anywhere else—the below-sea-level advantage. I also made records by New York's Holmes Brothers (coproduced with

Andy Breslau) and soukous star Tabu Ley Rochereau at Dockside Studio, where the unhurried and "place apart" atmosphere gave the music both focus and time to develop.

In the forty years I have spent recording Southern roots music, I have been privileged to observe and to occasionally be a part this changing landscape. I miss the iconoclasts and bigger-than-life characters such as James Booker, Beau Jocque, Sleepy LaBeef, and Boozoo Chavis, and I am disappointed that the record business is generally no longer able to support the higher-end level of the production of noncommercial, niche artists. Yet the music endures, and I have continued to make Southern roots records, such as Samantha Fish's *Kill or Be Kind* (at Royal Studio in Memphis) and the McCrary Sisters' *A Very McCrary Christmas* (at the Sound Emporium in Nashville). I have also enjoyed performing Louisiana roots music for children with my wife, Johnette Downing. Our 2019 record, *Swamp Romp*, offers an overview of Louisiana roots music styles, with contributions from dozens of the musicians I have worked with over the years. It is a microcosm of my career.

Were there downsides or regrets along the way? My single-minded focus on making records or on whatever song was playing in my head at any given moment took a toll on my relationships, and my partners often deserved better. My focus could be keen, but it was not always balanced. With my constant bouncing back and forth between New England and New Orleans, I missed and perhaps even consciously avoided the rootedness of place and family, although I was able to maintain a steady presence in my daughter's life. Today, Johnette and I often embark on our roots music adventures together, and I am glad to have found a sense of home, along with time to pursue interests such as gardening and hiking.

I was fortunate to have begun my adventures I the record business when I did, because it might be difficult to repeat my career if I were starting out today. The second half of the twentieth century may have been the defining time for American roots music, as the cross-cultural sharing of musical ideas and the exposition of various roots music styles barreled along at an ever-increasing speed. My father's dream of working as a curious cultural explorer was realized in the records I made. I hope my stories about them can impart the joy of the discoveries I experienced along the way.

ACKNOWLEDGMENTS

Thank you to Johnette Downing for her expert editing and proofreading, and for encouraging me to complete this book.

Thank you to Rosario Del Nero, Peter Guralnick, Steve Reynolds, and Dennis Paul Williams for their continuing inspiration.

Thank you to Mary Katherine Aldin, Bill Bentley, Nicholas Bergin, Andy Breslau, Renée Brown, Bruce Bromberg, Tony Daigle, Tom Dent, Sabra Dow, Jake Eckert, David Farrell, Rob Feaster, Herman Fusilier, David Gaar, Jay Gallagher, Craig Gill, Ed Goodreau, Michael Goodwin, Philip Gould, Jean Hangarter, Jeff Hannusch, Henry Horenstein, Ken Irwin, Rob Jaczko, Valerie Jones, Bob & Janet Lawson, Marian Leighton-Levy, Gragg Lunsford, Bill Nowlin, Steve & Wish Nails, Rick Olivier, Meredith Ragucci, Jan Ramsey, Kermon Richard, Barbara Roberds, Steve Rosenthal, Ben Sandmel, Hammond Scott, James Singleton, John Snyder, Joe Sunseri, Michael Tisserand, Graziano Uliani, John Virant, Mark Wessell, Kalamu ya Salaam, and Lee Allen Zeno.

The chapters on Beau Jocque, James Booker, and Boozoo Chavis were published in abbreviated form as liner notes for Rounder Records.

The chapter on Solomon Burke was previously published in different form in *Blues and Rhythm*.

DISCOGRAPHY

There Is Always One More Time (Rounder Heritage Series 11582)
Compilation

Man of My Word (Rounder 2155)
Ultrasonic Studio, New Orleans, 1998
Engineers: David Farrell and Steve Reynolds
OffBeat (New Orleans) 1997 Rhythm and Blues Album of the Year

Mood Indigo (Johnny Adams, Germaine Bazzle, and George French with the New
    Orleans CAC Jazz Orchestra, conducted by David Torkanowsky) (Rounder 2145)
Contemporary Arts Center, New Orleans, 1996
Engineers: Keith Keller and Jim Albert

One Foot in the Blues (Rounder 2144)
Ultrasonic Studio, New Orleans, 1996
Engineer: David Farrell

The Verdict (Rounder 2135)
Ultrasonic Studio, New Orleans, 1995
Engineer: David Farrell

Good Morning Heartache (Rounder 2125)
Ultrasonic Studio, New Orleans, 1993
Engineer: David Farrell

Sings Doc Pomus: The Real Me (Rounder 2109)
Ultrasonic Studio, New Orleans, 1991
Engineer: David Farrell

Walking on a Tightrope: The Songs of Percy Mayfield (Rounder 2095)
Southlake Studio, Metairie, LA, 1991
Engineer: David Farrell
National Association of Independent Record Distributors Rhythm and Blues Album
    of the Year

Room with a View of the Blues (Rounder 2059)
Southlake Studio, Metairie, LA, 1991
Engineer: David Farrell

After Dark (Rounder 2049)
Studio Solo, Slidell, LA, 1985
Engineer: David Farrell

From the Heart (Rounder 2044)
Ultrasonic Studio, New Orleans, 1991
Engineer: Jay Gallagher

DUANE ALLMAN

Skydog: The Duane Allman Retrospective (Rounder) (executive producer)

ALLONS EN LOUISIANE

The Rounder Records Guide to Cajun Music, Zydeco and South Louisiana (Rounder
    6093)
CD-ROM (author and producer)

ALL THAT

The Whop Boom Bam (Upstart UPST 039)
Magazine Sound and Ultrasonic Studio, New Orleans, 1999
Engineers: Chris Finney and Steve Reynolds

CHRIS ARDOIN AND DOUBLE CLUTCHIN'

Best Kept Secret (Rounder 2162)
Ultrasonic Studio, New Orleans, 2000
Engineers: David Farrell and Steve Reynolds

Turn the Page (Rounder 2157)
Ultrasonic Studio, New Orleans, 1998
Engineers: David Farrell and Steve Reynolds
OffBeat (New Orleans) 1998 Zydeco Album of the Year

Gon' Be Jus' Fine (Rounder 2127)
Ultrasonic Studio, New Orleans, 1997
Engineers: David Farrell and Steve Reynolds

MARCIA BALL

Hot Tamale Baby (Rounder 3095)
Studio Solo, Slidell, Louisiana, 1986
Engineer: David Farrell

BEAU JOCQUE AND THE ZYDECO HI-ROLLERS

The Best of (Rounder Heritage Series 11603)
Compilation

Give Him Cornbread, Live! (Rounder 2160)
Big Mo Mobile Recording Truck, 1993
Engineers: Ed Eastridge and Steve Reynolds

Check It Out, Lock It In, Crank It Up! (Rounder 2158)
Ultrasonic Studio, New Orleans, 2000
Engineers: David Farrell and Steve Reynolds

Gonna Take You Downtown (Rounder 2150)
Ultrasonic Studio, New Orleans, 1996
Engineers: David Farrell and Steve Reynolds
OffBeat (New Orleans) 1996 Zydeco Album of the Year

Git It, Beau Jocque! (Rounder 2134)
Big Mo Mobile Recording Truck, 1993
Engineers: Ron Freeland and David Farrell

Pick Up on This! (Rounder 2126)
Ultrasonic Studio, New Orleans, 1994
Engineers: David Farrell and Steve Reynolds

Beau Jocque Boogie (Rounder 2120)
Ultrasonic Studio, New Orleans, 1993
Engineers: David Farrell and Steve Reynolds

THE BLUERUNNERS

To the Country (Rounder 6073)
Dockside Studio, Maurice, LA, 1998
Engineer: Tony Daigle

BLUES COMPANY

From Daybreak to Heartbreak (in-akustik INAK 9071)
Bauer Studio, Ludwigsburg, Germany, 2003
Engineer: Johannes Wohlleben

JAMES BOOKER

Classified, Remixed and Expanded Edition (Rounder 9175-2)
Coproduced with John Parsons
Ultrasonic Studio, New Orleans, 1983
Engineers: Jay Gallagher and David Farrell

Resurrection of the Bayou Maharajah (Rounder 2118)
Coproduced with John Parsons
Live at the Maple Leaf Bar, 1980s
Engineers: John Parsons, Steve Reynolds, and Joe Gastwirt

Spiders on the Keys (Rounder 2119)
Coproduced with John Parsons
Live at the Maple Leaf Bar, 1980s
Engineers: John Parsons, Steve Reynolds, and Joe Gastwirt

Classified (Rounder 2036)
Coproduced with John Parsons
Ultrasonic Studio, New Orleans, 1983
Engineers: Jay Gallagher and Paul Muffson

CLARENCE "GATEMOUTH" BROWN

Texas Swing (Rounder 11527)
Coproduced with Jim Bateman
Compilation

One More Mile (Rounder 2034)
Coproduced with Jim Bateman
Studio in the Country, Bogalusa, LA, 1982
Engineer: David Farrell
Grammy nomination

Alright Again! (Rounder 2028)
Coproduced with Jim Bateman
Studio in the Country, Bogalusa, LA, 1981
Engineer: David Farrell
Grammy winner

RUTH BROWN

A Good Day for the Blues (Bullseye Blues and Jazz BB 9613)
Ultrasonic Studio, New Orleans, 1999
Engineers: Steve Reynolds
Grammy nomination

R+B = Ruth Brown (Bullseye Blues BB 9583)
Ultrasonic Studio, New Orleans, and the Magic Shop, New York, 1997
Engineers: David Farrell, Steve Reynolds, and Steve Rosenthal
Grammy nomination

CLARENCE BUCARO

Sense of Light (Rounder 3232)
Ultrasonic Studio, New Orleans, 1997
Engineer: David Farrell

BUCKWHEAT ZYDECO

Buckwheat's Zydeco Party, Deluxe Edition (Rounder Heritage Series 11602)
Compilation

Waitin' For My Ya Ya (Rounder 2051)
Blue Jay Studio, Carlisle, MA, 1985
Engineer: Glenn Berger
Grammy nomination

Turning Point (Rounder 2045)
Blue Jay Studio, Carlisle, MA, 1983
Engineer: Gragg Lunsford
Grammy nomination

SOLOMON BURKE

Soul Alive! (Rounder 2042/43) mixing credit
Blue Jay Studio, Carlisle, MA
Engineer: Glenn Berger

A Change Is Gonna Come (Rounder 2053)
Studio Solo, Slidell, LA, 1986
Engineers: David Farrell and Gragg Lunsford

CHUCK CARBO

The Barber's Blues (Rounder 2140)
Ultrasonic Studio, New Orleans, 1996
Engineer: Steve Reynolds

BOOZOO CHAVIS

Johnny Billy Goat (Rounder Heritage Series 11594)
Compilation

Down Home on Dog Hill (Rounder 2166)
Ultrasonic Studio, New Orleans, 2001
Engineers: David Farrell and Steve Reynolds

Who Stole My Monkey? (Rounder 2156)
Dockside Studio, Maurice, LA, 1999
Engineer: Tony Daigle

Live at the Habibi Temple (Rounder 2130)
Big Mo Mobile Recording Truck, 1993
Engineers: Ed Eastridge and Steve Reynolds

Zydeco Live, Volume 1 (Boozoo Chavis & the Majic Sounds/Nathan & the Zydeco Cha
    Chas) (Rounder 2069)
Richard's Club, Lawtell, LA, 1987
Engineer: Mark Bingham

DAVELL CRAWFORD

Love Like Yours and Mine (Bullseye Blues and Jazz BB 9606)
American Sector, New Orleans, 1999
Engineer: Jim Albert

The B-3 and Me (Bullseye Blues BB 9603)
American Sector, New Orleans, 1998
Engineer: Jim Albert

Let Them Talk (Rounder 2139)
Ultrasonic Studio, New Orleans, 1995
Engineer: David Farrell

TONY DAGRADI

Dreams of Love (Rounder 2071)
Studio Solo, Slidell, LA, 1988
Engineer: David Farrell

THERYL "HOUSEMAN" DE'CLOUET

The Houseman Cometh (Bullseye Funk and Soul BB 9637)
Ultrasonic Studio, New Orleans, 2001
Engineers: David Farrell and Steve Reynolds

GENO DELAFOSE AND FRENCH ROCKIN' BOOGIE

La Chanson Perdue (Rounder 2151)
Ultrasonic Studio, New Orleans, 1998
Engineer: David Farrell

That's What I'm Talkin' About (Rounder 2141)
Ultrasonic Studio, New Orleans, 1996
Engineer: David Farrell

French Rockin' Boogie (Rounder 2131)
Ultrasonic Studio, New Orleans, 1994
Engineer: David Farrell

JOHN DELAFOSE AND THE EUNICE PLAYBOYS

Blues Stay Away from Me (Rounder 2121)
Ultrasonic Studio, New Orleans, 1993
Engineer: David Farrell

Pere e Garçon Zydeco (Rounder 2116)
Ultrasonic Studio, New Orleans, 1992
Engineer: David Farrell

Zydeco Live, Volume 2 (John Delafose & the Eunice Playboys/Willis Prudhomme & the
    Zydeco Express) (Rounder 2070)
Richard's Club, Lawtell, LA, 1989
Engineer: Mark Bingham

JOHNETTE DOWNING WITH SCOTT BILLINGTON

Swamp Romp (Wiggle Worm Records 011)
Coproduced with Johnette Downing
NOCCA Studio, the Rhythm Shack, New Orleans, 2019
Engineer: Steve Reynolds

THE DIRTY DOZEN BRASS BAND

This Is Jazz (Columbia Legacy CK 65046)
Compilation

Twenty Dozen (Savoy Jazz 17891)
The Music Shed, New Orleans, 2012
Engineer: Steve Reynolds

Jelly (Columbia CK 53214)
Ultrasonic Studio, New Orleans, 1993
Engineer: David Farrell

Open Up—Whatcha Gonna Do for the Rest of Your Life (Columbia CK 47383)
Ultrasonic Studio, New Orleans, 1992
Engineer: David Farrell

The New Orleans Album (Columbia CK 45414)
Ultrasonic Studio, New Orleans, 1990
Engineer: David Farrell

Voodoo (Columbia CK 45042)
Southlake Studio, Metairie, LA, 1989
Engineer: David Farrell

SAMANTHA FISH

Kill or Be Kind (Rounder 888072100459)
Royal Studios, Memphis, and the Rhythm Shack, New Orleans, 2019
Engineer: Steve Reynolds

GIRL AUTHORITY

Girl Authority (Zoe 1088)
Dockside Studio, Maurice, LA, and Camp Street Studio, Cambridge, MA, 2006
Engineers: Steve Reynolds and Paul Q. Kolderie

Road Trip (Zoe 1109)
Piety Street Studio, New Orleans, and Camp Street Studio, Cambridge, MA, 2007
Engineers: Steve Reynolds and Paul Q. Kolderie

WOODY GUTHRIE

My Dusty Road (Rounder 1162)
Reissue producer with Michael Creamer and Bill Nowlin
Grammy nomination

COREY HARRIS

Daily Bread (Rounder 2219)
Coproduced with Steve Reynolds
Crystalphonic Studio, Charlottesville, VA, Ultrasonic Studio, New Orleans, 2005
Engineer: Steve Reynolds and Trip Faulconer

THE HOLMES BROTHERS

The Essential Collection (Rounder Heritage Series 11588)
Coproduced with Andy Breslau
Compilation

Promised Land (Rounder 2142)
Coproduced with Andy Breslau
Dockside Studio, Maurice, LA, 1997
Engineer: Tony Daigle

Jubilation (Real World 92127)
Coproduced with Andy Breslau
Real World Studios, Wiltshire, England, 1992
Engineer: Richard Evans

Soul Street (Rounder 2124)
Coproduced with Andy Breslau
The Magic Shop, New York, 1993
Engineer: Steve Rosenthal

Where It's At (Rounder 2111)
Coproduced with Andy Breslau
Blue Jay Studio, Carlisle, Massachusetts, 1991
Engineer: Mark Wessel

In the Spirit (Rounder 2056)
Coproduced with Andy Breslau
Sorcerer Sound, New York, 1990
Engineer: Glenn Berger
Winner of the French Academie du Jazz Prix Big Joe Turner

J. B. HUTTO AND THE NEW HAWKS

Slippin' and Slidin' (Varrick VR 006)
Blue Jay Studio, Carlisle, MA, 1983
Engineer: Glenn Berger

BURKE INGRAFFIA

Waves (Point Clear Media)
Coproduced with Steve Reynolds
The Rhythm Shack, New Orleans, 2020
Engineer: Steve Reynolds

CANDYE KANE

The Toughest Girl Alive (Bullseye Blues and Jazz BB 9606)
Your Place or Mine, Glendale, CA, 2000
Engineer: Mark Linnet

PAUL KELLY

Gonna Stick and Stay (Bullseye Blues 9523)
Ultrasonic Studio, New Orleans, 1992
Engineers: David Farrell and Steve Reynolds

THE KLEZMER CONSERVATORY BAND

Old World Beat (Rounder 3115)
Coproduced with Hankus Netsky
Blue Jay Studio, Carlisle, MA, 1992
Engineers: George Hicks and Mark Wessel

A Jumpin' Night in the Garden of Eden (Rounder 3105)
Coproduced with Hankus Netsky
Blue Jay Studio, Carlisle, MA, 19887
Engineers: Mark Tanzer and Mark Wessel

SLEEPY LaBEEF

Rockabilly Blues (Bullseye Blues and Jazz BB 9631)
Compilation

Nothin' but the Truth (Rounder 3072)
Harper's Ferry, Allston, MA, 1985
Engineers: EJ Ouellette and Gragg Lunsford

Electricity (Rounder 3070)
Dimension Sound, Jamaica Plain, MA, and Blue Jay Studio, Carlisle, MA, 1980
Engineer: Paul Muffson

LIL' BRIAN AND THE ZYDECO TRAVELERS

Z-Funk (Rounder 2146)
Coproduced with Lee Allen Zeno
Dockside Studio, Maurice, LA, 1997
Engineers: Tony Daigle and David Farrell

Fresh (Rounder 2136)
Coproduced with Lee Allen Zeno

Dockside Studio, Maurice, LA, 1995
Engineers: Tony Daigle and David Farrell

LIL' BUSTER AND THE SOUL BROTHERS

Right On Time (Bullseye Blues BB 9562)
Coproduced with Andy Breslau
The Magic Shop, New York, 2006
Engineer: Steve Rosenthal
National Association of Independent Record Distributors Rhythm and Blues Album
   of the Year

ROBERT JR. LOCKWOOD AND JOHNNY SHINES

Mr. Blues Is Back to Stay (Rounder 2026)
Coproduced with Peter Guralnick
Dimension Sound, Jamaica Plain, MA, 1982
Engineer: Paul Muffson

Hangin' On (Rounder 2021)
Coproduced with Peter Guralnick
Agency Recording Studio, Cleveland, OH, the Mixing Lab, Newton, MA, 1980
Engineers: John Nagy and Paul Muffson
W. C. Handy Award: Traditional Blues Album of the Year

THE McCRARY SISTERS

A Very McCrary Christmas (Rounder Records 1166100649)
Sound Emporium, Nashville, 2019
Engineers: Steve Reynolds and Rachael Moore

VAN MORRISON WITH THE HOLMES BROTHERS

"That's Where It's At" (track from sampler) (Real World)
Coproduced with Andy Breslau
Real World Studios, Wiltshire, England, 1992
Engineer: Richard Evans

BILL MORRISSEY

The Essential Collection (Rounder Heritage Series 11595)
Compilation

You'll Never Get to Heaven (Philo 1194)
Coproduced with Ellen Karas
Ultrasonic Studio, New Orleans, 1996
Engineer: David Farrell

NATHAN AND THE ZYDECO CHA CHAS

Hang It High, Hang It Low (Rounder 2164)
Ultrasonic Studio, New Orleans, 2006
Engineer: Steve Reynolds

Let's Go (Rounder 2159)
Ultrasonic Studio, New Orleans, 2000
Engineer: David Farrell

I'm a Zydeco Hog: Live at the Rock 'n' Bowl, New Orleans (Rounder 2143)
Rock 'n' Bowl, New Orleans, 1997
Engineer: Steve Reynolds

Creole Crossroads (featuring Michael Doucet) (Rounder 2137)
Dockside Studio, Maurice, LA, 1995
Engineers: Tony Daigle and Mark Wessel

Follow Me Chicken (Rounder 2122)
Ultrasonic Studio, New Orleans, 1993
Engineer: David Farrell

Your Mama Don't Know (Rounder 2107)
Ultrasonic Studio, New Orleans, 1991
Engineer: David Farrell

Steady Rock (Rounder 2092)
Southlake Studio, Metairie, LA, 1988
Engineer: David Farrell

THE NEW ORLEANS NIGHTCRAWLERS

Funknicity (Rounder 2154)
Ultrasonic Studio, New Orleans, 1997
Engineers: David Farrell and Steve Reynolds

LAURA NYRO

Angel in the Dark (Rounder 3176)
Post production with Eileen Silver-Lillywhite
Sorcerer Sound, New York, 2001
Engineer: Steve Rosenthal

The Loom's Desire (Rounder 3186)
Live recording, edited and mixed at Ultrasonic Studio, New Orleans, 2002
Engineer: David Farrell

DALTON REED

Willing and Able (Bullseye Blues BB 9547)
Coproduced with Lee Allen Zeno
Ultrasonic Studio, New Orleans, 1994
Engineers: David Farrell and Steve Reynolds

Louisiana Soul Man (Bullseye Blues BB 9517)
Coproduced with Lee Allen Zeno
Ultrasonic Studio, New Orleans, 1994
Engineers: David Farrell and Steve Reynolds

JIMMY REED

Mr. Luck: The Complete Vee-Jay Singles (Craft Recordings)
Reissue producer
Living Blues 2018 Historical Release of the Year

CHARLIE RICH

Pictures and Paintings (Sire)
Sam Phillips Studio, Memphis, 1992
Engineers: David Farrell, Mark Wessell, Tina Hanson

STEVE RILEY AND THE MAMOU PLAYBOYS

La Toussaint (Rounder 6068)
Dockside Studio, Maurice, LA, and Blue Jay Studio, Carlisle, MA, 1995
Engineers: Tony Daigle and Mark Wessel
National Association of Independent Record Distributors Cajun/Zydeco Album of
    the Year

DUKE ROBILLARD

Rockin' Blues (Rounder 11548)
Compilation

You Got Me (Rounder 3100)
Arlyn Studio, Austin, TX, 1988
Engineers: Rob Feaster and Gragg Lunsford

Swing (Rounder 3103)
Blue Jay Studio, Carlisle, MA, 1988
Engineer: Gragg Lunsford

Too Hot to Handle (Rounder 3082)
Normandy Sound, Warren, RI, and Blue Jay Studio, Carlisle, MA, 1985
Engineers: Phil Greene and Gragg Lunsford

Duke Robillard & the Pleasure Kings (Rounder 3079)
Syncro Sound Studio, Boston, 1983
Engineer: Walter Turbitt

TABU LEY ROCHEREAU ET L'ORCHESTRE AFRISA INTERNATIONAL

Africa Worldwide: 35th Anniversary (Rounder 5039)
Dockside Studio, Maurice, LA, 1996
Engineers: Tony Daigle and David Farrell

Muzina (Rounder 5059)
Dockside Studio, Maurice, LA, 1994
Engineers: Tony Daigle and David Farrell

BOBBY RUSH

Porcupine Meat (Rounder Records)
The Parlor and the Rhythm Shack, New Orleans, 2017
Engineer: Steve Reynolds
Grammy winner
Blues Music Award: Album of the Year
OffBeat (New Orleans) 2018 Blues Album of the Year

Sitting on Top of the Blues (Deep Rush)
tracks: "You Got the Goods on You," "Bobby Rush Shuffle"
Dockside Studio, Maurice, LA, 2019
Engineer: Justin Tockett
Grammy nominee

JOHNNY SHINES

Hey Ba-Ba-Re-Bop (Rounder 2020)
Coproduced with Peter Guralnick
Boston Blues Society concert
Engineers: Durg Gessner and John Nagy

AMANDA SHAW

Pretty Runs Out (Rounder 3257)
Recorded at Piety Street Studio, New Orleans, 2007
Engineer: Steve Reynolds

SOUL REBELS

Unlock Your Mind (Rounder 9117)
Recorded at the Music Shed, New Orleans, 2012
Engineer: Steve Reynolds

SPANIC BOYS

Spanic Boys (Rounder 9022)
Recorded at A.D. Productions, Milwaukee, WI, 1990
Engineer: Dave Henszey

JOSEPH SPENCE

Living on the Hallelujah Side (Rounder 2021)
New Olympia Hotel, Nassau, Bahamas, 1978
Engineers: Bill Nowlin and Scott Billington

TANGLE EYE

Alan Lomax's Southern Journey Remixed (Zoe 1024)
Coproduced with Steve Reynolds
Ultrasonic Studio, New Orleans, 2004
Engineer: Steve Reynolds

IRMA THOMAS

Fiftieth Anniversary Celebration (Rounder 2214)
Compilation

If You Want It, Come and Get It (Rounder Heritage Series 11597)
Compilation

Simply Grand (Rounder 2202)
Piety Street Studio, New Orleans, and Camp Street Studio, Cambridge, MA, 2008
Engineers: David Farrell, Steve Reynolds, and Paul Q. Kolderie
Grammy nomination, 2009
Best of the Beat Award (New Orleans) Contemporary Blues Album, 2009
Blues Music Association Soul/Blues Album of the Year, 2009

After the Rain (Rounder 2149)
Dockside Studio, Maurice, LA, and Camp Street Studio, Cambridge, MA, 2006
Engineers: David Farrell, Steve Reynolds, and Paul Q. Kolderie
Grammy winner
French Academie du Jazz Prix Soul Best Soul Recording
Living Blues Critics Poll Best Contemporary Blues Album, 2007

My Heart's in Memphis: The Songs of Dan Penn (Rounder 2163)
Coproduced with Dan Penn
Sounds Unreal Studio, Memphis, 1999
Engineers: David Farrell and Dawn Hopkins
W. C. Handy Award: Soul/Blues Album of the Year

Sing It! (with Marcia Ball and Tracy Nelson) (Rounder 2152)
Ultrasonic Studio, New Orleans, 1998
Engineer: David Farrell
Grammy nomination

The Story of My Life (Rounder 2149)
Ultrasonic Studio, New Orleans, 1997
Engineer: David Farrell

"A World I Never Made" (track from Doc Pomus tribute album) (Rhino)
Ultrasonic Studio, New Orleans, 1996
Engineer: David Farrell

Walk Around Heaven: New Orleans Gospel Soul (Rounder 2128)
Ultrasonic Studio, New Orleans, 1993
Engineer: David Farrell

True Believer (Rounder 2117)
Ultrasonic Studio, New Orleans, 1992
Engineer: David Farrell

Simply the Best: Live (Rounder 2110)
Slim's, San Francisco, and Blue Jay Studio, Carlisle, MA, 1991
Engineers: Phil Edwards, David Farrell, and Mark Wessel
Grammy nomination

The Way I Feel (Rounder 2058)
Southlake Studio, Metairie, LA, 1988
Engineer: David Farrell

The New Rules (Rounder 2046)
Studio Solo, Slidell, LA, 1986
Engineer: David Farrell
French Academie du Jazz Prix Otis Redding

DAVID TORKANOWSKY

Steppin' Out (Rounder 2090)
Southlake Studio, Metairie, LA, 1988
Engineer: David Farrell

ALVIN "RED" TYLER

Graciously (Rounder 2061)
Southlake Studio, Metairie, LA,1986
Engineer: David Farrell

Heritage (Rounder 2047)
Studio Solo, Slidell, LA, 1998
Engineer: David Farrell

VARIOUS ARTISTS

Ain't No Funk Like N.O. Funk (Bullseye Blues and Jazz BB 9608)
Compilation

Box of the Blues (Rounder 2171)
Compilation

Cajun Music: The Essential Collection (Rounder Heritage Series 11604)
Compilation

Keep It Rollin': The Blues Piano Collection (Rounder Heritage Series 11601)
Compilation

Mardi Gras in New Orleans (Rounder Heritage Series 11600)
Compilation

Modern New Orleans Masters (Rounder 2072)
Compilation

Zydeco: The Essential Collection (Rounder Heritage Series 11605)
Compilation

Zydeco Shootout at El Sid O's (Rounder 2108)
Recorded at El Sid O's Zydeco and Blues Club, 1990
Engineers: David Farrell and Steve Reynolds

TUTS WASHINGTON

New Orleans Piano Professor (Rounder 2041)
Coproduced by John Berthelot and Jeff Hannusch
Ultrasonic Studio, New Orleans, 1984
Engineer: Jay Gallagher

WALTER "WOLFMAN" WASHINGTON

Funk Is in the House (Bullseye Blues BB 9599)
Ultrasonic Studio, New Orleans, 1997
Engineer: David Farrell
OffBeat (New Orleans) Funk Album of the Year

Wolf at the Door (Rounder 2098)
Ultrasonic Studio, New Orleans, 1991
Engineer: David Farrell

Out of the Dark (Rounder 2068)
Southlake Studio, Metarie, LA, 1988
Engineer: David Farrell

Wolf Tracks (Rounder 2048)
Studio Solo, Slidell, LA, 1986
Engineer: David Farrell

DOC WATSON

Life's Work: A Retrospective (Craft Recordings)
Reissue producer, with Ted Olson and Mason Williams

MICHELLE WILLSON

Wake Up Call (Bullseye Blues and Jazz BB 9639)
Q-Division, Somerville, MA, 2001
Engineer: Matthew Ellard

Tryin' to Make a Little Love (Bullseye Blues and Jazz BB 9610)
Ultrasonic Studio, New Orleans, 1999
Engineer: David Farrell

CLAUDE "FIDDLER" WILLIAMS

Swingin' the Blues (Bullseye Blues and Jazz BB 9627)
Coproduced with Russ Dantzler
Nola Studio, New York, 1999
Engineer: Jim Czak

INDEX

ABOUT THE AUTHOR

Photograph by Rick Olivier

SCOTT BILLINGTON is a three-time Grammy-winning roots music producer who has worked with such artists as Irma Thomas, Charlie Rich, and Bobby Rush. For many decades, he balanced his roles of producer, art director, musician, and A&R executive at the highly regarded Rounder Records label, where he was responsible for hundreds of recordings. A former Recording Academy trustee, he lives in New Orleans, where he teaches music production at Loyola University. He often performs with his wife, the children's musician Johnette Downing.